Rise of the Nerds

How a Technocratic Elite Manipulates Your Life and Gambles With Your Future

Steffen Blaese

MARTYR TO SCIENCE

Who Makes these Changes?

I shoot an arrow right.
It lands left.
I ride after a deer and find myself
chased by a hog. ...
I dig pits to trap others
and fall in myself.
I should be suspicious
of what I want.

– 13th-century Persian poet and mystic Rumi

We humans have come a long way since our ancestors entered the stage about two million years ago. Imagine some age from the dawn of humankind until now. We have mastered the shift from gathering and hunting to agriculture. We have passed the Middle Ages and three industrial revolutions, and the forces of globalization are still working. Try to imagine the reality back then, but not the citchy tales of Hollywood. Through much of our history, people lived in extreme poverty. They suffered from tyranny, plagues, and famines. Hostile neighbors and societal collapse posed a constant threat. Despite all challenges our lives today are easier, longer, and healthier. In the past 100 years, living standards have increased in the developed world. We eat better, know more, communicate over long distances, and are more mobile. We can cure diseases that have been a death sentence for many generations. The common teaching is that we owe our prosperity to the advances of science and technology.

But you can look at this story from another perspective. All scientific and technological innovations have potential for both – good and evil. This simple wisdom is the core of the Prometheus myth. In Greek mythology, Prometheus was the creator and advocate of mankind. After he created humans out of clay, he gifted them with various skills that he borrowed from animals. Among others, he gave them the intelligence of dogs and the diligence of horses, and he convinced the goddess Athena to gift them with reason. Yet Zeus denied them the use of fire because it's a very powerful element that can harm humans, animals, and nature. Prometheus stole it and secretly brought it to the people. To punish him, Zeus has Prometheus chained onto a rock on Mount Caucasus for eternity and put him to relentless torture by denying him food, drink, and sleep. A vicious eagle (Ethon) fed on his liver, which constantly regenerated. But Zeus punished not only Prometheus, he also punished the humans. He gave Pandora a box from which sorrow, disease, suffering, and pain spread all over the world. The wrath of Zeus symbolizes the dual nature of technology. Technological progress has brought us astonishing political, social, and material wonders. But it has also brought us weapons of mass destruction, lifestyle diseases, and mass unemployment. Our ingenuity has now placed us on the very edge of extinction. But it's not always about life and death. Technological downsides are often more subtle and difficult to grasp.

X-ray research is a prime example: In 1895, while experimenting with gases, the German physicist Wilhelm Conrad Röntgen discovered an invisible radiation that could penetrate through matter. To distinguish it from other known rays, he simply named it X-ray. At first, he only told his wife about it because the effects of this radiation were so strange that he was afraid people might think he had gone mad. A few weeks later, he realized the usefulness of these rays for medical diagnostics. On 23 January 1896, he gave his only public presentation to an enthusiastic crowd of scientists, government officials, military, and celebrities. The response to his discovery was overwhelming. To get first-hand information, the German Kaiser Wilhelm II. invited Röntgen to Berlin, they named streets after him, he received many honors, e.g. the first Nobel Prize in Physics, and to this day, the Germans simply call X-rays Röntgen-rays.

Röntgen remained a humble person and didn't patent his discovery, so that it could spread more quickly. He meant well, but this decision had an unwanted side effect. Savvy salesmen found a way to exploit the new technology to make a fast buck with no regard to the harm it may cause. The first mass-produced X-ray device – the Vitascope – became the highlight of upper class parties. People x-rayed their fingers, sport injuries, or unfortunate nearby pets. In 1921, the Boston doctor Jacob Lowe introduced a commercial X-ray machine at an industrial fair in Milwaukee. With the shoe-fitting fluoroscope you could view the bones and soft tissues of a foot inside a shoe. Milwaukee became the center of the fluoroscope production, and the bulky machine became a prominent feature of shoe stores. From the mid-1920s to the 1950s, more than 10,000 fluoroscopes made their way into shoe stores all over the country. Children loved to play with the machines. It was as exciting for them as «free balloons and all-day suckers» – as a company advertised in a sales brochure. «Foot examination for children [is a] source of profit, » announced a shoe retailer in 1935. And indeed it was. The trick was simple as it was effective. The devices increased the fear of poor fitting shoes, thereby enhancing sales. We know little about the medical problems and possible deaths caused by the shoe-fitting fluoroscope. It didn't cause any immediate irritation. Parents would never have accepted injuries to her children during a visit to the shoe shop. But they spent little thought on the long-term effects. X-ray quacks vouched for the safety of those devices, and a manipulative rhetoric seized on the ideal of 'scientific parenthood' and the faith in progress.

X-rays save lives, no doubt, but they damage the genetic material of cells and can cause cancer. The higher the radiation dose, the higher the risk of developing cancer after years or decades. Every schoolchild now knows about these side effects. Since the lethal effect of X-rays was not yet known, some early researchers unfortunately died. Voices of reason early warned against the careless use of X-rays. In 1925, the London Times published a letter by Christina Jordan (née Brumleu), wife of the British X-ray pioneer Alfred C. Jordan. «We admire a 'martyr to science', » she wrote, «but a 'martyr to commerce' stands on a different footing. » The powerful and wealthy lobbyists vehemently dismissed any concerns. In conformity with the scientific zeitgeist, no one wanted to learn about the dangers. The Canadian historians Jacalyn Duffin and Charles Hayter concluded that the promotional literature from that period «sidestepped the thorny problem of truth in advertising. » The rise and fall of the shoe-fitting fluoroscope «was just one more manifestation of the promise of science and technology» – a tale of cutthroat competition, the «triumph of capitalism over common sense. » Effective legislation came slowly; the last devices disappeared from the shops only in the 1950s.

Activist and author Jerry Mander explains why it took so long: «The first waves of description are invariably optimistic, even utopian [because] in capitalist societies all early descriptions of new technologies come from their inventors and the people who stand to gain from their acceptance. » We get our first insights into technology by its biggest beneficiaries. In their myth technology cannot cause any harm. They seduce us with best case scenarios and dismiss warnings of the negative consequences as pure hysteria. Environmental devastation, damaged health, wars, and tyranny are, in their narrative, merely undesirable side-effects. Slogans like 'Progress is good,' 'There's no turning back,' and 'Technology will free humans from disease, strife, and unremitting toil' are ciphers for an attitude to life, a kind of brainwashing. The similarities with the history of computers are stunning. In 1948, IBM placed an early computer in a shop in New York for marketing reasons. What the public didn't know: The computer calculated hydrogen bomb simulations for the scientists in Los Alamo.

For a long time, computers served mainly mysterious calculations in science and industry. Today, they are restructuring all areas of our lives – our homes, businesses, and relations. The rise of the computer goes hand in hand with the rise of a technocratic elite: ultra-smart people, computer scientists, engineers, and hackers … Our parents used to call them nerds: pale homebodies with thick glasses, pimples, and greasy hair, sloppy dressed, and mincingly unsporty. They can always bore you with an endless lecture on a fringe theory. They feed on cold pizza and speak a few programming languages. They are into role-plays, and they idolize Spock and Data, the two emotionless characters from Star Trek. The physicist and author Carl Sagan interviewed a schoolgirl in the early 1990s, and her judgment was devastating:

«Nerds wear their belts just under their rib cages. Their short-sleeve shirts are equipped with pocket protectors in which is displayed a formidable array of multicoloured pens and pencils. A programmable calculator is carried in a special belt holster. They all wear thick glasses with broken nose-pieces that have been repaired with Band-Aids. They are bereft of social skills, and oblivious or indifferent to the lack. When they laugh, what comes out is a snort. They jabber at each other in an incomprehensible language. They'll jump at the opportunity to work for extra credit in all classes except gym. They look down on normal people, who in turn laugh at them. … There are more boy nerds than girl nerds, but there are plenty of both. Nerds don't date. If you're a nerd you can't be cool. Also vice versa. »

I don't like bashing people, but her description isn't only a cliché. Think of Bill Gates or Mark Zuckerberg. One wears thick glasses and is rocking back and forth in his chair whenever he contemplates about something. The other cannot look you in the eye and likes to show off with inappropriate classic quotes.

Nerds, geeks, and hackers – they have many positive characteristics. In their self-conception they talk about passion, tolerance, and creativity. But I would like to talk about some negative, less frequently discussed personality traits of nerds. A typical nerd biography often begins at school with experiences of humiliation, exclusion, and bullying. Some nerds can work through and overcome their injuries and free themselves from the victim mentality. But that rarely happens. Rather, behavioral and thought patterns are consolidated into generalized habitual action patterns that stay with them throughout their lives.

It has often been suggested that the term nerd is a circumscription for people with Asperger's, a moderate form of autism. Its symptoms include problems in social contact, speech, and articulation disorders, persistent occupation with activities incomprehensible to outsiders, and a preference for fixed routines and rituals. You can find such behavior also with the nerd. Larry

Page unnerves people by simply not talking. His partner Sergey Brin admits about himself that he is «not a very social person.» Canadian novelist Douglas Coupland wrote in his 1995 novel Microserfs: «I think all tech people are slightly autistic.» Eugene Jarvis, Berkeley graduate and one of the first computer game developers, explains: «Most computer people are nerds. If you're a true nerd, you can't deal with people at all, only machines.» In 2001, Steve Silberman, from the tech magazine Wired, called Autistic Spectrum Disorders the 'Geek Syndrome.' But the symptoms of Asperger's syndrome are rather soft, i.e. they also fit well to other syndromes or don't mean anything at all. Bill Gates could very well be a somewhat shy and sometimes choleric brainiac with some quirks.

Nerds have been around long before computers. One of the most famous nerds ever was Archimedes. The brilliant Greek mathematician first calculated the number Pi, discovered the laws of the lever, and designed some quite sophisticated machines. When he gained a mathematical insight, he is said to have jumped out of the bathtub and ran naked through Syracuse. Nerds have always been attracted to science. In fact, the whole history of science is a history of nerds. Chemistry and physics are particularly appealing to them, as is mathematics, although strictly speaking it's not a natural science. On the other hand, they tend to harbor a certain disdain for the humanities, in which structures and laws tend to be less strict. The Irish academic John Naughton has repeatedly called the bosses of Microsoft and Facebook half-educated nerds who studied only computer science but skipped the important lectures in liberal arts, history, and social sciences.

Over the past decades, the former insult has turned into an ironic self-description that is proudly used. Since the 1984 college movie Revenge of the Nerd, nerds are part of Hollywood's standard repertoire. The nerd has become the secret hero, who succeeds only by virtue of his intellect. Successful television shows such as The IT Crowd or Big Bang Theory celebrate socially inept, fantasy-enthusiastic, and computer-obsessed heroes. William Gibson's novel Neuromancer presents the nerd as a hard-boiled antihero. Nerd aesthetics and nerd culture are now mainstream. The death of Apple cofounder Steve Jobs was mourned as strongly as that of Michael Jackson. Nerds show off with their poorly fitting black hoodies as confident as with their powerful notebooks. It's no surprise that the image of this species is changing.

Everyone is happy to know a guy who can fix computer problems. In recent years, they have become absolutely indispensable. Companies need them because they are perfect employees: highly skilled and extremely frugal. Never before have so many nerds been billionaires. With their ability to control the flow of information and the technical progress, their economic power grew, and so did their influence. They meet with top politicians and have enormous influence on world affairs through their products and their wealth. They have programmed our social networks and thus define the rules of our relationships. Twitter, Facebook, Google and Co. have become powerful beyond measure. In terms of market value, Google and Facebook exceed the six largest marketing companies – combined. Facebook has more advertising revenue than all American newspapers – again, combined. And Google has twice as much advertising revenue as Facebook. They know that the real power lies with them. Their lobby has the deepest pockets. If nerds join the dark side, so to speak, they can do enormous damage and at worst turn into ruthless technocrats.

Some peculiar characters like Peter Thiel, Trump's favorite techie, and Travis Kalanick, founder of Uber, have become extremely influential people. As technocratically oriented individuals, they surrounded themselves with other technocrats. They even have a fancy name for their group of «misfits»: the PayPal mafia, because nerds think that's cool. The «Mafiosi» are well-connected, a messianic sect that sees itself as the harbinger of progress. They are infiltrating the mainstream and occupying key positions of global power. Thiel, the «Don, » estimates that about 220 people belong to the PayPal mafia. Many of them icons of the tech elite. There are Max Levchin, the «Consigliere, » and the «capos» Ken Howery, Elon Musk, and Keith Rabois, to name a few.

A famous characteristic of nerds is their rebellious attitude towards authorities. Think of Archimedes, who, according to legend, shouted «Don't disturb my circles! » to a Roman soldier and was subsequently killed with a sword. But these guys aren't rebels; they resented their parents or families very little. What separates this group from others is their will of power. They have dedicated themselves to shape humanity in their image with the means of technology. Almost three decades after its rather casual start, the downsides of the digitization are obvious. But they are blind to the ramifications of their doing, or they don't care. As high priests of their technocratic ideology, they lead the collective. If you raise concerns, they turn that collective into a mob. They relativize the risks, and doubts are dismissed as hysteria, no matter how coherent and eloquent the arguments are. Their companies control what billions of people read and watch and make sure that we hear everywhere every day how mega-toll-crass their gadgets and platforms are. It has become almost unthinkable to say no to technology, any technology.

My book is intended for anyone who is curious about these forces. Since I'm a history-minded person, you'll get some non-boring history lessons. The historical perspective provides a backdrop for the more controversial parts that follow. But it's not a work of history in the strict academic-scientific sense. I am neither a scientist nor a historian; I do the same as historians do. But they have a harder job because they can be faulted for what's left out. Writing on my own meant that I could pick only what I deemed important.

Don't expect this book covering everything and all. My story is only a small piece of this complex puzzle. I have covered what I believe is needed to understand the role of technology. I don't presume to have come up with 'The Answer' here. But I offer some thoughts that I hope will make a contribution to the debate.

I am not against computers. I wrote this book on a computer with the help of translation programs and spellcheckers. As a word processors, computers are a gift. I used the Internet for research. It saved me much time and drudgery. I have no illusions about my writing skills. But it's irrelevant as long as the message gets out. I focus on the United States because technology has taken hold more deeply there than anywhere else. The USA is the dominant force of the Internet. All important organizations that govern the infrastructure of the Internet are American, as well as almost all important tech companies.

Unfortunately, in the current political climate, science is under siege. Populist movements are thriving on an increasing distrust and are more than happy to use any criticism directed at science and technology to undermine its credibility. Science is the best available method to gain knowledge about the world. Those who reject scientific findings unsubstantiated either don't know what they are talking about or tell lies on purpose. As an author, I thus had to make a difficult choice. Should I censor myself to avoid getting approval from the wrong side and risk that my work could be used by anti-scientific circles to reinforce their views, or be called a Luddite and conspiracy theorist? Or should I tell my story?

I grew up in a socialist regime where freedom of speech was suppressed and science had to submit to the social utopias of the ruling party. Thus, I chose free discussion over self-censorship, regardless of the consequences. Without criticizing the technological revolution, we cannot repair its faults. The technophiles must speak for themselves and do so all the time. This book is about the ideas that fuel these nerds and their companies and the imperative of resisting them.

«This is your last chance. After this, there is no turning back. You take the blue pill the story ends, you wake up in your bed and believe whatever you want to believe. You take the red pill you stay in Wonderland and I show you how deep the rabbit-hole goes. » – Morpheus's warning to Neo

GARDEN OF EDEN

«Humans did not evolve from apes, even if this is repeatedly claimed: He's an ape. »
– André Langaney

«Man is an exception, whatever else he is. … If it's not true that a divine being fell, then we can only say that one of the animals went entirely off its head. » – G. K. Chesterton

We humans are rather strange animals. We walk on two legs instead of four. We have lost our fur and wear clothes. We have weak muscles, but a large brain. We have an extended childhood and a long lifespan. We are resourceful, compassionate, and caring, but sometimes also reckless and brutal. We are sentimental, we cry when we are sad and sometimes when we are happy. This list could be considerably lengthened. For the longer time in evolution, there has been no sign that human beings will appear one day. Thirty million years ago, our ancestors were one of a dozen different species of monkeys that thrived in the African tropical forests. They were hanging out in trees and eating leaves and fruits for free. But deep inside them, in their genes, the destiny of humanity was already dawning. On their way to become human they could rely on various valuable skills. Swinging from branch to branch demands a good stereoscopic vision and skilled hands, and both required a capable brain.

The hominine journey started with a climate change. Woods formed a large belt across the African continent from the Atlantic to the Indian Ocean. Over the next fifteen million years, geological events caused dramatic environmental changes. The climate became drier and chillier, the forests shrank, and open savanna landscapes expanded. These changes appear to have been incisive in our evolution. As competition grew in their shrinking habitat and taking refuge in the trees grew more difficult, our ancestors made their way into the expansive river valleys that stretched along the edges of the rainforests. If the Garden of Eden was a real place, these valleys with their lavish plant growth would come closest to it. The German anthropologist Carsten Niemitz believes that it was there where the apes learned to walk on two legs – another skill that would become useful later. Since apes usually cannot swim, they had to stand upright on their hind legs in the shallow water while searching for food. The water stabilized their unsteady attempts to walk. If they had not learned to walk on two legs, their descendants – we – would have been great apes and only an ecological fringe group like chimpanzees and gorillas.

About fourteen to eight million years ago, the climate in Africa became even drier, and large parts of the rainforests disappeared in favor of grasslands. Our ancestors finally left the forests for the savanna. The grass of the savanna is often more than one meter high. With a better overview, you have a greater chance of survival. Able to stand on two legs now, our ancestors could watch for food or enemies. Bipedalism may have also triggered another decisive development: Since the head is now balanced on top of the body, the facial skull could shrink, the brain skull grew which in turn gave more space for the brain. While the legs took on almost all the responsibility for locomotion, the hands were free for various tasks, like carrying food and babies and using tools, drawing and writing. The free use of the hand also changed the interaction between the body and the mind. Evolution equipped us with finely tuned muscles and nerves in hands and fingers which enable us to perform filigree activities. The more skilled their hands became, the more successful were our ancestors. Monkeys can walk on their hind-legs too, carry objects and use tools. But our hands with a fully opposable thumb and our arms are better designed for these activities. In turn, we had to sacrifice our climbing skills. Eating fruit is cognitively much more demanding than eating leaves. You need an «inner map» to remember where to find fruits, and you need to know exactly when they are ripe. The new diet – fruits and grains from the grass – provided more energy which allowed the brain to become even larger. As a result, humans became smarter.

Bipedalism comes with trade-offs: Back pain and stiff necks are part of the deal. Women had to pay a particularly high price. Standing upright and walking on two legs requires narrower hips which leads to a narrower birth canal. Meanwhile, the heads of the babies were getting larger, and giving birth became more painful and risky for the life of the women. Thus, it became an advantage to give birth to the young earlier, when the head was still small and malleable. That's why human babies are completely helpless at birth. To survive they need support from relatives and neighbors for many years. Raising the offspring requires cooperation in the group.

Group formation, which also occurs in monkeys, is another inherited characteristic of human beings. To understand complex human relationships you have to keep much information in mind. But a large brain not only brings advantages. It's also a burden because of its high energy consumption. The more complex a brain is, the more time it takes to mature and develop its full potential. Compared to many of our fellow earthlings our physical abilities are not very impressive. Other animals have developed special skills and are outdoing us in it, e.g. in jumping, running, climbing, swimming, or diving. Many of them have also developed more precise senses, can see, smell, and hear better. Humans are highly specialized creative beings because of our brains. We compensate many physical deficits with the use of complex tools. The oldest evidence of the use of tools from Gona in Ethiopia dates back almost 2.5 million years. Almost 70,000 generations, each thirty years old, have passed since then. Homo habilis, meaning 'skilled human', is credited as the manufacturer of these tools. An important milestone on the way to becoming human was the control of fire. We do not know exactly when, where and how people managed this. But about 300,000 years ago the use of fire seems to have been part of everyday life for many humans. They thus had a reliable source of light and heat and combined with other tools an effective weapon against the lurking carnivorous predators.

Each new discovery changed our way of living to a certain extent. With tools, fire, and fur clothing, we have gained some independence from the forces of nature. Previously uninhabited areas became habitable for human beings. According to the British ethnologist William Thorpe, it was fire that turned caves into dwellings. Fire is a 'force' that by far exceeds the strength of our bodies and with which we could clear away dry forests or steppes, creating «a chasm separates us from the rest of the animal kingdom, » as the Israeli Historian Yuval Noah Harari put it. But humans also became dependent on their tools. With every tool that we have invented, we distanced ourselves a little from other living beings. With technology, we expanded our abilities to perceive the world and to intervene in it. If the groundbreaking achievements brought relief to mankind for the time being, it did not take long for them to take their toll.

When Charles Darwin published his book The Descent of Man in 1871, the statement that humans and apes could have evolved from a common ancestor was a scandal. The theory of evolution didn't fit to the religious world view of many of his contemporaries and earned him much mockery and their rage. It still causes an outrage when people talk about «human and non-human animals» instead of «humans» and «animals. » Darwin himself was without a doubt a nerd: As a child he carried out chemical experiments, which is why they nicknamed him «gas» at school. He collected stones, fossils, mussels, insects, and bird eggs. But not because he loved animals. Occasionally he killed birds for fun and once he beat a dog puppy just to feel some control and power. He was physically a wreck and struggled all his life with various ailments. Darwin changed the world forever, although he only worked four hours a day. His genius was to prove that natural selection is a blind force and evolution follows random paths. Before Darwin, it was a common belief that God had created humans in His image and gave them the right to rule over nature, a still widely accepted idea in the Judeo-Christian tradition. Many philosophers, psychologists, anthropologists, and even biologists consider humans to be unique within nature.

If we look at the structure and physiology of the human body, it's difficult to accept any such claims. You only have to look into the faces of chimpanzees to see the similarities. Two parallel eyes, a bulge reminiscent of eyebrows, a nose, a mouth, and prominent ears on the side of the head. Then there are the two arms with hands that can grasp. And when they sit and put food in their mouths with these hands or hold a child in their arms, then you can't deny it. Of course, there are also differences. All the apes are so much hairier than we are, and finally they walk on all fours. But the similarity is there – and it needed explanation.

Already in antiquity people recognized the anatomical resemblances between humans and animals. The Greek physician Asklepiades was the first who discovered that the function of an organ determinates its design. His transformation theory – a theory of descent – predates that of Darwin by 1,900 years. According to Asklepiades, animals are natural beings like humans, only on a less complex level. It was Aristotle who denied that animals are able to reason. He claimed that all actions of animals are mere expressions of a low life of instinct. The Church of the Middle Ages has embraced his opinion. Anthropocentrists claimed man's superiority to animals by emphasizing alleged differences. Our language and cultural capacity would separate us from animals, it was said. Only humans are able to suffer, it was said. Only humans have consciousness, individuality, dignity, or whatever the difference was called.

Seventeenth-century French philosopher Rene Descartes was the shining star of Anthropocentrism. His epoch is marked by hexenwahn as well as the birth of modern science. In a poorly ventilated chamber, he contemplated about life, the universe, and everything. According to him, only man has a soul and the ability to think. A living being that cannot think – i.e. the animal – is nothing more than a somewhat sophisticated machine. Of course, we humans are unique – every species is. But the idea of a fundamental gap between the abilities of humans and apes has no scientific support. Yet we still tend to underestimate our fellow earthlings. Homo sapiens is not separated from the rest of the world of nature. We are blessed with special skills, yet these are not unique, but characteristics of life itself. We owe them to our ancestors whom these skills developed gradually. Many studies have confirmed a close relationship between humans and chimpanzees. The differences between us are quantitative, not qualitative. The similarity of our biology is amazing. Organs, senses, even the chemistry of blood – almost identical. On our biological nature, there is no uniqueness.

Researchers compared key genes in humans to the corresponding genes in chimpanzees. Main result: The genome of humans and chimpanzees is 93.5 - 99.4 percent identical, depending on the used method. The fewest genetic differences were found in the brain. These small differences evolved during human evolution. Chimpanzees and humans are much closer related to each other than both are to the gorillas or other great apes. Some scientists even suggest that chimpanzees should belong to the genus Homo. The evolutionary biologist Jared Diamond calls humans the «third chimpanzee. » Although we are close relatives of apes, we are not descended from the apes we know today. Rather, humans and chimpanzees have evolved from a distant common ancestor about six million years ago. Since then, our ape cousins seem to have changed their bodies and behavior much less than we have.

As a young woman, Jane Goodall spent months alone in the wilderness to study the behavior of chimpanzees. She discovered that chimpanzees use tools – a skill previously only attributed to human beings. Her discovery that chimpanzees, like humans, are prone to outbursts of brutality is the most shocking of all. Chimpanzees are capable of waging war. Goodall observed extreme violence, mutilation, murder, and even cannibalism. There is probably no cruelty and evilness of the human, which cannot also be found with chimpanzees. Gorillas and orangutans, on the other hand, are much more peaceful.

Chimpanzees are intelligent, they live in a complex social fabric. Experiments show that they can plan and be creative. They are able to reflect about themselves, feel pain, and compassion. There are great personality differences between them – as with humans. They have a culture which differs between groups. Their younger ones learn through observation, imitation, and practice. They can also solve simple arithmetical problems. They are aware of death and mourn for their deceased companions. In reaction to death, they show feelings of anger, denial, and finally acceptance – like humans. Our knowledge about them is the mirror in which we can see who we are: a random product of evolution, a bright, sick, eccentric, mostly shaved primate.

THE TALKING AND WRITING APE

After thirteen years as mayor of Bordeaux, the 38 years old French philosopher Michel de Montaigne retreated into his famous tower at Montaigne Castle in the Périgord to focus on writing. At that time, the situation in France was tense. Famines, epidemics, and religious tensions between Catholics and Protestants shook the country. Although he himself was a Catholic and a loyalist to the king, Montaigne remained skeptical throughout his life about any claim to absolute truth. In his famous Essais he demands tolerance towards the various ways of life. With his ideas he didn't make friends in the Catholic Church, and his writings ended up on the Vatican index of forbidden books. In his essay Man is No Better Than the Animals he reflects on the arguments of anthropocentrists. He points to the similarity of non-verbal communication and its significance for animals as well as humans:

«As to speech, it's certain that if it be not natural it's not necessary. Nevertheless I believe that a child which had been brought up in an absolute solitude, remote from all society of men (which would be an experiment very hard to make), would have some kind of speech to express his meaning by. And 'tis not to be supposed that nature should have denied that to us which she has given to several other animals: for what is this faculty we observe in them, of complaining, rejoicing, calling to one another for succour, and inviting each other to love, which they do with the voice, other than speech? And why should they not speak to one another? They speak to us, and we to them. In how many several sorts of ways do we speak to our dogs, and they answer us? We converse with them in another sort of language, and use other appellations, than we do with birds, hogs, oxen, horses, and alter the idiom according to the kind. »

Part of the reason apes cannot talk to us is that they lack certain anatomical prerequisites. The anatomy of the mouth and pharynx of chimpanzees and gorillas doesn't allow any well-modulated sounds. Their laryngeal muscles and vocal cords are not as flexible as to produce as clear sounds as we do. Apart from that, the communication behavior of the apes resembles that of humans. Much of our communication effort is unconscious and non-verbal, like animal gestures.

There is a fascinating anecdote about the famous bonobo Kanzi, who was born in captivity at the Yerkes Primate Center in Georgia in October 1980. Kanzi learned to communicate with people through symbols and also appeared to understand a significant amount of spoken language. Once, when Kanzi and the psychologist Sue Savage-Rumbaugh were on an excursion in the forest, he pointed to the signs for «marshmallow» and «fire. » As requested, he received the sweets and matches. He then collected a few branches, lit a fire, and roasted the marshmallows on a stick. But his taste for grilled marshmallows isn't the most amazing part of the story. It proves that the Bonobo could express his wishes. It's also surprising how he mastered cooking, a cultural technique that is regarded as only human. The scientists conducted a careful study about Kanzi's ability to comprehend spoken language and equaled it to the ability of a human child who appeared to understand approximately as much as Kanzi. Given the many similarities between the brains of humans, chimpanzees, and bonobos it's no surprise. Kanzi and many other primates are evidence that the first glimmerings of language must have appeared in the mind of our common ancestor.

We all learn at least one language as children, which guides us through our entire lives. It defines our perception, ideas, dreams, and actions. It's the key to our outer as well as to our inner world. Children need no instructions to learn to talk. Language is, as a popular book by Stephen Pinker claims, an instinct. Linguist David Crystal notes in How Language Works: «Unless there is something wrong with the child or something lacking in the child's environment, speech will emerge towards the end of the first year and develop steadily thereafter. » And from the day we say «Mommy and Daddy» for the first time, we never run out of talk. When two or more people meet, they are likely to start talking to each other. When we are alone, we talk to ourselves.

The development of language was a decisive factor for the success of human civilization. It's so intertwined with human experience that our life is hard to imagine without it. With language, members of a group can share information with each other. Through spoken language we express emotions, experiences, thoughts, desires, and needs. It's also a medium for shaping relationships with our fellow human beings. With words, we can ask others to do something or to refrain from doing something. Through language that we create ourselves. Unfortunately scientists can't pinpoint the exact time of language development. The lack of archeological record leaves us completely ignorant of its origins. There is, however, a proven coherent link between the development of the upright gait and the anatomical position of the larynx. The tongue now had room for speaking and singing. The origin of our language lies in Africa. Anatomical characteristics show that our ancestors probably had a language already 500,000 years ago. Homo erectus may have developed a kind of sign language, maybe even an early phonetic language. The earliest graves of Homo sapiens in present-day Israel are more than 100,000 years old. We don't know for sure what these people exactly believed in, but they obviously already contemplated mythological matters. It's unlikely that such ideas can be developed without communicating with others about it. According to this, human language developed at the latest 100,000 years ago. Today, there are about 6000 different languages in the world. Some scientists believe that all languages have a common origin. Others argue that several primitive languages have evolved into complex languages.

Already around 500 BC, the Greek physician and philosopher Alcmaeon of Croton performed animal sections. He recognized that nerve tracts run from the sensory organs to the brain and assumed that the brain was the center of sensory perception and thinking. However, he considered the brain to be a gland which excretes the thoughts like a tear gland. More than 2500 years later, we know better, but the brain is still a mystery. We know that it consists of billions of nerve cells (neurons), which exchange chemical and electrical signals via billions of connections (synapses). We know which areas of the brain are active when learning, speaking, or dreaming, and we know that the human brain regulates body functions such as digestion, heartbeat, sleep, breathing, and other vital functions. It's also responsible for emotions such as joy, grief, pride, boredom, anger, and aggression.

We can learn to speak only because of the brain's plastic design. The brain changes itself permanently through its use, and it's almost infinitely malleable. Nerve cells constantly break old connections and form new ones. All nerve cells are already present at birth, but the human brain doesn't stop adapting. Though this plasticity is most obvious in early childhood, it remains with us throughout our entire lives. The transformation of the brain in response to life experience can take place in periods ranging from decades to days and hours to seconds. Without its plasticity, the brain would be hard-wired like a computer and lack adaptability.

Yet the spoken word is, as soon as it is uttered, blown away by the wind. Already the Stone Age man showed the desire to make thoughts more permanent. In Les Eyzies, a village in France, they left many signs of their presence. Archeologists found stone tools, weapons, and graves with burial objects. In about 140 caves there are paintings of animals, like mammoth, rhino, wild horse, cave bears, and ibexes. Some show abstract motifs, such as groups of dots and grid patterns with colored fields – a kind of rudimentary writing. Writing seems to be known to Stone Age people all over the world. Some abstract drawings in South Africa are 75,000 years old. Some symbols in the form of pearls in the Skhul cave in Israel even 100,000 years.

Our ancestors had lived as foragers for some hundred thousand years. Since they preferred certain plants as food their natural environment began to change. About 10,000 years ago, they came up with the idea of sowing the first seeds and domesticating animals. Everywhere on the planet people turned their back on their nomadic roots in favor of a sedentary way of life. They cultivated the land, built the first houses, and permanent settlements. For the incipient trade, they needed reliable systems to monitor quantities of livestock and goods. Around 8500 BC, the Sumerians started to use small clay tokens engraved with simple symbols. Later they advanced the pictographic writing into a system with single syllables – the first phonetic scripture, the Sumerian cuneiform. Sumerians were living in what is now Iraq. The Greeks called it «Mesopotamia: «land between rivers. » The two large rivers Euphrates and Tigris had created a very fertile region. For their neighbors, Mesopotamia was the land of milk and honey, or «Paradise in Eden, » as the Bible says. «Eden» is a Sumerian word and means «desert. » But the Bible translators later misinterpreted it as «Paradise Eden. » In his book Tristes Tropiques the French ethnologist Claude Lévi-Strauss notes: «If my hypothesis is correct, the primary function of writing, as a means of communication, is to facilitate the enslavement of other human beings. » That sentence is disturbing, but he has a point. The clay token consists of lists, lists, and more lists. The Sumerians traded slaves like goods and indeed used writing to organize slavery.

During most of our early history, humans stored their knowledge only in their brains and traditions were passed down only by word of mouth from generation to generation. Writing ended the dominance of orality. Unwritten poetry and the unwritten sharing of information or oral contracts became rare. Now they could write religious ideas as well as scientific findings. It's no coincidence that the development of writing and mathematics began around the same time. Writing fell within the realm of administrative bodies of the early kingdoms. Their reign was increasingly based on the collection, storage, processing, and transmission of data. Writing schools were the first schools ever, but few people learned this skill. The scribes became a privileged class, vital to the rulership, much like programmers today. Until the Middle Ages, only priests could reach a broader audience, be it in the church or on large squares. Literacy was low and books were worth a fortune. This changed from the 15th century onward.

Gutenberg's printing press set off another round of social upheaval. The printed book radically changed the traditional habits of reading and writing. The writing culture of the monasteries with their scriptories and libraries became obsolete. Publishers and booksellers now duplicated and distributed the manuscripts. Books became affordable for lower social classes, and education was no longer a privilege of the ruling elite. The low priced books undermined feudal authority and spread the ideas of humanism and science. Bible translations started to circulate, and the Church feared losing its power and influence. Not surprisingly, the strongest criticism came from the clergy. In 1515, Pope Leo X issued an edict that strictly censored all new prints – not only in Rome. In Venice, an army of snitches was spying in the printing houses for the Church. Only one generation after Gutenberg, dozens of printing businesses had settled there. The feverish start-up atmosphere in Venice at the time reminds one of the mythical garage companies in Silicon Valley. For the experiments in the emerging market, you did not only need skilled typesetters and proofreaders, but also a large amount of money. Venice was the richest trading metropolis. People founded print shops with partners and split up again after fierce battles over profits. Hapless entrepreneurs sank into poverty as quickly as others became as rich as Nabob. A few worried people warned of the unforeseeable consequences. They argued that the printing press would demean the work of scholars and scribes. Others complained about the lack of care in printing and the lower quality compared to handwritten texts. The Italian humanist Hieronimo

Squarciafico lamented: «An abundance of books makes men less studious; it destroys memory and enfeebles the mind by relieving it of too much work. » And from their perspective, they were right.

New York University professor Clay Shirky noticed: «Most of the arguments made against the printing press were correct, even prescient. » It was hard then to imagine the many blessings that book printing would bring to people. The Canadian philosopher Marshall McLuhan considered the printed book as a step backwards. It has made modern man unfree and emotionally and mentally depleted, ended the age of orality and the mythical wholeness of the world. He considered reading to be an antisocial act, isolating us from our fellow humans. «The alphabet is a technology of visual fragmentation and specialization, » he said. His followers regard McLuhan as a prophetic genius. He praised the «Global Village» when the Cold War was still tearing the globe in half. In the 1960s, McLuhan was the most covered scientist in the world. He was in touch with influential writers such as James Joyce, T.S. Eliot, and Ezra Pound. Andy Warhol and the Beatles asked him for audience. It was actually McLuhan who speculated that «everyone could become famous for 15 minutes. » Warhol later worshiped that phrase. McLuhan was a gifted self-marketer. Probably his most famous slogan is: «The medium is the message. » According to him, it is not so much what we watch on television that is important, but that television itself as a medium changes our perception.

Already the ancient Greeks had feared that books not only deliver specific content, but also influence cognitive skills. 2,000 years ago, Plato wrote the collected dialogues of Socrates on the important topics of that time and let him say:

«The discovery of the alphabet will create forgetfulness in the learners' souls, because they will not use their memories; they will trust to the external written characters and not remember of themselves ... You give your disciples not truth but only the semblance of truth; they will be heroes of many things, and will have learned nothing; they will appear to be omniscient and will generally know nothing. »

Socrates may have been right. People didn't have to memorize everything anymore, but could look it up. Writing was a new form of the external storage of knowledge and promoted new methods of organizing thought and communication. The standardized typography of the printing press standardized the public communication, and a unified written language emerged. Typography created formal thinking, logical analysis and trust in the human 'ratio'. From now on, uniformity, repeatability and precision determined human perception and thinking. The printed book pushed everything that is not printed in books into the realm of the irrational. The eye became the central and most strained organ. Only the visual can comprehend the written and thus help the human being to gain knowledge. All other senses, such as hearing and feeling, are neglected and dismissed by the book. Typography would later also create a uniform society with the assembly line and the tract housing as its icons, the society of the «mechanical man» without depth of experience, without mystique.

«Print culture has long been blind to most other kinds of causation, » McLuhan said. This horror scenario explains his obsession with data streams. He welcomed «The Electronic Age» as a Golden Age, the dawn of the future over the 'graveyard of the alphabet'. He glorified television and computers as salvation, and his disciples continue to do so to this day. The new communication technologies would enable the return of modern humans to the original tribal society, to the global village. But the printed book made modern science possible. The development of television and computers would not have been possible without it. Modern communication empowers you to liberate yourself from the tribe without fearing the total loss of contact.

The spread of literacy resulted in another evolutionary step. We are not born to read. While the spoken language has left its evolutionary footprints in our monkey brains, writing is too young for that. There is no genetically specified reading area in our brains. Our modern brains don't differ from that of the earliest cavemen who could not read and write. The cultural development of reading must thus have taken place within our biological boundaries. The brains of the literate differ from the brains of the illiterate. «Learning how to read, » reports the Mexican psychologist Feggy Ostrosky-Solís, has been shown to «powerfully shape adult neuropsychological systems. » Neurons, which were initially responsible for recognizing faces and forms, now recognize letters and words. Reading takes place in a brain region whose strength is the visual identification of objects. These changes extend as far as the thalamus and the brain stem − evolutionary rather old parts of the brain. When symbols become words, a radical mental transformation begins. Learning to read has a lasting and profound effect on thinking and knowledge. It's a prerequisite for the analysis of complex problems and for a flow of ideas and critical thinking.

In 1892, the French neurologist Joseph-Jules Déjerine discovered that damage to a part of the visual areas in the left hemisphere of the brain caused a loss of the ability to read. As modern brain imaging techniques show, this region plays a crucial role in reading. This area, which is in the same place in all individuals, reacts to written words, even if they are shown only briefly so that they are not consciously recognized. In fractions of a second and without conscious effort, it identifies the word without being distracted by changes in shape, size or position of the letters. The brain thus exceeds by far all computer programs in visual recognition. The result of this visual analysis is then passed on to two large brain regions that encode the phonetic image and meaning of the words. All humans, no matter what language they speak, use the same regions of the brain for reading. Reading and writing are, at least in industrial societies, basic skills in daily life. When reading and writing can change our brains, it must without a doubt leave its mark when we spend a considerable amount of time in front of a screen.

THE DESERT BLOOMS

«When Adam delved and Eve span, Who was then the gentleman? From the beginning all men by nature were created alike, and our bondage or servitude came in by the unjust oppression of naughty men. For if God would have had any bondmen from the beginning, he would have appointed who should be bond, and who free. » – John Ball, Sermon preached during the English peasants' revolt at the end of the 14th century.

«Science has promised us truth...It has never promised us either peace or happiness. » – Gustave Le Bon

The emergence of agriculture is the most controversial turning point in the history of mankind. The standard version – in the myth of civilization – tells us a tale of an era of progress and prosperity. But the agricultural revolution was the biggest fraud in history. The daily life of an average farmer in Jericho 10,000 years ago was harder and less satisfying than that of their ancestors who lived in the area a thousand or three thousand years before him. People exchanged their unbound migratory life for hard field work, poor health, and a much lower life expectancy. Particularly the lives of women became more difficult. Instead of focusing only on household work and raising children, they had to work in the fields as well.

The gatherer-hunters knew the secrets of nature because their survival depended on it. They relied on a rich variety of food sources and could survive challenging times without building up stocks. When one food source failed, they knew plenty others. Sure, they also experienced seasonal hunger and periods of low food availability. But in sum they suffered less from hunger and disease. They had to work less and could engage in more interesting activities. In contrast, until recently, farmers depended on only a handful of crops, often only one. The wheat didn't offer any noteworthy economic security to them either. Peasants almost constantly suffered from hunger. Fungi could infest the crops, or swarms of locusts stripped the fields bare. When the rain failed for a season or two, thousands or millions of farmers starved to death.

Before the invention of agriculture, almost no grains were on the menu. A grain-based diet is poor in minerals and vitamins, difficult to digest, and harms teeth and gums. Since people lived in the vicinity of their livestock, they shared worms, fungal infections, viruses, and bacilli with them.

With the foundation of permanent settlements, the population started to grow. The more crowded a place was, the faster diseases could spread. Around 10,000 B.C., about four million people lived in the world. In 5000 B.C., the world population had risen to only five million. One of the reasons for this slow growth was epidemics.

To the migrating foragers, infants and young children were a burden. Children need much attention, and the tribe could only move slowly. Women had a child only every three or four years at most. After the people had settled down, women could give birth to a child every year. They stopped breastfeeding earlier and replaced the mother's milk with oatmeal and cereal porridge. In agricultural communities, all hands were needed in the field. Thus, people began to see some advantages in having more offspring. Over time, the «wheat trade» became increasingly burdensome. The extra mouths ate up the surplus and demanded more. Each generation of children were worse off on average than before. With the people living in dirty and germ-infested settlements, children getting more grain and less breast milk, and each child competing with more and more siblings for oatmeal, infant mortality skyrocketed. The children were dropping like flies, the adults literally ate their bread in the sweat of their faces. But the number of births rose faster than the number of deaths. So, people had more and more impoverished children. The «improvements» that should make people's lives easier led to a drastic decline.

How could people make such miscalculations? There are two schools of thought. The first is that agriculture was born out of necessity. With the warmer climate following the ice ages, Mesopotamia dried up. Before this, people could simply pick the fruits from the trees. But then, the harvest had to be brought in with heavy labor. The other school of thought is that our ancestors could not grasp all consequences of their decisions. Every generation lived almost like their parents, only slightly different. The society was already too far down the agricultural pathway before anyone could have realized that it was not going as planned. No one could remember that life had ever been any different. Whatever you may think of the agricultural revolution – once it had begun, it could not be undone. People would no longer have been able to feed the whole population if they had returned to foraging. The trap was snapped.

Gatherer-hunters live in small egalitarian groups. Cooperation is crucial for survival. They know almost no private possession. The sedentary way of life enabled individuals to accumulate greater wealth. Private property was a prerequisite for the formation of rigid hierarchical societies. Property multiplied and with it the concentration of wealth and power in the hands of a minority. Inequality led to a dramatic change in relations between men, women, and their offspring. The question of inheritance began to take on significance. The result was conflict and disharmony.

Over the next 13,000 years of human history, poverty, hunger, and wars were the rule. Life expectancy increased only slowly. I was not until the 18th century, when it returned to the level before the invention of agriculture. The dream of a better life chained people to misery. It should not be the last time: Today, we can see for ourselves what that means.

MACHINE BREAKERS

«Those engines of mischief were sentenced to die by unanimous vote of the trade, and Ludd who can all opposition defy was the grand executioner made. » – Luddite song

«I say break the law. Let your life be a counter-friction to stop the machine. What I have to do is to see, at any rate, that I do not lend myself to the wrong which I condemn. » – Henry David Thoreau

The invention of printing press was followed by a series of industrial revolutions. It began in the second half of the 18th century in Great Britain in an almost imperceptible manner. Textile production was the most important industry in the country. One of its centers was in Lancashire, a county in the north-west of England. Homeworkers, mostly women, were spinning the raw cotton from the colonies of Brazil, the Levant, or the Caribbean into yarn. It was an arduous work, done by hand. In the late 17th century, the demand for cotton textiles has increased in Europe. After the discovery and colonization of America, Europe had become more prosperous. The nutrition of the common people improved and the population grew, so did the demand for textiles. The trade boom attracted thousands of people from England, Ireland, and Scotland. Even children worked, and farmers earned some extra money in their free time. But the possibilities of increasing the production were limited. The craftsmen and homeworkers were independent and decided their working hours themselves. Many preferred more leisure time to a higher income. On weekends, the men spend their wages on booze, and on Mondays, they were often too hungover to go to work.

The expanding demand for cotton clothing and a growing competition from cheap products from India triggered a race for technical innovations to increase productivity and reduce labor costs at the same time. A successful invention promised huge profits. Around 1764, James Hargreaves invented a multi-spindle spinning frame. His «Spinning Jenny» was the first industrial spinning machine. With up to 100 spindles operating simultaneously, it replaced eight spinners and one weaver. It was a commercial success. Many workers bought the device to set it up in their homes.

Four years later, Richard Arkwright built a machine that worked almost without human intervention. The «Water Frame» was powered by water, and it was so large that it could no longer be installed in a living room. The first small cotton factories emerged. In the five-storey cotton factory that Arkwright had built in 1771, he introduced a strict work regime. One shift lasted 13 hours. Supervisors watched over the workers, imposed fines for any late arrival or threatened to fire them. The employers were particularly fond of hiring women and children, because they worked at a much lower wage than men. Children as young as six years old picked up cotton waste from the floors or crawled between the machines to clean them. Production shifted from homework and craftsmen to industrial machine manufacturing. A new source of power further accelerated the change: the steam engine patented by James Watt in 1769.

By the late Middle Ages, firewood had become scarce in Britain due to the loss of forests. The English had begun to mine coal on a large scale as a major source of fuel. As a result, the mines had become so deep that they flooded with water. Pumping stations were needed. Already in 1712, Thomas Newcomen had developed a steam engine to pump out the water. In 1769, the Scottish inventor James Watt patented two decisive improvements which increased the efficiency sixfold. Within a few decades, the steam engine became an all-purpose industrial machine. From 1785, the factory owners used steam powered spinning machines. Now the factories no longer needed to be located near rivers, but could be built anywhere.

When the nineteenth century dawned, Britain was in turmoil. It was at war with France, again. Prices rose, the economy declined. Political meetings and the press were restricted. The new industrialists plotted no longer to buy goods from the small textile workshops. The starving textile workers were not allowed to emigrate, since England did not want to lose their expertise to the competitors. During this time of transformation, a boy named Ned Ludd appeared. Legend has it that he damaged two textile machines out of sheer clumsiness. Yet he became a myth. Wherever a machine was sabotaged, the alleged perpetrator defended himself with the words: «Ned Ludd must have been here. » In 1811, the weavers founded a secret society. When asked who their leader was, they replied, «General Ned Ludd of course, who else? »

On 12 April 1811, 350 men, women, and children stormed a spinning mill in Nottinghamshire, smashed the looms and set them on fire. The factory belonged to William Cartwright, a low quality yarn manufacturer using the new machines. Seventy more looms were destroyed that night in the surrounding villages. Later the revolt spread to the neighboring counties of Derby, Lancashire, and York. For two years, the rebels were persecuted by an army of ten thousand (!) soldiers under the command of General Thomas Maitland. He commanded more soldiers than Wellington at the beginning of his campaign against Napoleon in Portugal. That indicates the difficulty for the government to fight the Luddites — as they called machine wreckers from now on. Maitland and his soldiers were desperately searching for their leader — a certain Ned Ludd. But of course they did not find him.

February 27, 1812, was a memorable day for the history of capitalism. Prime Minister Perceval introduced the «Frame Breaking Bill. » From now on, breaking spinning machines could end your life. In January 1813, George Mellor, one of the few captured leaders, was hanged. A few months later, fourteen other poor people were executed. Their crime was to attack the property of Joseph Ratcliffe, a wealthy industrialist. Never before in England have so many people ended up on the gallows on a single day and never afterwards. Only a few people today remember James Towle: In 1816, he was the last «machine wrecker» who was hanged. He yelled a hymn to Luddism when he fell through the gallows trap door. A funeral procession of 3,000 people sang the end of it instead of him.

For Karl Marx, who is notorious for his dogmatism, the Luddites were doomed to failure. According to him, they were backward naysayers who confused cause and effect. Marx believed that it's not the machine that steals jobs, but the capitalist conditions under which it's used. He concluded that the workers should not fight the machines, but seize them and establish a just form of economy. But he overlooked the fact that technology is not neutral. It forces its use in a certain way and promotes inequality and autocratic structures. After all, the industrial revolution created the working class, which he considered as the only revolutionary force. He didn't imagine that within the capitalist system mechanization could reach a level that would make the worker completely dispensable. He was in no way a Luddite, but a great admirer of technology. During a walk in London, Marx caught a glimpse of the future. In August 1849, he discovered an electric model railway in the window of a fashion shop. He hurried home to note that the age of steam would soon be over. Like King Steam changed the world, the electric spark would trigger a new technological revolution. He told his friend Friedrich Engels: «Now the problem is solved – the consequences are indefinable. » At least with the second part of this statement he was apparently right. Marx emphasized that the development of technology not only brings about changes in one industrial sector, but in many others as well. E.g., new means of production require new means of transport, like ships and railways. As a result, the steel and mining industry, the engineering, and others were pushed forward.

The Luddites did not succeed in creating a permanent movement. It was a rebellion with a mythical leader and without a centralized organization. Their aim was not political, but social, and moral. They did not want to take power, but to redirect the dynamics of an unleashed industrialization. The Luddites rarely issued any philosophical statements. Instead, they wrote threatening letters to the industrialists or composed ballads on the victories of Ned Ludd. They were pursuing an unusual cause: to negotiate at eye level with the new industrialists. An impossible endeavor. Yet they remain a powerful symbol as machines continued to destroy jobs. Their questions are still relevant today. Are there any boundaries for the greed of the industrialists? Is it possible to withstand new technologies or work processes if they harm the society? What are the social consequences of technical violence?

Today the term «Luddite» is used to discredit critics of the technological progress as technophobic. They would not be savvy enough to adequately appreciate the potential of new technologies. In fact, the original Luddites were skilled English workers and their worries were justified. In the end, it turned out that they had a point. The machines and factories awarded their owners richly. But hundreds of thousands of skilled craftsmen became unemployed. These people poured into the rapidly growing industrial cities. This influx was exacerbated by the rural exodus of impoverished peasants, victims of the progress in the agrarian sector. The surplus of labor resulted in a massive wave of impoverishment. During an unprecedented economic boom, millions of people suffered grinding poverty.

London was the most modern city in the world at that time. More than 3.2 million people crowded the city and its suburbs. One of them was the very same stateless and often broke failed revolutionary from Prussia: Karl Marx. Marx lived in London from 1849 and worked as European political correspondent for the New York Daily Tribune. During this time he gathered documents on the living conditions in England, especially the excesses and abuses of child labor in the textile industry. In his major work on political economy, Das Kapital, he wrote in 1867: «Children of nine or ten are dragged from their squalid beds at four a.m. and compelled to work until ten, eleven, or twelve at night, their limbs wearing away, their frames dwindling, their faces whitening. »

Such factories were built all over England. Slums spread in the big cities. Their inhabitants lived under miserable conditions. Many families dwelt in an attic or a damp cellar. Sometimes five people shared a bed. Property speculators raised houses fast and so close that they robbed each other of light. There was no running water nor a sewage system. Earth holes in the courtyard served as toilets, cleaned from time to time with wheelbarrows. A civil servant reported that the houses were so dirty, damp, and crumbling that you wouldn't let a horse live there. After visiting Manchester, the French historian Alexis de Tocqueville described the city as a «fetid sewer,» a «dirty pool,» in which «civilized people are returned to the beasts.»

The factory system demanded inhumanly long working hours of more than twelve hours per day from the workers. Except for the sleep breaks, there was not much left of their time. Many of these descriptions remind me to today's slums in Mumbai, Manila or Nairobi. The people in the slums of London or Manchester, as well as their successors today, were not victims of global impoverishment and scarcity, but victims of an unprecedented increase in wealth: «During the industrial revolution, the fruits of automation were first used solely to enrich the owners of the machines. Workers were often treated as cogs in the machine, to be used up and thrown away,» said the computer book publisher Tim O'Reilly.

The hellish factory system, its cruel working conditions, the stinking fumes, poisonous waste water, and lack of hygiene took its toll: The workers at the beginning of industrialization generally lived in worse conditions and had a shorter life expectancy than the average medieval peasant. Epidemics spread like fires. In October 1831, cholera broke out for the first time in the north-east of England.

Wages stagnated at such low levels that people suffered physical degeneration. Between 1830 and 1860, the average height of English soldiers sunk by two centimeters. Their health worsened so dramatically that the British army administration sounded the alarm. Infant mortality in all the major industrial cities of Europe reached alarming levels. It took many generations before the poor got their share to some extent of the prosperity they created, almost the entire first century in which capitalism began its ruinous march. It was not until 1880, that the wage level in England and on the continent slowly began to rise. And the one percent certainly did not share their wealth voluntarily. This phase, in which the living conditions of the common people gradually improved, lasted only short. It ended for the moment with the outbreak of the World War I.

LATE BLOOMER

«The greatest of America's homegrown religions – greater than Jehovah's Witnesses, greater than the Church of Jesus Christ of Latter-Day Saints, greater even than Scientology – is the religion of technology. » – Nicholas Carr

Compared to Europe, America was a late bloomer and lacked twenty or thirty years behind in its industrial development. Prior to the Civil War, it was an agricultural country, a land of small farms, small towns, and small businesses. Farmers and artisans produced for subsistence and the local markets. The transformation from a rural to an urban industrial society began with the construction of a dense railway network. Within forty years, it expanded from about 35,000 to over 200,000 miles. In the same period, import doubled, and exports tripled. The abundance of natural resources such as coal, iron, minerals, oil, and gold favored this development. In 1890, industrial production had already twice the value of agriculture, and the USA had become the strongest capitalist power. The change was first felt in vibrant places such as Los Angeles and San Francisco, where the first economic and political centers in Western America emerged. Stories of modern and pompous lives attracted innumerable settlers. Despite a massive influx of migrants, the country was constantly short of labor. Machines and equipment were needed that saved time and labor. Many migrants came from more advanced European countries and from a variety of professions. Their dexterity and creativity were priceless. It was an era of inventions that founded the American belief in technological progress.

America is not only the home of technical obsession, it's also the home of fundamental doubt about it. Henry David Thoreau was an eccentric – a nerd. But he was not seeking fulfillment in technical progress, he was seeking it in nature. In 1845, he made an experiment: On a lake plot in an extensive forest near the small town of Concord, Massachusetts, he built a simple house by his own strength and own means to live in it off the grid for a few years. Thoreau was an escapist, for a limited time only, who was looking for an attentive and conscious way of life. But Thoreau discovered something completely different. Concorde, where he was born and where he spent most of his life, was suddenly connected to the rail network. «The whistle of the locomotive penetrates my woods summer and winter, sounding like the scream of a hawk sailing over some farmer's yard, informing me that many restless city merchants are arriving within the circle of the town, » he wrote. Thoreau saw more than a technical development in the railway. He sensed a tremendous social change. Not only you could get everywhere now, but to make the trains run, different people must work at different places on the same project. The individual was no longer autonomous. In every area of life it is connected with other people and with machines. Thoreau didn't believe that technology can improve inner human nature. Rather, he saw feared that humans would become slaves of technology. The individual, as a part of the machinery, was reduced to their market value. And instead of serving all people, technological progress enriches only a few and crushes the masses. Humans would alienate themselves from their spiritual roots, he warned prophetically.

In 1851, Thoreau witnessed the construction of a telegraph line. Of course, he didn't see any use in it: «We are in great haste to construct a magnetic telegraph from Maine to Texas; but Maine and Texas, it may be, have nothing to communicate. » Aside from his doubts, Thoreau enjoyed the sound of «the string of the telegraph harp. » In his diaries, he explained: «We have no need to refer to music and poetry to Greece for an origin now. (...) The world is young and music is its infant voice. »

Samuel Morse was the driving force behind the telegraph. Morse was neither a technician nor a scientist, but a painter. He wasn't even untalented, but it didn't earn him money. He built his first telegraph in 1837 from the rest of an easel. The device still lacked the technical elegance. A clockwork pulled a strip of paper through the apparatus, and a pen attached to it drew a line on the paper. When an electric impulse came, the pen flickered and a spike appeared in the line on the paper. To send a message, you had to search for the words in a number list and enter the numbers digit by digit. The recipient had to count the spikes on the paper and look up the meaning of the numbers. For example «214-36-2-58-112-04-01837» means «Successful attempt with telegraph, September 4, 1837. » The system was a bit complicated. Much too complicated, thought his assistant Alfred Vail and created a system of simple short-long impulses, dots and dashes. Thus, he introduced the binary system into mechanical engineering. It's still the basic architecture of all modern data-processing machines. Today we call Vail's system «Morse alphabet» because Morse was not quite as good at inventing as Vail but much better at self-marketing.

Prior to the telegraph, information could only travel as fast as the fastest means of transport available. In 1860, that was the Pony Express. It transported documents with 153 intermediate stations, 80 couriers, 500 horses, and 200 grooms over a distance of 2,000 miles across North America.

If all went well, the horsemen needed ten days for a tour. Bill Cody – Buffalo Bill – was the most famous of them all. After only one and a half years, the expensive service was discontinued because the Western Union completed the first electric transcontinental telegraph line between Missouri and California. With the telegraph, news could now pass from one place to another without any delay. Oceans, deserts, and mountains were no longer obstacles. For the first time, the speed of information was much faster than that of people or goods. All you needed was a cable.

The idea that you could be up to date about anything and everyone in the world around the clock was both exciting and disturbing. Perplexity was the common reaction to the telegraph. The New York Herald declared it «the new age of miracles.» According to the New York Times, this new age would pulverize those who resisted its blessings: «Those who do not mix with this movement – those who do not become part of this movement – those who do not go on with this movement – will be crushed into more impalpable powder than ever was attributed to the car of Juggernaut. Down on your knees and pray.» Does this sound familiar? We hear the same about digital technologies. The Utica Gazette predicted that the telegraph would bring an «immense diminution» in crime and bring democracy and justice into the world. «Fly, you tyrants, assassins and thieves, you haters of light, law, and liberty, for the telegraph is at your heels,» it wrote. It has not quite worked out that way. Instead, many unscrupulous individuals have found new ways to commit crimes. We owe the word 'wire fraud' those days.

The customers' satisfaction depended to a large extent on the waiting times for the transmission of a telegram. To cope with peak traffic, the companies hired many telegraphers. These operators spent much of their time with the new communication network. During slow times, they chatted with each other, played virtual checkers, told jokes or the newest gossip from the neighborhood. They organized virtual meetings and discussion boards, creating the first virtual community, held together without physical presence only through communication. To signal faster, they developed abbreviations that remained an unintelligible secret code for outsiders. With this code you also could indicate moods, very much like with ASCII or emoticons today. LID meant «Poor operator» (Licensed Idiot), 73 meant «Best regards,» Nalime meant «Will only do what is absolutely necessary.» Thoughts chopped up into syllables.

The work required concentration but was not physically demanding. A large part of the telegraph operators were women. They worked more accurately and were more customer-friendly than men. In the telegraph community, it was not uncommon for man and woman to work together on the both sides of the wire. Any telegrapher using the line had access to all messages of the others and even had to listen to them to figure out when the line was free again so that they could send their own messages. Soon these rural telegraph lines were called «party lines. » People flirted without ever having seen each other. Friendships developed and virtual love affairs. Some relations even led to marriage. Around 1866, the Union Telegraf decided to restrict the private use of telegraph lines, which indicates what was really going on there.

Telegraphy and commerce thrived in a virtuous circle. The cable companies were pioneers of a new managerial capitalism, in which capital and control as well as investors and managers were separated from each other. According to Karl Marx the telegraph was transforming the whole world into a single stock exchange. It also created a new type of information gathering company. In mid-19th century, the three big news agencies were founded: Agence Havas in 1832 in Paris, Wolff's Telegraphisches Bureau in 1849 in Berlin and Reuter's Telegram Company in 1851 in London. Their business was the collecting, managing, and marketing of information. These three companies controlled the world market. Each company collected news from predefined regions in the world and exchanged it with the other two companies. This agreement created a cartel that existed until the outbreak of World War II.

The high costs of telegrams and of the global networks of correspondents not only accelerated the economic concentration of the journalism sector, but also had linguistic and stylistic consequences. The encoding of letters into electrical pulses resulted in long pulse chains, even when the messages were short. Telegraph cables were expensive to install and maintain, and their transmission capacities were low. This made communication by telegraph expensive, and the cost increased with the length of the message. Thus, the aim was to achieve shortness and efficiency. A message should get straight to the point and not contain any linguistic ornaments or unnecessary annotations. Grammar and punctuation were negotiable. Shortness was more important than proper grammar, politeness, or protocol. News were delivered without explanation and discussion. Stories were broken up into small chunks and lacked background information. That made it difficult to grasp the overarching connections between events. Some telegrams were downright incomprehensible, creating confusion and misconceptions. A problem that still exists in the media today.

When the telegraph and railroad networks emerged, the understanding of communication and of thinking changed. Now, the «news» was a value in itself. It shapes the consciousness of the recipient, even if the message turns out to be false or only half-true. Alexander von Humboldt called it the «wiring of thoughts. » The newspaper became the mass medium as we understand it today: available to everyone, cheap, fast, up to date. While books are the result of laborious work with various phases of planning and realization, the telegraph created the «raging reporter» and an endless stream of news. The value of information was no longer measured by its function for social and political action, but only by its novelty. Wars, crimes, crashes, fires, floods became «the news of the day. »

«Message follow each other in quick succession. Joy spreads on the track of sorrow. The arrival of a ship, news of a revolution, or a battle, the price of pork, the state of foreign and domestic markets, missives of love, the progress of courts, the success or discomfiture of disease, the result of elections, and an innumerable host of social, political and commercial details, all chase each other over the slender and unconscious wires which carry the heaviest intelligence with as much alacity and unconcern, as the news of a wedding, or the rhapsodies of a lover, » complained the New York Times in 1852.

A new type newspapers emerged – the tabloid pres or «Yellow Press. » Their aim was to deliver the latest and most exclusive news to its readers as fast as possible and ahead of the competition. Confronted with a sensationalist press, Thoreau groused: «Is there any dust which their conduct does not lick, and make it fouler still with its slime? »

The high prices prevented 99 percent of the population from sending telegrams. So they invented the phone, then the radio, then the e-mail. The seafaring industry continued to use the Morse code for some time. But on July 12, 1999, the telegraph was declared lifeless, and America's last commercial Morse transmitter went off the air.

CLOCK WHISPERERS

«If a man does not keep pace with his companions, perhaps it is because he hears a different drummer. » – Henry David Thoreau

«... and likewise all parts of the system must be constructed with reference to all other parts, since, in one sense, all the parts form one machine. » – Thomas Edison

When William Shakespeare wrote his play Julius Caesar, he made a slight mistake. When Caesar asked for the time, Brutus answered: «Caesar, 'tis strucken eight. » This answer presupposes a technical invention – the mechanical clock – that was not yet known in ancient Rome. No matter which device they used to measure time, it could certainly not strike. Until the Middle Ages, most people didn't even know a clock. They experienced the passage of time in a fundamentally different way than we do today. The rhythm of nature determined daily life. The eternal cycle of sunrise and sunset defined the working day. To define a specific time, people said: «when the rooster crowed, » «at nightfall, » «after sunset, » or «at midnight. » Most people were farmers, and these general pattern of time measurement were completely sufficient. The German historian Peter Borscheid wrote: «In the beginning there was slowness. The agrarian world did not know haste. Why hurry when the almighty nature never gives up her own slow pace of growth? » In the Middle Ages, Christian-Jewish teleology reinforced a different perception of time and introduced a quite random structuring that didn't depend on nature.

In 529, the Italian abbot Benedict of Nursia had founded the Benedictine Order. He specified exact times for seven daily prayers, each had a particular meaning. He further introduced a strict time frame for reading the Scriptures, meals, work, and sleep. With the necessity to ring the bells for prayer at exact times, the monks became increasingly concerned with the construction of instruments to measure time more precisely and in smaller units. To do so, they have used candle clocks, water clocks, sundials, and finally they invented mechanical clocks.

The «Munich Computus» is an important source for medieval concepts of time. The term Computus derives from the Latin verb «computare, » meaning «to calculate. » In the Middle Ages, it meant generally «calculation» and specifically the «calculating of time. » The «Munich Computus» begins with the question: «What is time? » The author delivers the answer himself: «Time is the interval extending from the beginning to the end» – a remarkably telling definition. Now people believed that the course of the world would follow a predetermined path from its creation to its end. They began to perceive time as linear.

Friedrich Nietzsche harbored a strong aversion to Christian destiny mentality. He presented his idea of eternal recurrence in a sharp contrast to Christian teleology, or any teleology (from the Greek 'telos' – 'end', 'purpose' or 'goal'). The cyclical understanding of time was for him the highest affirmation of life. Throughout the Middle Ages, people waited for the apocalypse. «The nature of the End had been revealed by Christ and through the Apocalypse of John, the nature of the future before the End had not, » notes historian Elizabeth Boyle.

The harbingers of doom also invented a new sin: wasting time. Wasting time became a «sin against the Holy Ghost, » as Aldous Huxley put it. Though the Bible doesn't mention it, you would surely go to hell for it. The monk Domenico Cavalca even doubted that those people who waste time deserve to be regarded as human beings and compared them with animals.

With the beginning industrialization around 1800, our lifestyle accelerated. Steam engines, railways, and telegraphs boosted production and consumption. People freed themselves from their dependence on natural rhythms and for the first time experienced the collective rush of speed. They began to follow «the rhythm of spinning and printing machines, railways and steamships [...] to think and act with their speed, to live according to their heartbeat,» explains Borscheid.

Leo Marx, Professor of the History and Philosophy of Science, noted that Henry David Thoreau saw the watch as the epitome of the capitalist system: By chaining production to a stopwatch, the stopwatch chained the industrial apparatus to the consciousness of the individual. The imperative of the rationality of progressive industrialism turned the old time rhythms into an abstract system. The division of the day by the clock submitted human perception to a mathematical scheme.

In 1882, the earnest young engineer Frederick Winslow Taylor began a series of fateful experiments in the Midvale Steel plant in Philadelphia. Armed with a stopwatch, he aimed to figure the optimal workflow for labor processes. He considered the workers «phlegmatic and stupid. » «College-bred men» should do all brain work in the «planning department, » strictly separated from the manual labor of the workers. Each job should be broken down into a sequence of small steps, and the management should define the exact amount of work in advance. Though he was using the term «science» inflationary, his «scientific» methods were a rather crude set of instruments. The definition of «the one best way» was based on the experience of the best workers. Then the «apostle of efficiency» modified it rather arbitrarily. It's an obvious contradiction that his «system, » as he liked to call it, was partly based on the cumulative experience of the workers, but at the same time denied them any ability to organize their work.

His method never fully succeeded. It was too strict and ignored human factors important for business success. His system degraded workers to interchangeable mechanical components and discharged them of any creative or intellectual effort. The authoritarian management replaced the judgement of the skilled individual craftsman with the rules of «science. » The strong specialization and low responsibility decreased the identification of the employees with the working place. They lacked any motivation to contribute to improvements with their ideas. The strict separation of labor and management created a huge administrative bottleneck. Taylor focused on the process instead of defining and controlling reasonable goals. There was no feedback of an error to the person who caused it, which led to high scrap rates. When the workers met the goals, profits increased. But the payment system did not reward them. Taylor claimed that payments are not subject to negotiation between employers and employees. Instead, wage conflicts and other issues should be solved – you guessed it – scientifically. He even believed that his teachings could be applied in every aspect of public life – in the churches, universities, and governments.

Taylorism became synonymous with work stress, surveillance, and disempowerment. A century later, we have plans for workflows in which even hand washing is meticulously timed. In 2008, Nicholas Carr concluded: «Taylor's system is still very much with us; it remains the ethic of industrial manufacturing. And now, thanks to the growing power that computer engineers and software coders wield over our intellectual lives, Taylor's ethic is beginning to govern the realm of the mind as well. »

Henry Ford applied Taylor's principles in a modified form in his factories by combining the division of labor with mechanization. For his goal to motorize humankind, he had to reduce production costs, and thus, he introduced the assembly line in his factories. But the assembly line work was meaningless and monotonous. The workers quit so quickly that replacing them was almost impossible. In other factories, ten to twelve-hour days at a daily wage of one dollar were still the norm. In Ford's factories nobody had to work more than eight hours a day, five days a week. Ford believed that well-rested and focused workers would perform at their best – a new concept. From 1914, he paid a minimum wage of five dollars a day and a few years later even six. He employed many workers who were not hired elsewhere at the time, such as African Americans or immigrants from Eastern Europe. His plan worked.

For many unskilled workers, social security and time for the family were more important than a meaningful job. But the workers entered a system of strict control. The processes in Ford's factories were standardized and rationalized down to the last detail. The manufacture of the Tin Lizzy, e.g., was split into 84 steps. Everyone could master each these steps after an only short training. A worker performed the same operations every 79 seconds. Henry Ford described in My Life and Work: «We expect the men to do what they are told. The organization is so highly specialized and one part is so dependent upon another that we could not for a moment consider allowing men to have their own way. Without the most rigid discipline we would have the utmost confusion. »

Rigid rules deeply interfered with the private lives of his workers, e.g. how they should furnish their homes, what they should eat, and how they should spend their leisure time. Those who did not conform to his ideal of an American worker were disciplined with wage deductions. Obsessed with control, he created a 'service department', headed by the shady ex-boxer Harry Bennett. Bennet turned the department into a private army. It not only spied on workers, but also brutally attacked trade unionists and peaceful strikers. For its brutality, the troop was – secretly – called «Ford's Gestapo» in the mid-thirties. A 1928 article about Ford in the New York Times headlined «The Mussolini of Highland Park. » Likely neither Ford nor Benett were offended by that.

Ford was a friend of Germany since the twenties, when his company competed with General Motors for the lucrative German market. Hitler himself admired the American way of mass production, and he particularly admired Henry Ford, whose anti-Semitic writings inspired him.

The assembly line was not a technological revolution. Ford used known technology from the stockyards of Chicago, the largest meat factory in the world. At the beginning of the 20th century, it stretched over an area of 475 acres. It was a city of its own with a bank, a hotel, a steam power plant, and an electricity plant, a boiler making facility, a large cooperage, a lard can factory, and a soapbox factory, 13,000 pens, fifty miles of road, 130 miles of track, ninety miles of pipelines, 10,000 hydrants. And animals as far as the eye could see. 75,000 pigs, 20,000 cattle, just as many sheep – penned up in small stalls.

Every few minutes a horde of animals was pushed into a dark hall. Once there, a hell of a squeak and howling began. Then it was quickly quiet. The smell of burnt flesh and bone meal lingered over the place – the smell of death. Literally hell on earth. Every day, an army of unskilled workers dismantled thousands of animal corpses, separating skin from flesh, bones from waste – a work process that has been known to humankind for thousands of years. A traditional butcher dismembered one cow per day and charged three dollars for that. In Chicago's slaughterhouses, the process took only a quarter of an hour and cost 42 cents. Industrialized death is as brutal as it is efficient.

In 1906, the young writer Upton Sinclair published his novel The Jungle. He had spent seven weeks undercover in the slaughterhouses. The workers, he concluded, had to work at a speed as if the devil was breathing down their necks. The work was dangerous: They had to handle their knives so quickly that the blades often cut into their fingers. Their hands soon turned into a raw lump of meat. No one could survive here for longer than a few years. There were no precautions. Injured people were simply replaced by fresh employees. Any human quality that was not useful for the machine was doomed to die. The slaughterhouses not only processed cows and pigs, but also the employed men, women, and children.

The assembly line stands for efficiency and an unleashed enthusiasm for technology. And for exploitation and despair. Ford's rationalization set a precedent. Work became a commodity, and the worker entered into a futile competition with the machine. Mass production created an unseen prosperity. The masses earned higher wages, which they could then spend on mass products. The consumer society was born, which still influences everyday culture. Charlie Chaplin found an impressive symbol of the dehumanization of industrial production in Modern Times: His famous Tramp suffers a mental breakdown as a result of the stress caused by his work. In his autobiography he noted that the film was actually inspired by reports of young workers from the Ford factories.

DAWN OF THE DIGITAL AGE

«But they are useless. They can only give you answers. » – Pablo Picasso on computers in 1964

For 36 days and nights election workers had counted punched card ballots, examined them with magnifying glasses, or held them up to bright neon lights to determine whether a legitimate vote had been cast. In December 2000, the Supreme Court ruled: The 537 vote advantage of Republican George W. Bush over his Democratic rival Al Gore in Florida is valid. Bush had won the Electoral College and became the 43rd President of the United States of America. The election was problematic not only because of the narrow lead. A 100,000 votes were declared invalid, since the ballots were not punched out properly and could be counted one way or the other. The history of punched cards began in the 19th century. They have been used in barrel organs and mechanical pianos, e.g. Around 1805, the French inventor Joseph-Marie Jacquard developed the first mechanical loom that could be programmed by punched card. Thus, «he was the first to separate the software from the hardware, » wrote the historian Hans G. Helms. Jacquard's loom inspired the polymath Charles Babbage. In the 1830s, he designed a calculating machine based on punched cards. His «Analytical Machine» mastered the four basic arithmetic operations. The programming language was written by Babbages' employee Ada Lovelace. She was the daughter of Anne Isabella Noel-Byron and the English poet Lord Byron. Anne was a hobby mathematician, Byron called her «Princess of Parallelograms. » Shortly after Ada's birth, their marriage ended. Anne feared that Ada could inherit the stormy and unpredictable temperament of her father. So she provided her daughter a scientific education. Ada developed a love for machines, which later formed the basis of her friendship with Charles Babbage. In 1848, at his request, Ada translated a French article about his Analytical Engine into English, adding her own explanations. The eight detailed notes are three times the length of the original article and explain what Ada saw as the potential of the machine. She understood that it was more than a numerical calculator and sketched a machine that could also process musical notes, letters, and images. Thus, she was 100 years ahead of computer science.

Data storage via punched cards began its triumphal march with the American census of 1890. In the late 19th century, the USA experienced a massive population growth due to the rising number of immigrants. The government therefore demanded a census every 10 years. The necessity of this census derives from the Constitution. Since the number of seats in the House of Representatives depends on the size of the population, it must be verified on a regular basis. The first census of 1750 was conducted by U.S. marshals literally by hand because they had no paper on which they could write the results. Between 1790 and 1840, the inhabitants were listed by households and categorized according to different characteristics, e.g. «white male, » under «16, » etc. The tenth census of 1880 covered more than 200 attributes to determine the status, property, household, and skin color. An army of 1,495 clerks was employed to count the questionnaires that were cartloaded to Washington in freight trains. The work was tedious beyond belief, prompting a journalist to write: «The only wonder . . . is, that many of the clerks who toiled at the irritating slips of tally paper in the census of 1880 did not go blind and crazy. » The analysis took almost seven years. The results became available when the eleventh census was almost due, and the data was no longer up to date.

One of the clerks was the entrepreneur, inventor and engineer Herman Hollerith. Born in 1860 in the state of New York to German immigrants, Hollerith showed an early interest in technical problems. To speed up the census, he invented the first commercially successful data processing device. With his punched card tabulator you could store information by punching holes in certain locations on a paper card. Hollerith's machine made it possible to process the 11th census of 1890 in only two and a half years. It cost a total of 11.5 million dollars. But without the Hollerith system, it would have been an estimated 5 million dollars more. Hollerith knew the machines of Jacquard and Babbage. He was not a deep thinker like the Babbage. But he was practical where Babbage was not. An observation in a train kicked off the development of the Hollerith machines: «I was traveling in the West and I had a ticket with what I think was called a punch photograph. [The conductor] punched out a description of the individual, as light hair, dark eyes, large nose, etc. So you see, I only made a punch photograph of each person. » Hollerith added two innovations. He used electricity for evaluation, and he translated information into a binary system of zeros and ones – power on, power off. His real achievement was combining these elements together in one machine. The German journalist Robert Jungk described the principle: «If these cards ran between a series of small electrically charged metal brushes, wherever the brushes made contact through a hole it closed an electric circuit, which set into motion an adding machine and an automatic typewriter. » This is how the information technology industry came into being.

A journalist noted, «The machine is patented, but as no one will ever use it but governments, the inventor will not likely get very rich. » But Hollerith turned out to be a quite savvy businessman too, and he found a new way of marketing his invention. Instead of selling the machines, he leased 56 machines to the census authorities. He presumed that the system, once established, would become indispensable to them. The initial rent of 1000 dollars per year per machine was very attractive; a service contract was already included. The clever engineer still made a profit. He could lease the machines several times because not all machines were in use at the same time. Yet the most lucrative source of income was the punched cards. They were needed in huge quantities, and since they could not be reused, they provided a steady money flow. The production price for 1,000 punched cards was only 30 cents. They were sold for almost 1 dollar per thousand. Hollerith later reduced the rent for the machines to 500 dollars and finally leased them for free.

But when the census ended in 1893, he was left with a warehouse full of census machines. The next census of 1900 was still seven years ahead. To maintain the income of his business, he needed to find new customers. As the industrialization accelerated, the amount of data could no longer be processed without machines. Railway companies had to manage their freight, insurances their customers, factories their orders, wages, and costs. With some small changes his invention could be used by other American businesses. Hollerith machines found their way into administrative institutions and companies everywhere. They were used in accounting, in human resources, for recording financial transactions.

In 1896, he founded the Tabulating Machine Company. It became a great success and made Hollerith a wealthy man. In 1911, he decided to sell it. He was fifty-one, his health was failing, and the business grew above his head. The buyer was Charles Flint. He merged Hollerith's company with three other companies: the Computing Scale Company, which produced calculating scales, the International Time Recording Company, which produced clocks, and the Bundy Manfacturing Company, a producer of coffee grinders. The name for the new company was Computing-Tabulating-Recording Company (CTR).

On the eve of the World War I, in May 1914, CTR appointed an ambitious new general manager, the 40-year-old salesman Thomas J. Watson senior. When Watson became Chief Executive Officer of CTR he changed the name of the company to the more impressive sounding International Business Machines – IBM. During the Great Depression, IBM was much better off than the average of the American companies. To implement Roosevelt's New Deal, the government and the companies required hundreds of punched card machines. With the introduction of social security in 1935, the government became IBM's largest customer. The social program of the 1930s could never have taken place if IBM had not developed some machines to carry it out. Watson was a supporter of Roosevelt and became a special advisor to the president. He «served unofficially as Roosevelt's representative in New York,» Watson jr. Remembered. And Roosevelt once remarked, «I handle ,em in Washington and Tom handles ,em in New York.» Roosevelt's election marked also the beginning of the career of George Horace Gallup, the pioneer of market research. In 1936, after interviewing some thousand eligible voters, Gallup had predicted that Roosevelt would win the presidential election. He was, of course, using Hollerith machines.

Punched card machines were also used for cruel purposes. In 1910, Willy Heidinger, an enthusiastic supporter of the Nazi regime, founded the Deutsche Hollerith Maschinen Gesellschaft, known under its acronym DEHOMAG. In the 1920, the DEHOMAG could no longer pay the license fees due to the high inflation. To compensate for that, Heidinger transferred 90 percent of the shares to IBM, and the DEHOMAG became a direct subsidiary of IBM. After the NSDAP came to power in 1933, the German IBM division was given a monopoly over data processing for German offices. Wehrmacht and SS belonged to their customers. Already in March 1933, the first concentration camp for political prisoners was set up in Dachau, Bavaria. Despite international calls for a boycott, IBM continued its business relations with the regime. In his book IBM and the Holocaust: The Strategic Alliance between Nazi Germany and America's Most Powerful Corporation the investigative journalist Edwin Black details the business relationships of IBM with the German government during the 1930s and World War II. A key message of the book is that IBM's technology helped at all stages of the persecution of Jewish people. In a first step, punched cards helped to collect all the information needed to identify them. On 12 April 1933, the Nazis announced a census in which they would use IBM's punched card machines. The census-listing developed by IBM Germany included the «race» in the sense of the fascist ideology. But it also included the bloodline over generations. Now Nazis could identify Jewish people by their ancestry. The estimated number of 400,000 to 600,000 Jewish people increased to 2,000,000. So the Nazis could remove Jewish people from all areas of public life.

IBM in America not only knew this, as Black claims, but promoted and supported it. In 1937, Hitler even granted Thomas Watson a private audience and awarded him a high German medal. Watson sent it back in 1939. Black points out that Watson was neither a fascist nor an anti-Semite, but a ruthless profiteer. The authoritarian German state offered lucrative opportunities. Watson recognized and used this without scruple. Even as war approached, Watson fought to keep IBM in the Reich.

With the occupation of Europe, censuses took place in the conquered countries. The German IBM branch played an important role there too. IBM's technology helped to carry out the mass expulsions of Jews from their homes to the ghettos. Later they helped to organize the transport of millions of people to the concentration camps. There were Hollerith departments in most concentration camps. They registered arrivals, allocated slave labor, and kept records of dead prisoners. Punched cards were also used to register soldiers and logistics in armaments production. But to say that the Holocaust would not have happened without IBM would be a false statement. David Martin Luebke teaches history at Bennington College in Vermont. Until April 1993 he served as staff historian with the United States Holocaust Memorial Museum in Washington D.C. He admits:

«The precise role played by punched-card tabulation technology in the bureaucratic apparatus of persecution is still partly speculative, and therefore our conclusions are tentative. ... Director Heidinger's vision of a totalitarian future in which every resident would be monitored and manipulated in a system of «comprehensive surveillance» was shared widely by Nazi party and German state officials. ... It must be emphasized that neither the Jewish Shoah nor the Romani Porrajmos was in any sense caused by the availability of relatively sophisticated census-taking technologies, including punched-card technology. Hitler's preoccupation with racial purity and the escalating radicalization of state policies of persecution, segregation, and coercion after 1933 were sufficient to bring about genocide, with or without punched-card technology. »

IBM's machines were essential for identifying Jewish people. But humans killed them, not machines. For the financial elite and industrial cartels wars were mere market opportunities. They received generous state funding and profited from a crisis-proof sales market. After the war, IBM was able to recover its assets, machines, and profits from Germany with surprising ease. In 1945, the U.S. military spending accounted for about 40% of the gross national product, and IBM got its share. And the best was yet to come. It was in business with exactly those customers who would later use electronic mainframes. For decades, no other computer manufacturer was able to catch up on this lead.

In the late Middle Ages, computer was a job title for people who performed calculations, like astronomers. Later, people who operated the mechanical calculating machines were called computers, a job usually done by women. Today, the term refers to the machine described by the mathematician John von Neumann in the 1940s. The history of computers is in part the history of machines, from the abacus to the code-breaking machines of World War II. Like the 1914-18 war, World War II was not only bloodthirsty, it was a scientific war too. Never before have so many new weapons been developed as in the two great wars of the 20th century. World War I brought us aircraft, poison gas and flamethrowers. World War II brought us nuclear weapons, radar – and significant progress in computer technology. The nuclear threat will never leave us, nor will the computers. The typical nerd was far from being the masculine hero needed in the army. But while the soldiers died in the trenches, the others made stunning careers. Their ingenuity not only produced the most terrible weapons, but ultimately decided who would win the war.

Before WWII, by far most of the American people tended towards isolationism. People still remembered very well the costs of WWI, the war mongering, and war profits of big business. The American intervention was considered a mistake. Now many talked about neutrality. In May 1940, events came thick and fast and the drama of the global war ran its course. German troops invaded the Netherlands, Belgium, and France. That eliminated any doubts in the U.S. about the necessity of mobilization. At the request of Roosevelt, Congress voted for the development of an aircraft industry with an annual output of 50,000 airplanes and an air force of the same size, which was ten times the existing capacity. He further demanded the approval of 1.2 billion dollars for the mobilization program; in July 1940, he asked for another five billion, and by December 1940, more than 10.5 billion dollars had been diverted into defense-related contracts. In June 1940, Roosevelt established the National Defense Research Committee and in 1941 the Office for Scientific Research and Development. Thus, he created the framework to organize the relations between the government, research institutions, the military, and industry.

The driving force behind this alliance was Vannevar Bush, who had ties to all these realms. Bush hailed from a rather humble family background and had to take his career into his own hands early on. His ambitions had no limit but the sky. After gaining experience at General Electrics and a stake in the radio pioneer AMRAD, he founded an armaments company which he euphemistically named Raytheon – the divine ray. The venture prospered and made him wealthy. His early financial independence reinforced his supercilious arrogance, which earned him a reputation for not mincing his words. In 1939, he resigned from his post as Dean of Massachusetts Institute of Technology (MIT) to become President of the influential Carnegie Institution of Washington. Soon after his arrival in Washington, he set the course for his future role in a scientific mobilization of the USA. With the help of Frederic Delano Roosevelt, uncle of Theodore Roosevelt, he got a 15-minute meeting with the president. During the conversation, Bush laid out his plan for a «centralizing agency» in the field of research. Roosevelt shared Bush's concern about the military backwardness of the country and affirmed his plan on a napkin: «OK FDR. » Vannevar Bush became head of the Office of Research and Development, a one-man army reporting only to the president. «No American has had greater influence in the growth of science and technology than Vannevar Bush, » wrote MIT president Jerome Wiesner later. According to Wiesner, Bush's most important decision was to funnel the government spending not into government-run labs, but corporate research centers and hybrid labs combining government, academia and industry.

Bush was also the brain behind the atomic bomb. For years, he had worked for the Manhattan Project without the knowledge of the public, or even his own wife. Not least because of his influence, the Americans feared that they would lose the race for the first atomic bomb to the Germans. But in fact there was no order to build an atomic bomb in Germany. Rather, they were fooled by the Nazis' megalomaniacal rhetoric. In December 1938, the German chemist Otto Hahn had succeeded in splitting uranium. Scientific articles described the enormous amounts of energy released when shattering atomic nuclei. Hahn received the Nobel Prize in 1945. But since he was imprisoned in a British internment camp that year, he could not take it that year. Hahn was meticulous and persistent. Shaking hands was taboo for him. His employees were only allowed to touch the door handles with toilet paper. In his Berlin laboratory, he paid scrupulous attention to cleanliness. It was not allowed to borrow the chair of a colleague. There were special chairs for employees working in highly radioactive environments and for those in low-level radioactive environments. But he was not concerned about the health of his colleagues, he rather wanted to avoid interference during his experiments.

Scientists who had emigrated from Germany in the years after Hitler's seizure of power reacted to Hahn's discovery with concern and fear. Soon there was talk of a super bomb. Hungarian researchers Leo Szilard, Eugene Wigner and Edward Teller, the later father of the hydrogen bomb, warned that such a weapon in the hands of the Nazis would be devastating. In the summer of 1939, the three men met with Albert Einstein, who was already a living legend. With his signature, their famous letter to President Roosevelt achieved the desired effect.

In the early 1940s, Roosevelt decided to push forward with the development of the atomic bomb and granted the MIT a contract for several research projects. In 1941, a report from the National Academy of Science on the feasibility of a nuclear bomb landed on Roosevelt's desk. The paper was based on the calculations and imagination of Otto Robert Frisch and Rudolf Peierls, who both worked in England. As scientific advisor to the president, Bush had handed this report over to him. This work was titled Manhattan Project.

The U.S. government provided enormous resources for the development of the first atomic bomb. An entire laboratory city was built in Los Alamos for

125,000 workers, including six current or later Nobel Prize winners. Robert Oppenheimer became the scientific director of the project. When he saw the first detonation of a nuclear bomb, he recalled a line of an ancient Hindu scripture: «Now I am become Death, the destroyer of worlds. » Asked for his thoughts about Sen. Robert Kennedy's efforts to urge President Lyndon Johnson to start talks to stop the spread of nuclear weapons, he answered: «It's 20 years too late. It should have been done the day after Trinity. » It seems like a confession from a remorseful individual. When Otto Hahn learned of the dropping of the atomic bomb on Hiroshima, he suffered a weakness attack. He is reported to have said: «I thank God on my knees that we didn't build the bomb. » Einstein later called the letter to Roosevelt a «big mistake. » It's not known of Bush that he showed any sense of remorse, shame, or guilt. On the contrary. With his limitless ambitions and arrogance, Bush never grew tired of teaching the world lessons.

The MIT was divided into different departments. There was, e.g., the Laboratory for Nuclear Science, which participated in the development of the atomic bomb, and a Servomechanisms Laboratory, where scientists developed control mechanisms for weapon systems. A servomechanism is a system that regulates itself based on its own functioning. Today, you can find these systems almost everywhere, in factories, airplanes, cars, etc. One of the scientists at the MIT was Norbert Wiener, according to the New York Times: «the original computer geek» – a nerd par excellence. His father, Leo Wiener, a professor of Slavic languages at Harvard University, educated Norbert at home with teaching methods he had invented himself. In his very personal autobiographical book Ex-Prodigy Norbert Wiener remembers his youth:

«He would begin the discussion in an easy, conversational tone. This lasted exactly until I made the first mathematical mistake. Then the gentle and loving father was replaced by the avenger of the blood. The first warning he gave me of my unconscious delinquency was a very sharp and aspirated «What! » ... By this time I was weeping and terrified. ... My lessons often ended in a family scene. Father was raging, I was weeping, and my mother did her best to defend me, although hers was a losing battle. She suggested at times that the noise was disturbing the neighbors and that they had come to the door to complain. »

Wiener went to college at the age of 12, studied philosophy, and received his bachelor's degree at 14, then studied biology, and finally mathematics. In 1913, Bertrand Russell wrote about his student Norbert Wiener in a letter to a friend: «At the end of Sept. an infant prodigy named Wiener, Ph.D. (Harvard), aged 18, ... The youth has been flattered, and thinks himself God Almighty – there is a perpetual contest between him and me as to which is to do the teaching. » The polymath showed all the faults of a genius: He was vain, rather blunt, and tactless. But his students adored him, and his colleagues liked him. He worked with the most brilliant minds of his time, and his path was set for a stunning scientific career. His book Cybernetics was the zenith of his scientific career. He was the first to find a definition and theory for the new science. He defined cybernetics as the science of the flow of information in open or closed loops. In this sense, his work is a prelude to major technological developments after the war. «It became the theoretical foundation for computers, microelectronics, and microelectronic-based and computer-controlled automation, » according to the historian Hans Helm.

His most important contribution was to describe the human being as a biological servomechanical system. Like artificial servomechanisms, the human body also strives to maintain or reach a stable state, the equilibrium. American physiologist Walter Cannon had already elaborated on this idea in his 1932 book The Wisdom of the Body. Later McLuhan borrowed heavily from the ideas of Norbert Wiener as he wrote: «The Eskimo is a servo-mechanism of his kayak, the cowboy of his horse, the businessman of his clock, the cyberneticist – and soon the world – of his computer. In short, to the spoils belong the victor. »

Wiener was, of course, aware of the ancient origin and meaning of the term Cybernetics. It's derived from the Greek word «kybernetes» meaning «pilot, » «steersman. » In church terminology, the word kybernesis means the leadership or administration of a church. Later it evolved into the Latin term gubernator and into the English governor. The term «Cyborg» is an abbreviation of the English «cybernetic organism, » which literally means «self-regulating organism. » It became popular in 1960 in the context of space travel. The two physicians Manfred E. Clynes and Nathan S. Kline introduced it into scientific parlance. In an article for NASA they argued that humans should be made fit to survive in space as «self-regulating man-machine systems. »

Wiener also gave the word «feedback» the meaning in which we use it today. He referred to it as a «chain of the transmission and return of information, » i.e. action – feedback signal – new action. Wiener's famous statement that the brain is a computer has created its own fatal feedback. The analogy that our minds operate like a computer has nothing to do with scientific knowledge about the brain, nor with human intelligence or consciousness. It's a modern myth and a sales argument for digital business models.

After the outbreak of the war, Wiener wrote to Vannevar Bush: «I ... hope you can find some corner of activity in which I may be of use during the emergency. » As the son of Jewish immigrants, he wanted to put his scientific skills at the service of the fight against the Nazis. The desire of the American anti-aircraft artillery to shoot fast maneuvering bombers was the key to the development of cybernetics. After the atomic bombing of Hiroshima and

Nagasaki, Wiener was plagued by doubts. On August 6, 1945, by order of President Harry Truman, the U.S. bomber «Enola Gay» dropped the first atomic bomb on inhabited territory. «Little Boy» detonated at 8.16 in the morning over the Japanese city of Hiroshima. Three days later another atomic bomb was dropped on Nagasaki. The two bombs killed immediately more than 80,000 people in Hiroshima and 70,000 in Nagasaki, hundreds of thousands died in the following years from radioactive contamination. Fireballs with a surface temperature of 10,800 degrees Fahrenheit turned Hiroshima and Nagasaki into apocalyptic landscapes. For humanity, it was an epoch break. From now on, the extinction of mankind was a terrifyingly realistic possibility. It would take no more than pressing a button.

Wiener feared that his cybernetics increased the potential for technical destruction. In an open letter he urged his colleagues to make their scientific work available to public and called on them not to sell themselves to the ruling power. He wanted to set an example and to decide from case to case whether the publication of his own research would be a danger to society. We don't know whether Wiener's letter had any impact at all. In his memoirs he reckoned with the scientific elite and the government: «The pressure to use the bomb, with its full killing power, » he wrote, «was not merely great from a patriotic point of view but was quite as great from the point of view of the personal fortunes of people involved in its development. » Wiener did not believe that the dropping of the bomb on Japan, on Asians, was random. «I was acquainted with more than one of these popes and cardinals of applied science, and I knew very well how they underrated aliens of all sorts, particularly those not of the European race. » For finding his conscience and speaking out, Wiener had to pay a price. From then on he was isolated from the research of his time.

In war, when you know the secret plans of your enemy, you have an enormous advantage. Never before the outcome of a war depended so much on information as in World War II. The Germans believed that their communications were completely safe – whereas in reality the Allies were often able to break and decode it without any problems. The Enigma (Greek for «secret») developed by Arthur Scherbius played a special role in technological warfare. It looked like a typewriter with 26 keys (or 29 keys with umlauts). The upper echelons of the Wehrmacht considered it uncrackable, because, depending on the version, there were between tens of billions and more than 150 trillion encryption possibilities. But the Germans had overlooked two important points: First, the machine could not encode a letter as itself. Hence, it was possible to crack the encryption with sophisticated mathematical formulas. Second, there were recurring elements in every message that hinted to the encryption setting.

When the global conflagration began, an atmospheric Victorian estate,

Bletchley Park, became one of the most important bases of the Allied secret services. Bletchley Park was Station X, the tenth station of the British Secret Intelligence Service, center of a worldwide network of listening posts. A group of eccentric thinkers tried to decipher the communications of the enemy here – messages sent by German government agencies, the NSDAP leadership, and the Wehrmacht. But it was the Polish government who first recognized the importance of the Enigma for the German military. Polish cryptologists were able to break into the Enigma system as early as 1932. But after the Wehrmacht attacked Poland, they could not continue the work. Two days after the attack, Great Britain and France declared war on the German Reich.

The British mathematician Alan Turing worked as a decoding specialist at Bletchley Park. Based on the polish groundwork, he developed the Turing Bomb and the first tube computer Colossus, which both served to encrypt German messages. This decoding success remained unknown to the Germans until the end of the war. With his Logical Computing Machine Turing had envisioned a universal calculating machine as a gedankenexperiment. The decisive work from 1937 is entitled On computable numbers with an application to the Entscheidungsproblem. His main idea was to separate software and hardware. According to this, the functioning of a program is dependent on some hardware, but it's not specified on which hardware. The hardware is not important, the inner logic of the program is. He transferred this idea to the human brain as well: If, as some philosophers claim, you can reduce thinking to logical operations, then machines can think, he concluded. Thinking is pure function (software) and does not depend on the medium which thinks, be it an organic brain or a silicon chip (which did not exist at that time). Turing believed that it was possible to build «thinking machines» by the end of the century that could perform almost all human mental operations. He even proposed a test to determine whether the intelligence of a system can be compared to that of a human being. His ideas influenced the mathematician John von Neumann, who, ten years later, developed the computer architecture on which all modern computers are based today.

Turing was not only a brilliant mathematician, he was also a nerd who, e.g., chained his teacup to the heating, so that no one could steal it, and who wore a gas mask while cycling to protect himself from flying pollen. He was as cranky and clumsy in many everyday things as he was ingenious in his science. On June 8, 1954, his cleaning woman found him dead in his house in Wilmslow near Manchester. Next to his bed was a half-eaten apple, likely poisoned with cyanide. Turing was driven to this death by the prejudices and discriminatory laws of his time. Turing was homosexual, and he was open about it. For him it was completely natural and no reason to hide. Herein too, Turing was far ahead of his time. In the narrow-minded milieu of the early

1950s being gay was not only «reprehensible, » relationships between men were also punishable. Turing was sentenced to chemical castration to «heal» his homosexuality. It consisted, bizarrely, of massive infusions of female hormones. His health suffered dramatically, both, mentally and physically. His body feminized and was completely out of balance. The social isolation and the constant surveillance by security forces also weighed on him. His merits at Betchley Park were classified and not made public. So he suffered the lack of recognition for his work.

The true function of Bletchley Park was kept secret until 1967. Although Turing has now been officially rehabilitated, his conviction has not been lifted to this day. «So, on behalf of the British government, and all those who live freely thanks to Alan's work I am very proud to say: we're sorry, you deserved so much better» – with these words the British Prime Minister Gordon Brown tried in 2009 to make up for what had happened to Alan Turing – 55 years after Turing's death.

After the war, the commander-in-chief of the Western Allies and later US president, Dwight D. Eisenhower, described the work of the decoding specialists at Bletchley Park as «decisive for the war. » Historians later calculated that the decoding work of Turing and his team shortened the war by two to four years. With over 50 million war dead, one can imagine how many lives they saved.

Germans are often attributed with some not very flattering characteristics: We are obsessed with punctuality, unfriendly, have no sense of humor, but schadenfreude (i.e. the misery of others cheers us up). Well, there is a grain of truth in every cliché, otherwise it wouldn't exist. Above all we are mocked for our pedantry. Germans love fixed structures and cannot imagine doing things any other way than the rules demand. Not all Germans, but some. This can be annoying, but it also means reliability. Not surprisingly, the taximeter is an invention made in Germany. We owe it to Friedrich Wilhelm Gustav Bruhn. When Bruhn developed it for horse-drawn cabs, the automobile had not yet been invented. Brunhuber's device counted the wheel rotations, so passengers could no longer be overcharged. But he could not claim the fame for himself alone, since the ancient Greeks were faster. In the 1st century AD, the mathematician and engineer Heron of Alexandria described a device to measure large distances. His nickname reveals his talent: mechanicus. His device used a cogwheel construction to drop a ball into a vessel after a specific distance; the number of balls gave the distance and thus the fare. This machine was one of the first analog computers in the world.

Analog computers are fundamentally different from digital computers. Analog computers solve the given problem by using a physical model, an analogon, which follows the same rules. Depending on the design, these can be electrical, mechanical, geometrical, or hydraulic parameters. In contrast to the Turing machine, analog computers are highly specialized computers.

There is no distinction between software and hardware. Their programs are not sequences of arithmetic rules stored in the memory as discrete numbers, but are in the wiring. They cannot do everything digital computers can do. But they can solve specific problems that digital computers have trouble with. In 1928, the serial production of analog calculators started in the USA. Until the 1960s, mostly the military used them, but also scientific institutions and industrial production. In the following decades, however, they were replaced with digital computers which are cheaper, easier to program, and more flexible.

In 1937, the engineer Howard Aiken from Harvard University sketched out a first concept for an electromechanical, program-controlled computer system. Aiken had studied the designs of other inventors and was in particular inspired by the Analytic Engine of Charles Babbage. Until his death in 1871, Babbage had continuously improved the Analytic Engine. But it was never built because of the deep distrust of his contemporaries and the enormous cost. Aiken saw himself in the position to complete the work of Charles Babbage. He turned to IBM for financial support and entered an agreement with the company. The project started in 1939 at IBM's Endicott plant in the state of New York. In 1943, it was tested and named IBM Automatic Sequence Controlled Calculator (ASCC). In February 1944, it was dismantled and rebuilt in the Harvard laboratory. It was a monster weighing 4.3 tons, 16 m long, and consisting of around 76,000 individual parts and 800 kilometers electric wire. The arithmetic instructions were punched into paper tape, and the output was done with punched cards and electric typewriters. From estimated 15,000 dollars, the costs had exploded to over 200,000 dollars. Even for IBM a large sum – so at least the marketing should be right.

IBM boss Watson arrived on August 7, 1944, in Harvard to present the ASCC and hand it over to the University as a gift from IBM. But two egocentrics had met here, and Watson figured that Aiken had stolen him the show. Aiken had already held a press conference the day before at which IBM was hardly mentioned. The New York Times headlined: «Algebra Machine Spurs Research Calling for Long Calculations» and «Harvard Receives Today Device to Solve in Hours Problems Taking So Much Time They Have Never Been Worked Out. » The article was not on the front page, which was devoted to the war in France and the Pacific. Next day, the article «Aiken's Calculator» provided more information. The readers learned that it was invented by Commander Howard Aiken and engineers of IBM. Aiken had managed to make history with the first American mainframe not as IBM ASCC, but as Harvard Mark I. Watson did not like the poor publicity, but couldn't do much about it. He made sure that the next IBM mainframe operated at IBM's New York headquarters.

The Mark I aka ASCC was the first American digital computer, if you count relay computers. It was programmed mainly by two women and two men:

Grace Hopper, Ruth Brendel, Richard Milton Bloch and Robert Campbell. By order of her supervisor Aiken, Grace Hopper had to write a manual. After the confidentiality period expired in 1946, Aiken and Hopper described the computer in three detailed articles in the journal Electrical Engineering. The performance of machine was limited: It needed 0.3 seconds for an addition, a multiplication took six seconds, a division eleven seconds. This prompted many engineers to abandon relay technology and turn to vacuum tubes. John von Neumann was one of the firsts to recognize the significance of these calculating devices for the course of the war. Already in March 1944, before its public presentation, he used the Mark I for calculations for the secret nuclear project. The Mark I operated until the 1950s and was partially dismantled nine years later. Aiken founded the Computation Laboratory in Harvard and constructed three more Mark computers for the U.S. Navy and Air Force without help from IBM.

At about the same time as Aiken was designing his device, John Atanasoff was developing the concept for a vacuum tube computer. In Ames, where he taught mathematics and physics, he used IBM punched card machines for scientific calculations and built himself a small analog computer. Eventually, he wanted to develop a calculating machine that would increase the speed and accuracy of scientific calculations. In the winter of 1937, Atanasoff had the decisive idea. After a trip with his car in the country in Illinois, he was having a drink in a roadhouse. He later recalled: «I had reached the Mississippi River and was crossing into Illinois at a place where there are three cities ... one of which is Rock Island. I drove into Illinois and turned o the highway into a little road, and went into a roadhouse, which had bright lights ... I sat down and ordered a drink ... As the delivery of the drink was made, I realized that I was no longer so nervous and my thoughts turned again to computing machines. »

In 1939, he pitched the idea to his college and received an initial funding of 650 dollars. With the help of his student Clifford Berry, he completed the first prototype in only seven weeks. It already had all the important components of a calculating machine. With further funding Atanasoff and Berry were able to construct a desk sized machine in 1940. The nameless calculator – the title Atanasoff-Berry-Computer or ABC was not introduced until 1966 – had a memory capacity of ca. 3,000 bits and could perform about 30 additions or subtractions per second. Tests showed that the arithmetic unit and the memory worked perfectly. Problems arose only with the input and output system by punched cards. America's entry into the war prevented Atanasoff and Berry from continuing their work, and so the problem remained unsolved. Both were drafted and worked on other military projects. However, the prototype found some use for military applications.

At a scientific conference in Philadelphia in December 1940, John Atanasoff met the 33-year-old John Mauchly, who taught physics at a nearby college. The two men soon discovered their common interest in arithmetic. Like his colleague, Mauchly had built an analog computer, but was dissatisfied with it. Atanasoff told him about his digital computer and invited him to Ames. Mauchly accepted enthusiastically. Their meeting in June 1941 had consequences for computer history. Mauchly could read a manuscript in which Atanasoff sketched the details of his computer. The two researchers met a few more times in Washington in 1943 and 1944. Already in 1942, Mauchly had published the essay The Use of High Speed Vaccum Device for Calculating. Later, Mauchly and John P. Eckert built the ENIAC (Electronic Numerical Integrator and Computer), a tube computer, at the Moore School for Electrical Enineering at the University of Philadelphia.

In May 1943, they signed an army contract for the construction of the ENIAC. Already in 1940, Atanasoff had submitted the manuscript of the ABC to his college for a patent application. But the Iowa State College somehow lost it and later scrapped the computer. This episode of computer history was almost forgotten if not, in 1947, Eckert and Mauchly were dismissed from their university in a dispute over the rights to the ENIAC. They later applied for a patent, which was initially granted in 1964. Atanasoff's role in its development was settled in 1973 after a lengthy court case.

The ENIAC was as huge as an apartment, weighed 27 tons, and did not even have a screen. It required 17,468 electron tubes and 7,200 diodes to operate it. Its electricity consumption was enormous, comparable to that of a small town. It generated a large amount of waste heat, which required cooling. Since almost constantly some tubes failed, the computer was rather unreliable. A group of technicians was assigned to find and replace defective solder joints (there were about 500,000) and burnt-out tubes. Yet compared to its mechanical predecessors the ENIAC processed calculations much faster. It was able to perform around 5,000 operations per second, which was about 1,000 times faster than mechanical computers. By comparison, your smartphone can handle more than 30 billion instructions per second.

The programming of the ENIAC was complicated, as it had to be rewired for each change in the program, a strenuous and demanding task, which was performed by the so-called ENIAC women. The talented women who mastered ENIAC were Francis Betty Snyder Holberton, Betty Jean Jennings Bartik, Kathleen McNulty Mauchly Antonelli, Marlyn Wescoff Meltzer, Ruth Lichterman Teitelbaum and Frances Bilas Spencer. Already in the early 1940s, the U.S. Army had hired female mathematicians and scientists at its research facility in Aberdeen, Maryland. When the USA entered the war in 1942, the army systematically began to recruit women with college degrees, preferably in mathematics. When the war was over, about 80 women worked as «computers» at the Ballistic Research Laboratory. Tragically, the rise of the computers devalued the skills of these women.

The ENIAC was completed right on schedule in autumn 1945 with 50 engineers and electricians in 200,000 working hours for almost half a million dollars. Everything was classified. On 15 February 1946, there was a public «dedication ceremony» with a demonstration of ENIAC's performance. The technology reporter T.R. Kennedy jr. described the hitherto secret computer in an article, but only vaguely indicated what its purpose was: «The machine was used for a problem in nuclear physics. » In fact, ENIAC calculated parameters for the first hydrogen bomb. None of this was allowed to become public, but it wasn't a secret for long.

Despite all confidentiality, John von Neumann visited the New York Times with his colleague Vladimir Zworykin and raved about the fantastic possibilities of the ENIAC. Their aim was to steer enthusiasm for the atomic bomb in war-weary America. The first report that appeared in the New York Times didn't call it ENIAC, but Von Neumann Zworykin device. The «development of a new electronic calculator, reported to have astounding potentialities ... might even make it possible to 'do something about the weather,'» the Times wrote. «Atomic energy might provide a means for diverting, by its explosive power, a hurricane before it could strike a populated place. » Crash boom bang – and you have good weather thanks to computer and atom bombs. Such prospects should spark off the public, von Neumann thought. Instead, the actual inventors and builders of ENIAC, Eckert and Mauchly, had a meltdown. Both were upset that their machine was not correctly mentioned.

ENIAC was the breakthrough into the digital age. But due to its cumbersome programming, von Neumann began work on an even more powerful machine: the MANIAC (Mathematical Analyser Numerical Integrator and Computer). The MANIAC finally made the production of the hydrogen bomb possible. In 1954, von Neumann was appointed a member of the U.S. Atomic Energy Commission by President Eisenhower. But he soon fell ill and died of cancer after long suffering in a hospital in Washington.

Eckert and Mauchly founded a computer company to produce Univacs (Universal Automatic Computers) for government and corporate use. In 1950, they had orders for six Univacs, each costing well over a million dollars each, but no money to produce them. They turned to IBM, RCA, National Cash Register, and General Electric but were rejected everywhere. The war was over, and the big high-tech companies were still hesitant since they did not believe that anyone other than the military and government agencies would buy computers.

«Where a calculator like the ENIAC today is equipped with 18,000 vacuum tubes and weighs 30 tons, computers in the future may have only 1000 vacuum tubes and perhaps weigh only 1½ tons. » – This enticing prophecy made Popular Mechanics in March 1949. With this predicted weight, computers would hardly have been a success.

In the late 1940s and early 1950s, computers were in deed huge technical devices. Their operation involved a whole team of technicians and programmers, which only large corporations and the government could afford. Only a few foresaw the full potential of the new tools. One of them was James Rand of the Remington Rand Corporation. He bought the Eckert-Mauchly Computer Company, and the first Univacs were a complete success. When IBM finally released its first mainframe computer, the Type 701, it was technically no better than the Univac. But IBM had a powerful sales organization and an unrivaled service.

It may be true that war is the father of all things, but in the case of the German Konrad Zuse, the war has not «positively» promoted the development of his technology. While American and British computer pioneers had considerable resources at their disposal, they were being beaten by the engineering student working rather in obscurity. In 1937, Konrad Zuse assembled the first fully mechanical calculating machine – the Z1 – from metal strips and steel cylinders in his parents' apartment in Berlin. The reason for his stroke of genius was laziness: Zuse hoped that the calculator would relieve him from arduous and tiring calculations. He was born at the right time but in the wrong place. He had to stop his work when he was drafted for military service. The German military judged that his scientific work was not immediately useful. Other than his British and American colleagues, he did not praise his invention for military use. Both, the Z1 and its successor Z3 were destroyed in the bombing of Berlin. Nobody in the USA knew about Konrad Zuse. Zuse, however, learned about the Aiken computer from the daughter of his accountant in his engineering office. She was a secretary in the German intelligence service and had seen a photo. But more than the words «Sequence Controlled Calculator» were not identifiable on it.

The most interesting aspect of Zuse's work was not the hardware but a programming language called Plankalkül. The name is a combination of two words «plan» and «calculus. » All essential aspects of later programming languages were already present in Plankalkül. Zuse developed dozens of example programs (e.g. a chess program) to show its functionality. It was the first advanced programming language in the world, but it was not implemented until recently. In 1957 Zuse wrote: «I hope that my Plankalkül will still be brought to life after twelve years [...] I should be pleased if this could possibly be made possible in cooperation with universities. » He did not live to see that happen, Zuse died in 1995. At CeBIT computer expo 2000 in Hanover, computer scientists presented an implementation of his programming language to a wider audience for the first time.

In 1944, fascist Germany was almost defeated, and Vannevar Bush was already thinking about the tasks ahead for the many scientists. When the war was over, he delivered a report to then president Truman explaining his ideas about a new science offensive. Bush chose an appealing and quite American title: Science, the Endless Frontier. «In this war it has become clear beyond all doubt that scientific research is absolutely essential to national security, » he explained. Science is where the next dangers lurk. The Cold War would break out on this front, and only those who win the decisive battles in this war can keep the enemy under control. Bush advocated the further consolidation of the alliance between government, industry, and science. After his wake-up call, government subsidies and contracts increased. Congress established the National Science Foundation (NSF). The Department of Defense and the NSF became soon the main sponsors of American research. Before the war, government spending on research and development was in the range of a hundred million dollars per year, with the military share accounting for less than half. During the war, this funding grew to several billion dollars, with military expenditure accounting for around 90% of the total. And this was by no means the end of the boom. Scientists pampered with research money entered the «megabuck era»: Between the 1950s and the 1980s, the government spent as much money on research as industry. Its expenditure more than doubled from less than 20 to over 40 billion dollars. The return on these investments was immense. It brought us the Internet and many other milestones of the post-war economic boom.

GARAGE IN, GARAGE OUT

As Alexis de Tocqueville noted long ago, there is «no country where the love of money has taken stronger hold on the affections of men … Love of money is either the chief or secondary motive in everything Americans do. » Tocqueville had written about America from his own experience. In 1830, he and his friend Gustave de Beaumont went on a mission to study the prison system in the United States. After the completion of their research, they travelled the continent: 7,000 miles in less than nine months on steamboats, stagecoaches, and horseback. The two enthusiasts aimed to collect evidence for the superiority of democracy to encourage their home country to carry out some overdue and urgent reforms. Tocqueville's «De la Démocratie en Amérique» is probably the most quoted book about the United States. After the success of his America book, Tocqueville went into politics. From 1839 to 1848, he was a member of the Chamber of Deputies in his home constituency. Fearing socialist conditions, he initially met the February Revolution of 1848 with skepticism. While blood was flowing in the streets of Paris, the telegraphs were spreading a sensational message around the world: The worker James W. Marshall had found a gold nugget at Sutter's Mill, the building site for a sawmill on the ranch of the Swiss Johann August Sutter. The news triggered one of the largest mass migrations in the history of America. Until then, far-off California was of little importance to the rich American East. Now many hopeful adventurers and settlers wanted to move as quickly as possible to the new promised land to make their fortune. They came from the USA, Asia and Europe, no way was too far or too arduous. The Gold Rush was a boost for California, putting it on a path to become the world's sixth largest economy. San Francisco evolved from a small settlement to a large busy commercial and economic center. One of the first millionaires of the Gold Rush was a man who bought canvas from ships in San Francisco to make tents for the gold seekers. When he noticed their worn trousers, he started to produce cotton trousers called «jeans. » His name was Levi Strauß. Most miners did not find great fortunes, but the mine owners, traders, and shopkeepers – a small minority. Since those days, many people have come to California to follow their dream of happiness and success. The historian Larry Baumgardner summed it up: The actual Gold Rush turned to the farmer's Gold Rush in the 20th century. Then came Hollywood and the entertainment industry and finally Silicon Valley and the Gold Rush of the computer guys in San Francisco. It never ends, California will always be the country where apparently everyone can easily become a millionaire.

A valley south of San Francisco has for decades been home to the most important companies in the tech industry. The legendary Silicon Valley includes the Santa Clara Valley and the southern half of the San Francisco Peninsula. Highway 101 runs through a blooming landscape, past Palo Alto and Mountain View to San José. On the left is San Francisco Bay, with hills and palm trees on the horizon. The Silicon Valley looks, at first, like a small paradise, about fifty miles long and twenty miles wide. Of these, ten miles are forests and grass land, only ten miles are civilization. The whole area is barely larger than my hometown Berlin. San Jose is with about one million inhabitants the Valley's largest city, the third-largest in California. It emerged from the settlement of El Pueblo de San José De Guadalupe, founded in 1777. When John Muir walked across the valley, 150 years ago, he was stunned by the beauty of the rural scenery. «It was bloom time of the year..., » he wrote, «The landscapes of the Santa Clara Valley were fairly drenched with sunshine, all the air was quivering with the songs of meadowlarks, and the hills were so covered with flowers that they seemed to be painted. » «Valley of heart's delight» was the name of the region. An advertising spot from the

1950s shows farmers between apricot and plum plantations. Farmers settled there to grow food for the military bases and fortresses in San Francisco and Monterey. But that picture postcard California contrasts with the reality of the present day. The Valley has become a mecca for computer freaks. It's home for thousands of companies including almost all leading digital platforms: Alphabet, Apple, Cisco, Intel, Adobe, eBay, WhatsApp, Yahoo, Facebook, Airbnb, Microsoft, Oracle, SAP, Hewlett Packard, YouTube, Sun Microsystems, etc. The combined market value of these technology giants far exceeds that of traditional leading industrial companies, like General Electric, Exxon Mobile, or Volkswagen. Every day dozens of new business are started in garages and sheds. Yet you see no sign of the enormous corporate power. There are no factories or research labs, no skyscrapers, industrial zones or villas with huge gardens. The valley seems like a superpower on sleeping pills, as one pundit described it.

A reason for the Valley's success is the strong ties between the universities and their sponsors in business and the military. California is home to several universities, including three of America's absolute top addresses: Stanford, Berkeley, and the University of California. Stanford University, the «Harvard of the West,» is located in Palo Alto. Its lavishly spacious campus stretches along an evergreen chain of hills. A palm tree–lined avenue leads into the center. The architecture with its terracotta roofing reminds of a colonial Spanish complex. Elegant inner courtyards are framed by manicured lawns and shiny Rodin statues. It smells of fragrant flowers, even in January. Stanford is considered as one of the most beautiful universities in the world. But its present beauty is only a shadow of the wealth of its founder, railroad capitalist and former governor of California, Leland Stanford. The tragic story behind its founding was the early death of his only child, Leland Stanford Jr., due to typhoid fever at the age of only 15 in 1884. The way of business of this epoch was a hard-fought battle for money. It was characterized by ruthlessness, greed, and corruption up to the highest levels, as well as social inequality, and extreme poverty. Mark Twain's novel The Gilded Age gave its name to this era of rapid industrialization. It has become a synonym for the shallow shine of economic success. The men behind these economic battles were called robber barons. Among them was Leland Stanford. They grabbed enormous riches and political power in a relatively short time. The snobbishness and vulgar extravagance of these villains are legend. Rockefeller built himself a castle by the Hudson, and Cornelius Vanderbilt burned down fireworks every time he travelled to Europe with his wife, children, and countless servants. The railway barons Leland Stanford, Mark Hopkins, Charles Crocker, and Collin P. Huntigton – The Big Four – competed with each other in the decoration and splendor of their villas. That's how Nob Hill in San Francisco got its name. It's not clear whether the word «nob» is derived from «nabob» or simply refers to «snob. »

The earthquake and fire of 1906 destroyed their villas. The immense profits generated by their companies were not passed on to the workers. While few families with monopolies in boom sectors such as railways, oil, steel, and banks achieved immense wealth, the working conditions of ordinary workers worsened. The past is only the prelude to the present. Almost 150 years after Mark Twain wrote his socio-critical satire, the story is as relevant as it was then. The unscrupulousness and undisciplinedness are still the characteristics of American industry today. American society believed in the myth that anyone who works hard enough will be rewarded and that everyone who is rich deserves it. Social Darwinism was the basis of this view, spread by Rockefeller, Carnegie, and the like. The social struggle divides society into strong and weak. The weak are wiped out for the good of society, only the strong survive. In their world view, workers and unions were doomed to failure as were political controls over industry. Society is dominated by only two laws: the law of competition and the law of supply and demand. The gap between rich and poor was widening in the United States, and by the end of the 19th century 1/8 of all Americans were living below the poverty line. The age led to drastic reforms by President Theodore Roosevelt, who smashed corporate empires with the help of antitrust laws and taxes for the rich.

«Die Luft der Freiheit weht, » is the written on the seal of Stanford University. «The wind of freedom blows, » was the slogan of the German humanist Ulrich von Hutten. The choice for the materialistic philosopher is not a coincidence. Here, in the center of turbo-capitalism, «freedom» refers primarily to the material, the freedom of the wealthy who can do what they want, while the forgotten enjoy the freedom that no one cares about them. This 'air of freedom' has inspired generations of researchers to develop basic technologies and to start successful businesses, and it has made some of them incredibly rich. Stanford is the Almer Mater of bigwigs like Jawed Karim, founder of YouTube, David Packard and William Hewlett, founders of Hewlett-Packard, Larry Page and Sergey Brin, Benjamin M. Rosen, founder of Compaq, Peter Thiel, and many more.
It all got started in 1909, when David Starr Jordan, President of Stanford, raised the first 500 dollars in risk capital for the development of the audio tube. In the same year, the first American radio station went on air with regular broadcasts in San Jose. A little later, the Federal Telegraph Corporation settled in Palo Alto, providing the first commercially successful system of radiotelegraphy. In 1933, the U.S. Navy opened an airship base at Moffett Field Mountain View, a southern suburb of San Francisco. It was the kick starter of the Silicon Valley High Tech industry. The base created jobs and attracted suppliers and engineering companies. Many aerospace companies followed, settled around the airport, developed rockets and aircraft, later space technology such as the Hubble Space Telescope. After

the Navy abandoned airship technology, NACA, the forerunner of NASA, took over parts of the airbase as a research and testing site.

Stanford's most valuable asset is the enormous property of more than 8,000 acres. According to the will of Leland Stanford, the property cannot be sold, instead it should secure «a greater income than any other investment. » After World War II, Stanford began to lease large parts of its land, which is now the legendary Stanford Industrial Park. Frederick Terman, a professor at Stanford University, is often dubbed the «Father of Silicon Valley. » In the late 1930s, he encouraged two of his engineering students, Bill Hewlett and David Packard, to found their own company. The two started in a garage in Palo Alto – without a business plan and with 538 dollars in their bank account. Bill and David were lucky: Stanford and private research laboratories needed tons of technical equipment, and the U.S. Army requested electronics for modern weapons technology. During the war, Terman transferred from Stanford to Harvard University for several years. On behalf of the government he led a research group to understand and interfere with German radar systems. When he returned to Stanford he took eleven top researchers from Harvard with him. With his valuable connections to the American government he set up state-funded research laboratories specializing in military-relevant electronics. In 1946, he landed his first government contract – the beginning of a long and very lucrative relationship resulting in the first big wave of start-up companies. At the beginning of the Korean War in 1950, Stanford was the best prepared institution to provide the military with expertise.

The name «Silicon Valley» goes back to the company founded in 1955 by the student William Schockley in a storage shed for apricots. The fear of the Americans of a Soviet lead in the arms race accelerated research in the rocket sector. As the germanium-powered transistors melted at the extreme temperatures, researchers turned to silicon. Shockley had discovered how to use silicon to generate electrical currents by making some parts of the material conductive and using others as insulators – the semiconductor was born. The idea of using cold Silicon crystals instead of hot tubes triggered a revolution in electronics. The small semiconductors could emit incredibly fast electrical signals which made them useful for a wide variety of applications including watches and cellphones, street lights and fittings, steel factories and toys – and, of course, computers.

But the actual take-off of Silicon Valley dates back to the autumn of 1957: In a café in San Francisco, eight young researchers from Shockley Semiconductor Laboratory decided to quit their jobs. They turned to Wall Street banker Arthur Rock to ask if he knew of a company that would hire them. Rock proposed to start their own company and offered to finance it. At the time, this was outrageous. Workers did not simply leave their employer to start their own business. Shockley embittered called them «The Traitorous Eight. » To the young renegades it was more a compliment than a disgrace. The eight announced their intention by signing a one dollar bill, which was later dubbed as Silicon Valley's Declaration of Independence. The official reason for their decision was Shockley's irascibleness. In reality, it was greed, plain and simple. The start-up era had begun.

Head of the group was Robert Noyce, an Iowa-born physicist with a doctorate from MIT. Noyce was a man of both, research and earning. He introduced the typical corporate culture of Silicon Valley: flat hierarchies, no formalities, open offices with small cubicles, teamwork, and careful measurement of performance at all levels while working to the bone. Thus, he became a role model for an entire generation of entrepreneurs. By 1967, Fairchild Semiconductor had 11,000 employees and made 12 million dollars in profits. That they owed the technology to someone else was irrelevant. In 1968, together with Gordon Moore, Noyce founded the microprocessor company Intel. Intel would dominate the semiconductor industry in the years ahead.

«The future of integrated electronics is the future of electronics itself. The advantages of integration will bring about a proliferation of electronics, pushing this science into many new areas. Integrated circuits will lead to such wonders as home computers – or at least terminals connected to a central computer – automatic controls for automobiles, and personal portable communications equipment. The electronic wristwatch needs only a display to be feasible today. » These words were not published for the release of Apple Watch. These words are the introduction of Gordon Moore's essay Cramming More Components onto Integrated Circuits, which was published in the magazine Electronics on April 19, 1965. Only a nerdy engineer can come up with such a cumbersome title. The article became famous several years later, when a scientist summarized it as Moore's Law, plain and simple. Moore's Law has become the Valley's guiding principle, almost like a divine command. Initially it said that the calculating power of computer chips doubles every year while the chips become smaller and cheaper. In 1963, you could buy twice as much computing power for one dollar as in the previous year. Moore later corrected the assumption and suggested a doubling only every two years. Today, it takes about 18 months to double the current computing power.

The fact that Moore's law is still valid today – since 50 years now – is due to efforts by chip researchers to further shrink the structures on a chip, i.e. the thickness of the conductor paths and the size of the transistors. In 1965, Gordon Moore and his colleagues combined 50 transistors to form an integrated circuit. Today, more than a billion of these semiconductor components fit on a standard processor. Scientists don't know how long this development can continue. They don't even agree on exactly why Moore's Law or other similar patterns exist. «It can't continue forever. The nature of exponentials is that you push them out and eventually disaster happens, » Moore says.

Humans are incredibly bad at cognitively capturing exponential developments. This is illustrated by the famous chess board story. The inventor of the chess game allegedly asked an Indian king to reward him with rice: one grain for the first field on the chess board, two grains for the second, four grains for the third, eight grains for the fourth, and so on. The king agreed, because at first it sounded like a reasonable, even humble request. However, the number of grains on the last field of the chess board has 21 digits. When the king finally got it, the inventor was beheaded for his impertinence. We're all a bit like the king in this story. We've been in the middle of an exponential technological development for decades, but we're still incapable of grasping it.

Yet in terms of growth – or, to be more precise, in miniaturization – there are physical limits we can't overcome. Today's conductive paths are only a few atoms thick. With such small sizes, the laws of quantum mechanics come into play. These laws influence particle behavior. But chip manufacturers are developing new methods of printing small circuits in three-dimensional structures. So Moore's law doesn't need to level off anytime soon.

With the development of computer technology came digital companies. By 1970, there were already fifteen computer companies in Silicon Valley selling three hundred million chips. Over the years, the government has lost much of its dominant position in the region. The emergence of private venture capital companies in the 1970s made the technology industry more independent. In the following decades, the private sector and university structures became increasingly intertwined.

Today, Stanford is the nexus of Silicon Valley, the place where all networks of researchers, founders, donors, and corporate leaders converge. Whoever has connections to Stanford goes with a head start into the race for commercial success. That's why Silicon Valley became the seething cauldron of the digital revolution: Money flows here like nowhere else. And that's why it attracts the brightest scientists and engineers like a giant magnet. Each year, numerous Stanford students set up start-ups, and the university launches spin-offs in which it has a financial stake. This combination of inventiveness and entrepreneurial spirit creates a fertile ground that promotes explosive growth, and it rewards investors and scientists alike. The Valley has become the core of America's economic and cultural dominance.

In 1970, the former space scientist Niels Reimers founded the «Stanford Office of Technology Licensing. » The university had always been concerned with marketing its innovations, but there was no professional system. Between 1954 and 1967, Stanford received only 50,000 dollars from patent licenses, in 2017/2018 it was 40.96 million. The system is strict: When scientists make a groundbreaking invention that they would like to monetize, they first turn to the Office of Technology. Since the research was carried out with funds from the university, it reserves the right to license it. Their task is to look for promising partners. Katherine Ku, former director of the Office of Technology, has been quoted: «We feel we are a marketing office, not a legal office. » If an industrial partner is found, the revenues from the license fees are divided as follows: 15 percent is collected in advance by the Office of Technology. Of the remaining sum, one third goes to the inventor himself or the team, one third to the faculty where the innovation was developed, and one third goes to a special investment fund at Stanford. If, after some time, the Office of Technology does not find a licensee, it returns the rights to the scientists. Now they can do whatever they want with it. Naturally, they try to market it themselves, start a business or find a partner. Despite the success, Stanford's method is controversial. The critics call it a corruption of science as a result of a mania for start-ups. It's probably not a good idea to carry out science primarily to maximize profits. Those who distribute the money, the venture capitalists, are the real powerbroker of Silicon Valley. Dozens of investment firms spend billions of dollars every year on young companies. Without this start-up capital, Google, Facebook, and Apple wouldn't exist.

In America, third-party funding of universities has long played an important role. Concerns that the market mentality may have too much influence in academic decision-making are not new. Already in 1963, Clark Kerr, president of the University of California, complained that «Universities have become 'bait' to be dangled in front of industry, with drawing power greater than low taxes or cheap labor. » The orientation of research in a desired direction according to commercial objectives has serious long-term consequences. For what is researched and – equally important – what is not researched determines in which direction our society moves or does not move. Only rarely it's about fraud. But you can also lie with the truth. One-sided representation or half-truths are not refutable or only with difficulty. In many controversial issues there are arguments, figures, data, and facts for and against a certain point of view. If, in scientific studies, one looks only the side that favors a particular issue and neglects the arguments against it, political or social processes are directed in a specific way. After all, the arguments claim to be true and scientifically verifiable. Do we really want that?

The effects of corporate science are real. Many examples show where this can lead in the worst case. For decades, the tobacco industry paid well-respected researchers to claim that smoking or passive smoking is not harmful. While their profits increased, countless people died. The chemical industry has done the same in several cases. The results of studies on harmful chemicals were falsified by corrupt researchers. Thus, the manufacture and sale of such chemicals could go on for decades. In drug research, about 90 percent of all published studies are financed by the pharmaceutical industry. It's a common practice that negative study results disappear. The evidence on which our decisions in medicine are based is systematically falsified to exaggerate the benefits of the drugs and to trivialize the side effects. This may well have negative consequences for patients and for further research. If a clinical trial shows that a therapy is less effective than before thought, doctors and patients should know this so that they can take it into account when making future decisions. It's also important for other researchers, e.g. to plan further trials. These patterns can be applied to countless, much more subtle cases of industrial money influencing seemingly independent research. In his book «Gekaufte Forschung» («Bought Research») Christian Kreiß discusses some cases in which private companies exerted considerable influence on research through third-party funding. The scientists either derived direct economic benefits or could advance their careers. The costs for society are rather speculative and can rarely be expressed in money. How many lives are harmed because there was no research? How many careers were destroyed of researchers who were not corruptible? How do we know which scientific facts we are missing because they don't fit into the business model of the industry?

Universities that behave more like businesses pose a threat to academic principles. Researchers start to think more like entrepreneurs than scholars. The cultural anthropologist Wesley Shumar warns that if research is «to be valued in terms of their ability to be translated into cash or merchandise … eventually, the idea that there are other kinds of value is lost. » It also causes a considerable loss of confidence in research and universities. When confronted with scientific findings, many people rightfully ask: Cui bono – who benefits from it? How else can average people assess the validity of today's scientific research?

FLYING WINDOWS, SERIOUS BUSINESS

In the early 1950s, Robert Jungk worked as a correspondent for various newspapers in Los Angeles. He was particularly interested in the developments in science and technology that changed society. A research trip through the whole country resulted in the book Tomorrow is already here. It became a bestseller, and the title was prophetic. Its message was in a nutshell: Scientific and technical progress have highly negative effects. New technologies bring omnipotence, dominance over Heaven and Earth, Man and Nature, Spirit and Atom. At the same time, it causes powerlessness, a loss of personal freedom, and submission to the collective or dictatorial commander. His visit to IBM's factory Endicott in New York served as an example. At that time, it was IBM's most important production and research facility. Jungk found a company in a «state of bliss. » From the executive to the workers, he was given ready-made answers: «I am the most satisfied manager. » – «We are the happiest commercial representatives. » – «We are the happiest workers. » There were everywhere portraits of company boss Thomas J. Watson senior, «the head of a friendly elderly man with a priestly smile on the thin lips, and a gleaming white collar like a halo that has fallen down. » As omnipresent as the chief priest was his supreme command: «THINK gleams over every door, leaps at you from every wall. It's a command without an exclamation mark: THINK. The omnipresent imperative is planted in red tulips on green turf, chiseled in stone or marble, cast in bronze, embroidered on material, burned into the night in light-writing: THINK ... THINK ... THINK ... » The ambitious slogan didn't detract from a practical «materialism, » but rather promoted it. The almost missionary desire to make the world a happy place met with an incredible toughness on the sales front. An ideology of success and the pursuit of the monopoly made IBM the most modern and expansive company in the world. It grew faster and faster, and its profits exploded – despite the immense risks. Watson was initially skeptical about the future of computers. But after World War II, IBM entered the new computer market with the full support of the U.S. government. During the 1950s, the military and other branches of the state were IBM's largest customer. Under the aegis of Thomas Watson Jr., who took over the company in 1952, Big Blue secured many lucrative patents. It became the leading company in the segment, and U.S. taxpayers footed the bill. By today's standards, computers then were extremely inefficient. Mainframes had about 32 kilobytes of RAM, a hundred thousand times less than a smartphone. In April 1964, IBM laid the cornerstone of the mainframe era with the S/360. With development costs of about 5.5 billion dollars at the time (approx. 30 billion today), this bolide was the most expensive computer of all time. The age of mainframes began, computers conquered the economy. In the 1960s, there were eight computer companies in the U.S., somewhat ironically called Snow White and the Seven Dwarfs. IBM was Snow White, Burroughs, UNIVAC, NCR (National Cash Register), Control Data, Honeywell, RCA (Radio Corporation of America) and General Electric were the seven dwarfs. IBM's supremacy became so strong that the antitrust authorities repeatedly took action.

Yet in the early 1970s, still only few American people came in direct contact with a computer, not even programmers. They delivered their programs by hand to technicians, who took care of the input. Hours later, they picked up the results. The invention of the microprocessor changed all that. It allowed to integrate the central unit of a computer on a single chip. This made small and inexpensive workstations possible and created a completely new market segment for affordable microcomputers, small thinking machines, an in-between of pocket calculator and computer system. When IBM noted that it was missing out the opportunity, it released its first own personal computer in August 1981. Home computer had been around for five years already, mainly bought by hobbyists and gamers. About 200 manufacturers build them, such as Commodore, Atari, Sinclair, and Texas Instruments. But their operating systems were closed systems and hardly expandable. Within only a few months, a team in the IBM research laboratory in Boca Raton in Florida developed the 5150, the smallest IBM system to that date. The managers of IBM had no intention of writing a new chapter in computer history. It was a defensive maneuver to blow competition off the market. The time pressure was great, as the cost pressure, so they made a critical decision: Instead of developing its own technology, as usual, and thus setting the standard globally, IBM began looking for suppliers for the two most important components of each computer. The small chip company Intel delivered the microprocessor. It would have been a simple task to develop their own operating system. But they didn't really take it seriously. It was still unthinkable that every private household would need a computer. The operating system for the 5150 was supplied by a then quite unknown company of a certain Bill Gates, called Microsoft.

Gates was a nerdish twenty-five-year-old. To IBM's negotiators, he looked like an office boy. They probably thought they could fob him off quickly and cheaply. He is just a hacker, they assumed, a harmless computer freak. They didn't understand that they got involved with a person who came from an impeccable background and who was born to seize power and profit. The son of a successful lawyer understood the language of contracts perfectly. His mother, Mary Maxwell Gates, came from an old bankers' family in Seattle. Being the first female president of the United Way charity, she interacted with John Opel, IBM's president. That may have influenced IBM's decision to meet with Bill Gates. No one can say that charity isn't lucrative.

IBM negotiated an inconspicuous contract that turned out to be the most serious mistake in its history. Gates promised the East Coast guys a system that Microsoft hadn't developed yet. His partner, Paul Allen, negotiated an advance of 186,000 dollars with IBM. Allen and Gates have met in 1968 as students at Lakeside School, a private school in Seattle, where the two nerds had access to one of the first minicomputers. With IBM's money they bought an operating system from Tim Patterson which he called Quick and Dirty Operating System (QDOS). For 50,000 dollars it was a bargain. The programmer was bought with it and after some modifications QDOS was delivered to IBM under the name MS-DOS.

With the IBM contract, the small business had its breakthrough. In a smart move they did not sell the whole operating system to IBM, but only licenses for its use. While retaining the right to license it also to other manufacturers, Gates negotiated a clause that no IBM PC could be delivered without an operating system, which, in most cases, was Microsoft's operating system. It appears that IBM didn't understand the full consequences of their contract with Microsoft, and thus it sabotaged itself and its own supremacy in the sector.

On August 12, 1981, IBM presented the PC with MS-DOS. It was a typewriter-sized box to which you could plug printers, monitors, and keyboards. To IBM's surprise, it was a huge success. In 1982, Time Magazine awarded its «Person of the Year» award to the personal computer, naming it «Machine of the Year. » Competitors quickly figured out that the IBM PC was assembled from components they could get from their electronics store. Many copycats developed their own PCs, also opting for Microsoft's operating system, and fought a hard battle for market dominance. The strategists at IBM underestimated the rapid transformation in the computer world. The giant slipped into a paradox situation. With his own market power it helped its suppliers Intel and Microsoft to develop monopolies. Meanwhile, IBM had to defend itself against hordes of rivals shooting out of the ground like mushrooms. Due to the merciless price war, the PC boom never brought the hoped-for money into IBM's pockets. While the tiny boxes became ever more powerful the mainframe, profits disappeared. Management mistakes and the loss of market share caused a deep crisis in the early 1990s with losses running into billions. Microsoft made a fortune, and Gates became a billionaire at the age of thirty-one. The New Yorker wrote: «To many people, the rise of Bill Gates marks the revenge of the nerd. » He was the wealthiest person in the world, for a long time. As I write this, the trophy goes to Jeff Bezos.

A couple of years later, Paul Allen left the company after a malignant tumor was discovered in his lymphatic system. In an autobiography Allen writes that he left Microsoft not only for health reasons. He accuses his partner of having repeatedly disadvantaged him in the allocation of company shares. He also insists that many of the brilliant ideas that made Microsoft great actually came from him. Hence, for all of Bill Gates' business acumen, he owns almost everything to a combination of initiative and luck. He certainly has an above-average level of intelligence, yet without being in the right place at the right time, he would be, at best, a freelance computer programmer. In fact, he hasn't even developed any groundbreaking software. Hundreds of computer scientists do so every year, but I know of no significant work by him. There seems to be no program with the label «© Bill Gates. » Actually, not a single known Microsoft product was invented by the company itself. Microsoft is first and foremost a marketing company using some tough legal tricks to extend its dominance. When Windows 95 was published, Microsoft already had a market share of over 90 percent. In 1991, the U.S. Federal Trade Commission began investigating whether the company was exploiting its dominance, and in 2002, it received a negative verdict. In 2008, Microsoft and U.S. authorities again clashed. In the same year, Bill Gates announced that he was leaving his desk at Microsoft. Many people only now realized for how much this skinny guy with the oversized glasses had influenced their lives.

EVERYTHING IS CONNECTED

«*You can see what is happening in the world, in the Western world: technology, commercialism, and consumerism is the highest activity that is going on now.* » – Jiddu Krishnamurti

«*In an extreme view, the world can be seen as only connections, nothing else.* » – Tim Berners-Lee

Throughout World War II, President Roosevelt was a loyal ally of Stalin. But after 1945, Stalin ruthlessly tried to expand his power. The Soviet Union supported the communist takeover of Eastern Europe and East Germany. By 1949, it had established communist dictatorships in all countries occupied by the Red Army. In America and Western Europe this expansion of Soviet power provoked fear and mistrust. In 1957, the Soviet Union launched their Sputnik satellite into earth's orbit which shook America's self-confidence to the core. One month later, Eisenhower promised to set up a comprehensive research program. In his State of the Union speech, he announced his intention to catch up with the Soviets in the space race. He ordered the establishment of a scientific research facility with mythical dimensions. The «Advanced Research Projects Agency» (ARPA or DARPA) is one of the most influential research organizations in the world. For a group of ambitious scientific strategists led by Vannevar Bush, James Covenant, and MIT president James Kilian, it was the fruition of a long-cherished plan. Kilian was Eisenhower's science advisor and lobbied to ensure that the agency was set up properly. First director of ARPA was Roy Johnson, a businessman. ARPA didn't maintain its own research facilities, instead it funded and managed research in cooperation with academic and industrial partners. ARPA also encouraged the industry to transform research into products, and, at the same time, it encouraged scientists should start their own companies. In return, the military could get advanced technologies at a reasonable price. ARPA recruited employees from a pool of the brightest scientists and engineers. Ironically, it was 5-star General Eisenhower who warned of the «military-industrial complex. » He feared that this alliance would exert its influence on all cities, parliaments and federal authorities in the country. In his farewell address in 1961, he said:

«In the councils of government, we must guard against the acquisition of unwarranted influence, whether sought or unsought, by the military-industrial complex. The potential for the disastrous rise of misplaced power exists and will persist, » Eisenhower said. «We must never let the weight of this combination endanger our liberties or democratic processes. We should take nothing for granted. Only an alert and knowledgeable citizenry can compel the proper meshing of the huge industrial and military machinery of defense with our peaceful methods and goals, so that security and liberty may prosper together. »

His words were as accurate then as they are now. The USA continue to be the undisputed leader of global military manufacturing. Through aggressive lobbying the companies have turned the country into the world's armory. The ballooning of the military budget is a decisive factor for the entire American high-tech sector. Military applications are increasingly finding use in civilian markets. Radar, lasers in DVD players or in medicine, automatic vacuum cleaners, mobile phones, GPS navigation, or the Internet – all these products were first developed for the military.

In February 1961, a terrorist group had blown up several radio relay stations of the U.S. Army in Utah. Scientists and the military became concerned with the safety of communication networks. In his 1964 film Dr. Strangelove, Stanley Kubrick brilliantly satirized the paranoia of a military apocalypse, «the specter of wholesale destruction, » as Eisenhower dubbed it. The leitmotif of the film is repeated in various ways: the difficulty of communication. Not only one communication fails, but almost every communication. After ordering a massive nuclear strike, the commander of a bomber squadron cuts off all outside connections. The first step for the bomber crews in an emergency is to switch to a coded channel which is inaccessible to the enemy. Later, an explosion completely destroys one bomber's radio so that no one can contact it at all. But even telephone conversations suffer from serious disruption. In one case, the conversation is running through an incompetent middle person, in another case, the other person is drunk. Kubrick ridicules the naive myth of modern communication technology.

In 1962, Kilian established the Information Processing Techniques Office (IPTO) and recruited the psychologist Joseph Carl Robnett Licklider. «Humble and genius» is how companions described him. Licklider was a generation younger than Vannevar Bush and Norbert Wiener and heavily influenced by Wiener's ideas on cybernetics. In his article Man-Computer-Symbiosis, Licklider described the concept of a simpler interaction between man and computer:

«The hope is that, in not too many years, human brains and computing machines will be coupled together very tightly and the resulting partnership will think as no human brain has ever thought and process data in a way not approached by the information-handling machines we know today. »

The growing amount of data turned the exchange of physical data storage such as magnetic tapes or punched cards into a laborious task. Besides, many data storage were compatible only to computers of the same manufacturer and even the same model. Licklider outlined a plan to connect all the computers at the universities researching for ARPA. As head of IPTO, he was in the powerful position to propagate his ideas. Together with a group of like-minded scientists and engineers he presented the concept for an Intergalactic Computer Network. Their idea already contained almost everything that makes up the Internet. Freed from bureaucratic constraints, Licklider paved the way for two of the most important prerequisites of the Internet: decentralized networks and interfaces that enable human-machine interaction in real time. As one of his partners and protégés, Bob Taylor, put it: «He was really the father of it all. »

In April 1964, the IPTO computer scientist Paul Baran presented an eleven-volume study entitled On Distributed Communications. He described a network in which «blocks of information» can be redirected if parts of the network are damaged. This network would not be operated centrally, and thus remain capable of communication even after severe devastation. The study is regarded as the theoretical basis of the Internet. It was classified until the 1970s. Only a few people were allowed to view the study, one was Licklider. Baran's study is partly responsible for the myth that the Internet emerged to protect communication from nuclear bombing. But there is a much more practical motive: Via the network, researchers could make a more efficient use of the scarce and expensive data-processing machines. Baran couldn't claim the idea of packet switching for himself only. The Briton Donald Watts Davies had the same idea around the same time. So the Internet was not created in the USA alone.

In 1966, Barans successor at IPTO, Bob Taylor, funneled a million dollars into a project called ARPANET. He had developed a comprehensive concept for a computer network and – with the approval of ARPA – sent it to 140 companies. Most of them considered his proposal absurd, only twelve expressed an interest in building the network. In 1969, ARPA contracted BBN Technologies. The BBN team, which initially consisted of only seven employees, was headed by Frank Heart. They established a small network of computers that operated as Interface Message Processors (IMP) and which were connected by gateways (now routers). On October 29, 1969, Charley Kline, a student and programmer, sent the first message via ARPANET between a UCLA computer and a computer at the Stanford Research Institute. The letters LOG (for »Login«) were to be transmitted. Simultaneously, the technicians spoke over the telephone: «Do you have the L? » – «Yes! » – «Do you have the O? » – «Yes! » – «Do you have the G? » – Then the computer crashed.

In the same year, Licklider predicted that the network could connect about 14 computers and 2,000 scientists by 1978. When the year 1978 came, Licklider had to admit that his prediction was wrong. In a publication celebrating the 20th anniversary of ARPA, Licklider nevertheless dared to look ahead to the year 2000 and wrote:

«If we could look in on the future at say, the year 2000, would we see a unity, a federation, or a fragmentation? That is: would we see a single multi-purpose network encompassing all applications and serving everyone? Or a more or less coherent system of intercommunicating networks? Or an incoherent assortment of isolated noncommunicating networks? The middle alternative – the more or less coherent network of networks – appears to have a fairly high probability and also to be desirable. »

Over time, various universities and research institutions were integrated into the network, and ARPANET evolved from a military to a civilian application. In the middle of the 1980s, the Defense Department became concerned about possible security risks. It decided to create a separate network for specific military uses: MILNET, and ARPANET became ARPA-INTERNET. In 1984, the NSF set up its own network, NSFNet, for research and educational purposes. The NSF adopted a concept that would later shape the Internet: It did not finance the access of each individual research institution, but only the construction of the «backbone. » To connect to the NSFnet, the institutions had to set up their own regional network. ARPANET became more and more insignificant, as the majority of the data traffic was now handled via the NSFNet. At the end of the eighties, ARPANET, technologically obsolete, was decommissioned. The last IMPs were either transferred to other networks or switched off.

From the beginning, one of the goals of NSFNet was to open the network to commercial providers. The institutions should buy the necessary hardware and know how directly from commercial companies, and the NSF provided them with their own budgets. In the first years, however, there was a strict ban on advertising in the NSFNet, which made a commercial use impossible. In 1991, this advertising ban was lifted. Furthermore, the access to the internet was no longer restricted to universities and research institutions. With this decision the NSF opened a new chapter in the history of the Internet. At the end of 1992 there were only 50 websites in the world. Only five years later there were already a million.

The Internet seemed the realization of mankind's old dream of a universal library that contains all the knowledge of the world and is accessible for everyone. Many people dreamed of it: In the eighteenth century the French philosopher Denis Diderot created the first great encyclopedia. Around 1900, the Belgian bibliophile Paul Otlet wanted to preserve the world knowledge on index cards. In the late 1930s, science fiction author H.G. Wells predicted the creation of a «world brain. » In the mid-1940s, Vannevar Bush imagined it in the form of the Memex (Memory Extender). And in the early 1960s, an eccentric genius named Ted Nelson conceptualized it as Hypertext-Xanadu. To be buried under a mountain of scientific works was Bush's nightmare. In 1939, he formulated his angst in a warlike mood: «There is a growing mountain of research results; the investigator is bombarded with the findings and conclusions of thousands of parallel workers which he cannot find time to grasp as they appear, Iet alone remember. » His Memex would be a cataloging device, «in which an individual stores all his books, records, and communications, and which is mechanized so that it may be consulted with exceeding speed and flexibility. » Bush imagined that his machine could compress the entire Encyclopaedia Britannica to «the volume of a matchbox» or a million-book library into «one end of a desk. » «It consists of a desk, » Bush explained, «and while it can presumably be operated from a distance, it's primarily the piece of furniture at which [the user] works. On the top are slanting translucent screens, on which material can be projected for convenient reading. There is a keyboard, and sets of buttons and levers. Otherwise it looks like an ordinary desk. » Over time Bush developed an obsession with the Memex: In 1939, he laid out his plan for the first time, in 1941, he wrote a memorandum regarding Memex, and about 1945, he extended the memorandum to the essay «As We May Think. » In 1946, he adopted «As We May Think» into a collection of essays called Endless Horizons, in 1959, he wrote a manuscript with the title Memex II, in 1967, Memex Revisited was printed in the collection Science is Not Enough, and finally in 1970, he dedicated a whole section to Memex in his autobiography. From the very beginning, he has seen its realization within reach. After all, he only wanted to combine technologies that had long been developed: microphotography for information storage and cathode ray tubes with which data material could be reproduced immediately. In 1940, he presented a prototype called «Rapid Selector.» It was not the elegant and dexterous Memex. But it was used in the 1940s and 1950s by the intelligence service and American libraries.

The core of Bush's vision was an even more radical new idea. Instead of storing information linear, i.e. alphabetically, or according to subject, he proposed a network of smart links. According to Bush, the common indexing methods are harmful to humans because «the human mind does not work that way.» It «operates by association,» he claimed, «with one item in its grasp, it snaps instantly to the next that is suggested by the association of thoughts, in accordance with some intricate web of trails carried by the cells of the brain ... The speed of action, the intricacy of trails, the detail of mental pictures [are] awe-inspiring beyond all else in nature.» Influenced by this proposal, Ted Nelson coined the term «hypertext» with his project Xanadu. Nelson imagines Xanadu as a memory for all humanity. The linked content is broken down into small units: a definition of a term, a graphic, a photo, a note, a data set, etc. He hoped that hypertext will liberate people from the artificial linearity created by books. Nelson says: «We are striving to create a unified, universal literature, available to everyone both as readers and contributors, instantly available everywhere, with the ability to publish connections freely. That is, anyone may publish footnotes, comments, disagreements; and anyone may quote, republish, anthologies and otherwise re-use everything in the system -- provided that the republication stays within the Xanadu world.» Due to its complexity, his project has not yet been completed and perhaps never will. In 1995, »Wired» called Nelson's project in a not so nice article «the longest-running vaporware story in the history of the computer industry.» «Vaporware» is software that never gets any further than the announcement. In 1974, however, Nelson published the first book ever about the personal computer «Computer Lib/Dream Machines,» urging the reader «you can and must understand computers NOW.» Thus, he changed our understanding of what a computer was for and who could use it. Nelson's life has its own tragedy. Though he inspired generations of programmers, he has not made a fortune. His curriculum vitae doesn't contain any company foundations and no executive positions. Nelson had many ideas. But others earned the big money. In the past twenty years, Nelson has almost been forgotten. His story is a footnote in the history of a well-known hypertext protocol called the World Wide Web.

At the end of the eighties, a more sociable guy, Tim Berners-Lee, developed the WWW almost incidentally while he was working at the European nuclear research center Cern. Tim Berners-Lee had no intention whatsoever of changing the world. He only wanted to improve communication among his scientific colleagues. He developed a computer language, the web address, a browser and a server. Done was the World Wide Web in 1991. Tim Berners-Lee described it as «the marriage of hypertext and the Internet. » Without his simple innovation there would be no Google, Amazon, Facebook, Twitter, or any other online business. He considered his inventions as a vehicle for intercultural understanding, for the spread of knowledge and democracy. Berners-Lee, now professor at Oxford University and the MIT, is an idealist. He has never applied for patents on his work, although they would have made him rich. Today the terms «World Wide Web» and «Internet» are often used synonymous, which is not quite correct. Even Facebook celebrated «25 years of the Internet» in 2016. In short: The internet is the infrastructure, the World Wide Web is a specific service of the Internet. There are many more, e.g. various e-mail protocols and FTP, instant messaging, Voiceover IP, network games, and gopher – an early competition to the Web that no longer plays a role.

For a brief moment after Berners-Lee unveiled his invention, the Web was free of commercial activity. In 1993, hardly anyone outside academic circles had come into contact with the Internet. Many technology companies were still discussing whether to invest in it, or whether it was only a hype. During the presidential election campaign of Bill Clinton, his running mate Al Gore seized on the growing media coverage of the term Internet and called for the development of «Information Superhighways. » As vice president, Gore promised the companies that the «data highway» would be the most important and lucrative market of the 21st century. He emphasized that «from these connections we will derive robust and sustainable economic progress, strong democracies, better solutions to global and environmental challenges, improved health care, and ultimately a greater sense of shared stewardship of our small planet. » In his speech to the International Telecommunication Union in 1994, Al Gore made it clear that the costs for the network structure had to be assumed by the private sector. In view of the U.S. budget deficit, it's no surprise that the government was no longer willing to pay for the further expansion of the Internet. Thus, the infrastructure of the Internet has been privatized, and the basic idea of the Internet and the WWW as public institutions was abolished. The utopia of scientists and the computer elite was transformed into a distribution platform.

The WWW grew fast. While the architects of the telephone network had to create a complex new infrastructure, lay lines, hire operators, manufacture telephones, etc., the Web could thrive on an existing infrastructure. The apologists of the commercialization of the Web, such as MIT technology specialist Nicholas Negroponte, Bill Gates, and the journalistic entrepreneur Esther Dyson, were able to convince the public that it was in their interest to open the Internet to commerce. At the same time, these cyber luminaries tirelessly proclaimed the promise of «empowerment» with the help of the

Internet. It was precisely this attitude which met the neoliberal zeitgeist of the 1990s. As a result, a handful of corporations now controls what we read and see. We run the risk of losing sovereignty over our most important cultural asset and becoming dependent on those who operate the infrastructures and deliver the content. Berners-Lee recognized the growing concentration of power in the network early on and became a pioneer for a second time. In 2009, he founded his World Wide Web Foundation, which advocates an open, free and generally accessible Internet. It's an attempt to launch a digital counterrevolution: The network is to be decentralized again by giving individual users back control over their data – a radical approach that is far from today's reality.

WE OWE IT ALL TO THE HIPPIES

«The Internet is not a technology; it's a belief system. » – Joi Ito

«We Owe It All to the Hippies. » – Steward Brand

In 1949, George Orwell, a rather odd bird and loner with a difficult character, published his novel 1984. He described a gloomy future in which a totalitarian system with the help of surveillance maintains its power over the oppressed population. William Gibson published his novel «Neuromancer» in the same Orwellian novel year 1984. In 1984, there were still no PCs in the households. There was no Windows, no Google, no social media, and no smartphone. The Internet existed only for some IT freaks and for military purposes. In this technological vacuum Gibson invented a new world, the «cyberspace. » He defines it as «a consensual hallucination experienced daily by billions of legitimate operators. » People can explore the cyberspace with electrodes attached to their heads and bodies. The cyberspace as described in Neuromancer does not yet exist, but it's based on the idea of the virtual community. Its roots go back to an underestimated movement that shaped Silicon Valley more than anything else: the counterculture of the 1960s, a decade that was characterized by contradictions.
The American civil rights movement reached its peak in the early 60s. 1964 was an unusual year: Martin Luther King was honored with the Nobel Peace

Prize, the GNP rose stunning 6 1/2 Percent, and Congress green lighted President Lyndon B. Johnson's plan to engage in the Vietnam War. But before he sent soldiers to Vietnam, he signed the Civil Rights Act. It banned discriminatory election tests for black Americans and racial segregation in public institutions. In the southern states, however, the reality was different. In Mississippi, the most backward of all U.S. states, racism was the rule. During the semester break, hundreds of students from all over the country travelled to the south to protest racism. With the impressions and experiences gained there, the Free Speech Movement was born at Berkeley University. They wanted to deliver information about the racism in the south to the universities. The university administration reacted with a ban of any political activity. As the students didn't follow this instruction, the situation escalated quickly. The negotiations dragged on for weeks. The more stubbornly the administration resisted the students' demands, the larger their movement became. On December 2, 1964, more than 1000 students occupied the administration building of Berkeley. After 15 hours, about 800 squatters and sympathizers were taken into custody by the police. It was the largest mass arrest in Californian history. Five days later, Berkeley's professors decided by a large majority to implement the demands of the Free Speech Movement. But the movement had vehement opponents and the backlash came fast and heavy. Ronald Reagan, a second-rate actor, whom nobody had reckoned with, won the elections for governor of California. One of his first steps was the dismissal of Berkley's President Kerr, who – in his opinion – had been far too lax with the students. But in the end even Reagan was unable to stop the tide.

The success of the student revolt triggered a change of mood in the USA. The civil rights movement gained rapidly growing support and merged with other movements. In the Haight Ashbury district near Berkeley, the hippie movement gave the counterculture its characteristics.

Haight Ashbury was little more than a crossroads of two streets near Golden Gate Park in the western part of San Francisco. The 19th century wooden houses lend the district a European flair. Because of the increasing car traffic, the old, well-off inhabitants fled the city and settled in the suburbs. From about 1966, the place became the heart of a sociocultural revolution. A mix of artists, dropouts, and revolt groups began to populate the apartments on Haight Street. Countless young people united in protest against the Vietnam War and capitalism. The soundtrack of the movement came from Jimi Hendrix, The Who, Janis Joplin, Jefferson Airplane, Grateful Dead, and many others. Among their loyal fans, who were known for their drug use, were some techies who later ended up in Silicon Valley – Steve Jobs was one of them. Without drugs, there wouldn't have been a Summer of Love, above all LSD – an intoxicant with immense hallucinogenic effects: Colorful clouds of fog arise, smells seem visible, feathered snakes wind around swastikas.

Some people also suffer horror trips and whine in fright. Others are convinced they can fly and jump off the windowsill. Those who don't fall, feel tremendously wise and believe that they have gained insight into the blueprint of the universe. In the tristesse of reality, however, things are different:

LSD blocks social abilities, you become incapable of clear thinking and solving simple practical problems. The symptoms remind of an acute psychotic phase, like people who suffer schizophrenia experience them. «Every exertion of my will, every attempt to put an end to the disintegration of the outer world and the dissolution of my ego, seemed to be wasted effort, » described Albert Hofmann, the inventor of the drug, his first LSD intoxication. «A demon had invaded me, had taken possession of my body, mind, and soul. I jumped up and screamed, trying to free myself from him, but then sank down again and lay helpless on the sofa. The substance, with which I had wanted to experiment, had vanquished me. It was the demon that scornfully triumphed over my will. » Later, the symptoms of intoxication became more pleasant, and he began to enjoy «feelings of happiness and thankfulness. » Soon, he was dazzled by «a kaleidoscopic flood of fantastic images, spiralling as they opened and closed as fountains of colour. » LSD is the ideal drug for the visual age. It creates an endless flow of images devoid of meaning.

In October 1966, California banned LSD. Shortly afterwards, on the afternoon of January 14, 1967, about 30,000 young and young-at-heart rebels gathered at the Golden Gate Park in San Francisco for the first «Human Be-In. » Timothy Leary, a dismissed Harvard professor of psychology, encouraged the crowd to leave all educational institutions, true to the slogan: «Turn on, tune in, drop out! » It should become the motto of the counterculture. Leary established a weird cult around the drug and preached free access to mescaline and LSD. It was about something called «expanding consciousness» that should help to transform the «system. » For this shallow nonsense and for handing out psilocybin and LSD to students, a federal judge declared him «the most dangerous man in the world. » Leary's thoughts were inspired by the work The Doors of Perception by the English writer Aldous Huxley. Huxley describes an experiment with the psychedelic drug mescaline: «To be shaken out of the ruts of ordinary perception, to be shown for a few timeless hours the outer and inner world, not as they appear to an animal obsessed with survival or to a human being obsessed with words and notions, but as they are apprehended directly and unconditionally by Mind at Large this is an experience of inestimable value to everyone and especially to the intellectual. » From this book the band The Doors borrowed their name, and the hippies chose it as their Bible.

The hippie movement spread all over the country and soon merged with the Baby Boomer generation. Sociologists use this term to describe the postwar generation until the early 1960s. In the 1960s and '70s, the whole baby boom generation came of age. Suddenly, America had more teenagers than ever before. Many of them moved to the countryside to experiment with alternative ways of life. They did not want to get politically engaged, but formed small communities based on shared values and views. An essential aspect of that time was people's belief in technology and science. The atomic bombs dropped on Hiroshima and Nagasaki created a deep reverence for technology: A technology that could create an atomic bomb with such a destructive power could do anything. The country slid into a technocracy that was all about becoming more efficient, productive, and wealthy. The Cold War and the military armament of America created prosperity. While the military industry flourished, the job market boomed. The workers could use the money to buy consumer goods and thus other economic and industrial branches also prospered. Though the USA made up only 6% of the world's population, it produced half the world's economic goods. Yet tensions were brewing under the surface. In the 1950s, Eisenhower had declared self-sacrifice and obedience to national virtues. As a result, the land of freedom developed into a stronghold of bureaucracy, regulation, and conformity. There was only one path: You had to do what was expected of you. People had to function, adapt, and subordinate themselves, stamp their punched cards and take care of their families. It was at this time, when the media began to condition the masses. Almost every household had a TV. After a family evening watching one of the few channels, people had the same topics to talk about the next day at work.

This economic development also disempowered many people. Their personal responsibilities were taken away by large companies. Many young educated people from the middle class tried to get rid of these restraints. Millions left their homes to live in free chosen poverty according to the principles of the hippie ideals. The movement started with a big No: no to street cruisers and little boxes on the hillside, no to prudery and fear, no to safety nets and the bond for life, no to ties and bras, fake morals, discipline, and protestant work ethics. In short: no to the American Way of Life and everything that was normal. It was an escape from the idea that one day they might be living like their parents.

Harvey Cox, professor of theology at Harvard University, argues that the counterculture had all the characteristics of a quasi-religious movement. As with many religious splinter groups, the counterculturists opposed the religious institutions of the dominant culture. Though most of them denied religiosity, they asked for universal values and the meaning of life, searching for the same spiritual answers as any other religious movements. They tried to find new answers for the questions of life, on which, in their opinion, the established religions and their parents had failed. As one hippie couple wrote: «The young people we meet in the LSD-Underground appeal to be groping toward [...] a renewal of religion, a religion of loving, dancing and much music. Making a joyful noise unto the Lord! – A personal as well as group unifying religion [...] based on 'The unmediated Vision'. » The whole generation had grown up in a world plagued by massive armies and the real threat of thermonuclear annihilation. To some hippies, their vision could only come true by turning away from scientific progress, rejecting it as a false god and returning to nature. For The New Left, computers were a hated symbol of the military-industrial complex. Integrated circuits was something for nuclear power plants and ballistic missiles. At Berkeley, protesting students strung computer cards around their necks, with holes stamped through them to read STRIKE. They mockingly wrote, «Please do not fold, bend, spindle or mutilate me. » In contrast to the technology-skeptical left and the back-to-nature hippies, some communalists were up to something with the new technologies. They believed that technology could make their liberal principles an inevitable social reality and prepared themselves to make computers part of the individual life. Apple co-founder Steve Wozniak summed up their goals: We wanted «to bring computer technology within the range of the average person, to make it so people could afford to have a computer and do things with it. […] We wanted them to be affordable–and we wanted them to change people's lives. »

These technophiles, influenced by Marshall McLuhan's theories, among others, believed that the merging of mass media, computers, and telecommunications would lead to the appearance of an electronic Agora: a virtual space where everyone could express their opinions without fear of censorship. McLuhan preached the radical message that new technologies would empower the individuals to break the rule of large corporations and the government. His entertaining performances and a blessed mix of genius and higher nonsense caused the misunderstanding that he was a progressive, a liberal, and sympathizer of the hippies. The opposite was true. During his second studies at Cambridge he converted to Catholicism. He was a devout, elitist, misogynist reactionary, arrogant, and self-absorbed. His dislike of modernity was stunning. But he wanted to understand technological progress in order not to disappear in its all-consuming maelstrom. At the same time, he recognized the enormous monetary potential.

Strengthened by McLuhan's predictions, the West Coast radicals engaged in the development of new information technologies for the alternative press, collective radio stations, self-built computer clubs, video groups, etc. They believed themselves on the front line of the struggle to build a new America. The struggle would be tough, but «-kotopia» was near.

One of the most influential publications of this culture was the Whole Earth Catalog. Founder and central figure of the project was Stewart Brand. As son of academic parents with a degree in biology from Stanford University and two years of experience as a lieutenant in the army, Brand was a perfect candidate for a conventional academic career. But it came differently: From the hippie and eco movement to the parallel world of the Internet – Brand was always at the forefront. In the December 1972 issue of Rolling Stone magazine, Brand published an article about the computer game Spacewar, in which he also reports about the still young ARPANET. The article gives an exciting insight into the American hacker scene of the early 1970s, their fanaticism and how counterculture influenced it: «Ready or not, computers are coming to the people. That's good news, maybe the best since psychedelics, » he wrote.

Brand himself didn't start a California computer company that's among the top ten in the world, nor did he host the most prestigious series of conferences of our time. He didn't found a magazine that has accompanied every technological development for decades. And he didn't become the richest man in the world with an online shop. All this was done by his fans: Steve Jobs, TED founder Chris Anderson, Wired co-founder Kevin Kellyand, and Jeff Bezos. In the 1960s, Brand also had contact with futurists like R. Buckminster Fuller and computer scientists like Douglas Engelbart – the inventor of the computer mouse and the first graphical user interface. It was Brand who coined the term «personal computer, » which would make a great career. In an interview, Brand recalls his experiences in San Francisco, after he placed tabs of LSD on his tongue. He sat on the roof of a house and noticed that the skyscrapers in the distance did not look exactly straight, but a little crooked. He believed that this was due to the curvature of the earth. But you cannot see this curvature unless you are very high – like in space. Colored satellite photos of the Earth were not yet published at that time. But there were rumors that NASA had pictures of our planet. Brand believed that such a photo could make people aware of the uniqueness of the Earth and create an ecological awareness. He started a campaign for the publication of the NASA images. The core of his campaign were buttons, which he sold for 25 cents. They had the inscription: «Why haven't we seen a picture of the whole world yet? » NASA responded quickly: On November 10, 1967, a satellite took the first color photo of the planet. Brand used this image on the cover of the first issue of his Whole Earth Catalog. It gave people an idea that the earth is a small blue-white-green-brown dot surrounded by uninhabitable cold vacuum.

His experience in the army provided him with some practical and organizational skills. He doubted that the back-to-the-landers were prepared for their life experiments. Furthermore, they simply ignored the fact that technology was improving in all areas. Brand and his wife traveled to communities with a pickup truck, sold tools, lent books, and taught craftsmanship. Brand's goal was simple: His catalog was intended to provide «access to tools» in areas such as ecology, self-sufficiency, DIY, and education. The term «tool» was meant to be broad. In addition to machines and actual tools, the magazine also promoted clothing, seeds, the first programmable desktop calculator from Hewlett-Packard, and much more. But for the most part it presented books about the cybernetic contemplation of Norbert Wiener, system theory, psychology, and building instructions for Buckminster Fuller's geodesic domes. It was no mail order business, since Brand sold nothing but the magazine. The catalog merely had a guiding function. It included manufacturer and reference addresses as well as reviews, which were often written by experts. The catalog built heavily on the active participation of readers, who sent suggestions about what to include. They talked about their experiences with technologies, methods, or organization. In short, the Whole Earth Catalog was a printed version of the internet. Or as Steve Jobs later put it: «It was sort of like Google in paperback form, 35 years before Google came along. »

The effect of the catalog can hardly be measured today. It became the link between the social utopias of the hippies and a growing high-tech culture. In an early issue, it announced: «We are as gods and might as well get good at it. So far, remotely done power and glory – as via government, big business, formal education, church – has succeeded to the point where gross defects obscure actual gains. In response to this dilemma and to these gains a realm of intimate, personal power is developing – power of the individual to conduct his own education, find his own inspiration, shape his own environment, and share his adventure with whoever is interested. Tools that aid this process are sought and promoted by the WHOLE EARTH CATALOG. » The catalog was extremely successful. One edition, of which 1.5 million copies were sold, even received the National Book Award. The magazine was regularly published until the end of 1971, then only sporadically. The last issue was published in 1994.

In the early 1980s, the honeymoon of counterculture was over. Stanford professor Fred Turner describes Brand as a depressed man. Like many of his generation, he saw the failing of the counterculture. At least that's how the gradual disappearance of rural communities and countercultural lifestyles was interpreted. But as it turned out, the networks of that time had not disappeared, only their way of life had changed. Many technology-savvy hippies had become IT developers and scientists. The Whole Earth Catalog had brought together extremely diverse groups and individuals, creating a community that was constantly exchanging. Mostly, their communication took place in small groups or private conversations, by phone, or by mail. Then, finally, the necessary technology emerged. The new desktop computers and the Internet helped revive the spirit of counterculture. In the mid-1980s, Brand founded the computerized conferencing system Whole Earth 'Lectronic Link, The WELL for short, together with the physician Larry Brilliant. It was based on a solitary computer in California and the modems of the users, who could send text messages via telephone lines to which all users could respond. It was the world's first digital social network, discussion board, and job exchange. But not only that: It was a hub for the loose network of communes, a communication medium of the counterculture. There were sections for certain topics, ranging from «Agriculture» to «Writers, » from «Telecommunications Law» to «Spirituality, » special discussion groups for weapons freaks and gay people. The commune no longer needed a physical presence.

In the 1980s, the working world in the Californian technology sector changed fundamentally: The days of safe jobs in the aerospace industry were long gone. In the new computer industry people started talking about «projects» instead «jobs. » All the more important was networking, and The WELL provided the tools – like Brand's catalog. A large proportion of its users were journalists and authors who made their first experiences with cyberspace there and then enthusiastically wrote about it. One of them was Howard Rheingold, who invented the term «virtual community» explicitly for The WELL. At The WELL you could meet famous theorists and influential practitioners who later played a decisive role in the development of the Web. Craig Newmark, e.g., whose free Internet classified ad service Craigslist has almost completely wiped out the classified ad business of the entire American newspaper industry, or founding executive editor of Wired magazine Kevin Kelly, the cyberlibertarian political activist John Perry Barlow, media theorist and writer Douglas Rushkoff, to name a few.

As a business model, The WELL has never been financially successful. There was no advertising, as the technology was not yet available, and so the project financed itself with payments from its users. The investment was worth it. Journalists had free access to the network, which helped to spread the word. After many crises, The WELL still exists today. Larry Brilliant later joined Google, where he headed its charity Google.org. Stewart Brand became a business consultant. His impact on the culture of Silicon Valley and geekdom is hard to overestimate. «The '60s generation had a lot of power, but they didn't have a lot of tools, » explained Jane Metcalfe, cofounder and president of Wired. «And in many respects their protests were unable to implement longterm and radical change in our society. We do have the tools. The growth of the Internet and the growing political voice of the people on the Internet is proof of that. » The revelations of counterculture continue to this day: The technological paradise shimmers on the horizon...

THE NEW ROBBER BARONS

«The future is already here – it's just not very evenly distributed. » – William Gibson

«Silicon Valley made its siren call–a chance to change the world and get rich at the same time. We had been scrounging around for research funds to build our projects; now a new class of financiers–venture capitalists–came calling with their bulging bankrolls. » – Jerry Kaplan

Nerds are often interested in one thing only and show little empathy for other people. Some consider them amoral because they stick to their principles, even if these don't conform to those of society. It was no coincidence that the übernerd Friedrich Nietzsche constructed his own ethics: He speaks of the «Revaluation of all values» in the Antichrist. In the genealogy of morals he writes: «Nothing is true, everything is permitted. » Nietzsche had a certain contempt for the rest of humankind, coupled with plenty of arrogance: I'm smarter than you and I'll let you feel it. Almost unnoticed by the public, something Nietzsche like has happened in the Silicon Valley: a revaluation of all values and the rise of a new elite.

Two British media scholars, Richard Barbrook and Andy Cameron, wondered what had become of the «free-wheeling spirit of the hippies. » In their 1995 essay The Californian Ideology, they criticize a «bizarre fusion of the cultural bohemianism of San Francisco with the hi-tech industries of Silicon Valley» to form a radical dot.com neoliberalism. The hippies' dream of a better world merged with blind faith in the innovative power of business. A mixture of esoteric New Age utopias, raw individualism, an idealized free-market economy, and aims for the dismantling of the government and its institutions are core elements of the Californian ideology, culminating into a strange yet powerful worldview. Just as Nietzsche's philosophy claims universality, so does the belief in progress of the computer elite. Nietzsche praised a rugged individualism and dismissed democracy as the rule of the majority over the minority. People should be independent and self-reliant, define their own values and be compassionate out of an inner strength. The rights of the individual take precedence over those of the community. «True philosophers are commanders and legislators: they say 'That is how it should be!'» claimed Nietzsche.

Ironically, Nietzsche was the staple of some left-wing rebels. Emma Goldman, the grandmother of American anarchism, was an enthusiastic Nietzschean, and Jack London was one too. Nietzsche's polemic against the materialism and hypocrisy unmasked the façade-like nature of bourgeois virtues. By destroying the old theories of culture, morality, religion, and philosophy, he spawned new approaches based on completely new ideas and concepts. Accepting 'evil' as a force of life, he created the Übermensch, who is not bound by ethical norms. Nietzsche knew that his radical ideas pose a certain danger: «I am not a human being, I am dynamite, » he wrote in his autobiography. What he meant was the disruptiveness of his work. But if there was one thing that Nietzsche explicitly didn't care about, then it was the misery of the plundered masses. Whenever he criticized the bourgeois world, it was from an elitist perspective. The similarities with the Californian ideology are stunning, and the valleyists don't even try to hide it. They admit frankly: We want to shape the world according to our ideas. But how did the Summer of Love became the winter of greed and heartlessness?

With the arrival of tens of thousands of young people in Haight-Ashbury, chasing an illusion of freedom and adventure, it gradually went off the rails. The movement had fallen victim to commercialization, boredom, and crime. Motorcycle gangs and addicts besieged Haight Street. The end of the «Summer of Love» was marked by the «Death of a Hippie» on 6 October 1967. Several hundred flower children symbolically buried a hippie in a coffin full of flowers. The magic of Haight Ashbury, Monterrey, and Woodstock was followed by the horror of Altamont Free Concert in 1969, the «symbol for the death of the Woodstock Nation. » A member of the band Jefferson Airplane was beaten up, and a young man was killed with a knife. On May 15, 1969, Governor Reagan ordered armed police to take action against protesting hippies who had occupied People's Park. In the following fights, one man was shot dead, and 128 people needed medical treatment. The Johnson & Nixon CIA targeted the anti-Vietnam movement. The agency's mission was to erase everything that spoke of peace, innocence, and altruism. Civil rights activists, protest students, Martin Luther King, and the two Kennedys were murdered. The Black Panthers, the Beatniks, and communalists were infiltrated. The counterculture was flooded with containers full of cocaine and heroin. Under the influence of stronger and more dangerous drugs, the once so colorful and ecstatic movement darkens, and satanic sects in Charles Manson format appeared. Bad drug trips led to suicide, murder, or madness, happy trips to a bloated, foggy consciousness. Many heroes silently wasted away: Janis Joplin, Jimi Hendrix, Jim Morrison… Even the former prophet of the LSD movement, Timothy Leary, gave up. He married and declared that the selfish use of LSD «may be creating a new race of mutants. » Finally, most hippies went home. Probably few ever had anything else in mind.

«Throughout the centuries there were men who took first steps down new roads armed with nothing but their own vision, » wrote Ayn Rand in her novel The Fountainhead from 1943. It perfectly sums up the self-image of the Silicon Valley entrepreneurs. Ayn Rand has always denied that she was influenced by Nietzsche. Yet her novels deal with nothing but Nietzsche's «Übermensch. » In her main work Atlas Shrugged, she praised an unleashed market economy. Inventiveness and efficiency are the highest virtues. Egoism is good, selflessness is evil, since it leads straight into collectivist totalitarianism. Capitalism is the best of all possible economic forms. The more the government keeps its mouth shut, the better. Rand is full of contempt for those «scroungers» who demand to share the wealth which they allegedly did not help to create. She called them the «moochers and looters, » a formulation that Nietzsche certainly would have liked.

Silicon Valley has adopted its own variant of the fantasy of being chosen. Some of them have named their companies to reflect their limitless aspirations. Amazon, as in the most voluminous river on the planet, has a logo that points from A to Z. The name Google derives from googol, a number (1 followed by 100 zeros) that mathematicians use as shorthand for large quantities. Since 2015, Google has been operating under the name Alphabet, so that all doubts are eliminated as to where the company sees its place in history.

It's not only about what we consume or some small changes, but the total transformation of all areas of our lives. And they are confident that the changes of recent years were little more than an overture. A highly messianic technocracy has emerged in the Valley, an elite that is disconnected from the people outside the Valley. The new turbo-capitalists believe that their work really contributes to the welfare of humankind, and that they are somehow advancing civilization.

They want to change the world and not accept established rules. «The question we always have to ask is what problem are they trying to solve? Are they taking on problems that are important for the world? » asked City CarShare co-founder Gabriel Metcalf in an interview without any irony.

Steve Jobs still staged himself as a hippie and a rebel while he was running one of the toughest companies in the world. In the only extensive interview with him – conducted by journalist Bob Cringely for a television series entitled Triumph of the Nerds – the interviewer finally wants to know whether Jobs is a nerd or a hippie. With his yellowish skin, perhaps a consequence of his ascetic diet, and the greasy strands of hair in his forehead, Jobs rather reminds you of a hallucinating traveler who is stranded in the desert. Behind his round John Lennon glasses Jobs glares at his vis-à-vis with a piercing look: With Apple he always wanted to create something different than the standard world of job, family, and two cars in the garage. He wanted to create an intermediate realm, as Henry David Thoreau and the Indian mystics had explored … His former associate Steve Wozniak never gets tired to tell to people, how important the counterculture was to him: «We were participating in the biggest revolution that had ever happened, I thought. I was so happy to be a part of it.» In the meantime, their products have become a status symbol of the well-off rather than the poor.

Mark Zuckerberg has the chutzpah to claim that it's not about money. He repeatedly said that «we don't wake up in the morning with the primary goal of making money.» Facebook «was not originally created to be a company,» he declared to potential investors a few months before the initial public offering for Facebook in 2012. «The goal of the company is to help people to share more in order to make the world more open and to help promote understanding between people.» He almost religiously insists on the social importance of the network. But if this was true, and he really does not care about profit, why is Facebook then not a non-commercial platform and why does it use targeted advertising?

Larry Page delivered a similar statement: «If we were motivated by money, we would have sold the company a long time ago and ended up on a beach.» Google still prides itself as being an «uncompany» even though the 1 trillion dollar leviathan is, as of January 2020, the world's second most valuable corporation. In this context, Google's former motto «Don't be evil» seems either naïve or like a bad joke. Without any prior business experience, Page built the most successful money machine on the Internet in a very short time. As a child, he wanted to be an inventor, because, «I really wanted to change the world,» of course. All kids want that, which is why it's childish.

Spotify, a music streaming service, claims that its mission is «to unlock the potential of human creativity.» Dropbox, which lets you store your files in the cloud, has no lower ambition than «to unleash the world's creative energy by designing a more enlightened way of working.» Uber, which offers an app for mobility services, wants to «bring transportation – for everyone, everywhere.» From its beginning, Yahoo's mission (and slogan) has been the same: «It's the only place anyone has to go to get connected to anything or anybody.» Bill Gates once claimed: «Technology is unlocking the innate compassion we have for our fellow human beings.» What exactly would the world according to Bill Gates be like? Today, people spend already more time alone than any other generation. Amazon was once the «everything store,» now it's the «unstore» and produces television shows, designs drones, and powers the cloud. It's the largest online shop in the world and a notorious bully of small competing companies. «Our culture is to leave the world better than we found it,» said Bezos during a conference. Bezos earns 250 million dollars a day, while many of his employees depend on Medicaid and food stamps, and he is refusing to provide paid sick leave for all of them.

In the digital utopia everyone will be happy and rich. Rachel Botsman announces in her book What's Mine is Yours the end of all social problems. She is a former manager who today is only busy spreading the word of the Sharing Economy. This optimistic vision has, not surprisingly, been enthusiastically embraced by computer enthusiasts, lazy students, innovative capitalists, social activists, scholars, and bureaucrats everywhere in the United States. Siva Vaidhyanathan, professor of media studies at the University of Virginia and author, warns that the «naive vision that a company can do no wrong is unhealthy.» When a company goes public and is watched by analysts and investors, constraints arise which it cannot escape if you want to be successful, regardless of your political, moral, and other convictions. Steve Levy already described in his book Hackers how Apple evolved from a hacker company to the world's largest company by the gradual abandonment of its ideals. Levy believes that was inevitable since you can't run a large listed company like a hacker.

In 1975, 32 young computer freaks gathered in the garage of engineer and programmer Gordon French in Menlo Park, southeast of San Francisco, to share their hobbies. It was the first of a year-long series of events that would go down in technical history as the Homebrew Computer Club. One of its members was Steve Wozniak, called Woz. The 25-year-old had just been expelled from university for using the college's computer to display obscene messages. Woz was certainly not a rebel, but a nerd with a strange humor who liked to show off with his computer skills. Besides electronics, he was also interested in mathematics and natural sciences, but only as far as it could help him with his projects. Through a mutual friend Woz had recently met the five years younger Steve Jobs. Until his meeting with Woz, Jobs believed that nobody could hold a candle to him as a tinkerer. But his new friend showed him how limited his knowledge really was. What Jobs was really good at, however, was his talent for organization. Wozniak had designed a device with a monitor and a keyboard that was much more powerful than many other computers available at the time. He shared his idea with the Homebrew Computer Club and asked for advice. While Woz merely wanted to impress his buddies at the club, Jobs was also interested in making money: 'Don't give your ideas away for free,' was his advice. Jobs knew that the awakening computer age was their time.

In 1976, the two founded the Apple company in the garage of Jobs' parents in Los Altos and marketed Wozniak's machine as Apple I. The success was rather modest. Before Apple could outperform the other hobby shops in Silicon Valley, it needed a second, rather accidental encounter: In 1977, venture capitalist Mike Markkula met the two boys. With Markkula's management know-how, Apple became the hottest start-up in Silicon Valley. The Apple II blew away everything that had been on the American computer market until then. Apple became the epicenter of Silicon Valley, a multibillion dollar success story and the mecca of the nerds of this world.

For all their messianic rhetoric about changing the world for the better, the tech giants follow the ethos and priorities of business. Their business exist for the sole purpose of maximizing shareholder value. «If you really want to understand how Silicon Valley works today, you should watch the HBO series 'Silicon Valley', » recommends Bill Gates in a blog post. He is surprised at how rarely pop culture accurately depicts Silicon Valley, given its enormous influence. Gates points out that though «Silicon Valley» is a parody, it reflects many truths. Especially the characters are recognizable for him. The series follows a group of friends who try to build a successful startup, satirizing the stereotypical computer geek as well as the tech industry as such: Dotcom millionaires, venture capitalists, tech gurus and corporate sharks are represented as well as the tech press. «The programmers are smart, super-competitive even with their friends, and a bit clueless when it comes to social cues, » writes Gates. The show is not questioning their motives, instead it shows, a little exaggerated, what is going on. «We want to make the world a better place, » is the mantra for every product developed and introduced in this series, no matter how absurd it may be. And no matter how silly the product is, ultimately it still totally okay if you can make money with it.

Sorry, but selling people whatever it is does not mean that they care for the welfare of our community. The failed Internet entrepreneur Michael Wolff put it best, when he described an important component of any business discussion he had in Silicon Valley: «How we, the people at the table, could make as much money as fast as possible–even if that meant doing what we knew to be wrong or futile. » That is their real religion: materialism. What can't be measured has no meaning, which is why they almost always end up speaking in the language of markets and businesses. All their talk about «changing the world» is to deflect attention away from their own greed. Succinctly put, the Californian ideology equals their personal enrichment with social benefit for all. All their projects are carried out with one goal in mind: to fill our lives with their products and services and to drag us into their commercial realms. It would be easy to dismiss their ambitions as the prattle of some overambitious entrepreneurs. But that would be a huge mistake. This is not only the freakish world view of some Sheldon Cooper nerds. They are the spearhead of a global movement that is well connected with politics, business lobbies, and the media. They don't follow delusional fantasies, but have realistic materialistic goals in mind, and their entrepreneurial instinct has served them well.

The Gold Rush mentality is still there. A few smart and lucky people found a pot of gold, which encouraged everyone else to keep believing and wishing. One of Silicon Valley's most successful entrepreneurs is Marc Andreessen. He loves to brag that the basis for the success of a start-up is «courage and genius» – not less. In 1994, together with James H. Clark, he founded a company called Mosaic Communications Corporation. Clark was a venture capitalist who contributed nine million dollars. Very brave. Later, the company was renamed Netscape Communications Corporation. Its main business was the development of server software for the Internet. To make the company known, they developed the Netscape browser. Netscape went public in August 1995 and continuously increased in value. The 25-year-old Mark was suddenly passed around as THE prodigy of the Internet. In less than five years, he transformed himself from a computer scientist to a savvy businessman. In 1998, Netscape lost the so-called browser war due Microsoft's aggressive marketing. For this, Microsoft was later sued by antitrust authorities. In 1999, Netscape was sold for a whopping 4.2 billion dollars to AOL. In one fell swoop, Marc was really, really rich. But the fun for the valleyists was just beginning.

In 1994, thirty-year-old Jeff Bezos was the youngest senior vice president whom investment banker D. E. Shaw had ever employed. While surfing the Internet in search of new investment opportunities, Bezos stumbled upon a website that claimed that the numbers of web users grew at 2,300 percent per year – growth rates that every speculator dreams of. Without hesitation, he decided to leave his old career behind and to start his own online business. The company he founded was Amazon.com. Only five years later, the company had a stock market value of 36 billion dollars, and Bezos's own net worth was approaching 13 billion dollars.

The rise of these nerds symbolizes what the MIT economists Andrew McAfee and Eric Brynjolfsson call an economy of «stars and superstars.» Their motto is: The best wins, the rest loses. «Elite selection and a certain Darwinism, however, are central principles of Californian ideology: there are only a few victors, in the social sphere it's eliminative,» explains Peter Thiel. The fabulous successes of a small group seem like proof of the power of their free-market fundamentalism.

BILLIONAIRES AND BEGGARS

«An imbalance between rich and poor is the oldest and most fatal ailment of all republics. » – Plutarch

«Let me tell you about the very rich. They are different from you and me. » – F. Scott Fitzgerald

Barbrook and Cameron published their essay during the first boom of digital capitalism, the dotcom bubble. The mid-1990s were a time of optimism. The planned economies of the communist countries had collapsed, the Western world had proved to be superior economically and culturally. With the fall of the Iron Curtain, goods, services, and people could now move freely around the world. The «Big Four» – Amazon, eBay, Facebook, Google – did not yet exist. But the Digital Revolution provided the decisive impetus for globalization.

The promises of Californian ideology are so lofty that few people take note if they are not kept. In the 1990s, Wired – the key propaganda magazine for the Californian ideology – announced the «Long Boom»: decades of prosperity and the solution of environmental problems. The burst of the speculative bubble in the early 2000s could not curb their optimism. The crash spawned new radical-liberal theories. Former Wired editor-in-chief Chris Anderson declared that the economy of the future would 'inevitably' see a democratization of the market. With the Internet, people would make their living as micro-entrepreneurs. So far, his thesis hasn't come true. In fact, large digital corporations dominate the economy.

The technological faith of the Silicon Valley disciples has nothing to do with real progress. It's based on blindness towards racism, poverty, and environmental destruction. Even in the upper echelons of the Valley, there is no sign of their promises being fulfilled. There has been no democratization despite all their talk of an open and non-hierarchical corporate culture. Elon Musk, e.g., stands for extra-rigid management methods. Occasionally he spits coffee over the table or threatens to «cut off the balls» – like so many other mentally balanced people do. Jeff Bezos is not a feel-good manager either. He wanted to call his company Relentless.com. Relentless is Bezos outside and inside his company. He wants to destroy competitors, negotiates with business partners till they bleed, and he is also relentless towards employees. The only one who perhaps topped it was the now deceased Steve Jobs.

The Californian utopia, though still in its infancy, has already become a dystopian nightmare for many people. Every morning, there's an invasion coming over Silicon Valley. Thousands of employees of high-tech companies arrive from San Francisco. The big city is more attractive to them than the small towns where Apple, Google, and Facebook have their headquarters. They accept long drives to work every morning and evening. Typically, a one-way drive on the highway from Palo Alto to San Francisco takes about 40 minutes, but on the overcrowded highways in rush hour traffic, it sometimes takes two hours. The old diesel-powered suburban CalTrain is slow and has no Wi-Fi, and the train station in the Valley is poorly connected to the corporate headquarters. The big companies have solved the problem in their own way and set up private bus lines, which can use the Diamond Lane. Since the public sector lacks the money, public transportation is being transferred to the corporations. Google now operates America's largest private bus company. LinkedIn, eBay, Yahoo – they all shuttle their employees back and forth for free. The air-sprung buses with dark mirrored windows are equipped with W-LAN and air conditioning. The companies name comfort for employees as the decisive reason for the free buses. They also are stuck in traffic jams, but the programmers, data analysts, or social media experts can work while driving – every day up to three hours longer than in their cars. Silicon Valley organizes the lives of its employees with a lot of dedication. Every aspect of their private life is taken care of, everything is free: rooms for a midday nap, swimming pools and fitness clubs, dental treatment, flex time, hairdressing appointments on the company premises, and lactation programs for nursing mothers. The company's concierges handle every conceivable task. They get insurance policies, deal with authorities, apply for credit cards, go shopping, take the kids to kindergarten, etc. In the battle for talent, such incentives have become standard. Back in the day of Taylor, entrepreneurs had it easier. Our former masters could crack the whip over everyone. Today, it takes a more sophisticated torturous approach. The motivation of the companies is clear. By relieving employees of all tasks that detract them from peak performance, they can be fully utilized. Nothing should prevent them from achieving the highest possible productivity. In the 1930s, economist John Maynard Keynes boldly predicted that technological progress would allow people to work only 15 hours per week. We all know that didn't happen. The valleyists works around the clock. Every day they test their limits. And at night, the pressure to succeed robs them of their sleep. No rest for the improvers of mankind.

In 1880, George M. Beard, a neurologist from New York, described the clinical picture of neurasthenia, the «nervous weakness. » The symptoms range from general anxiety to impotence and depressive moods – much like today's burnout. In 1910, neurasthenia was the most often diagnosed disease in Germany. At that time, Germany was the technological powerhouse of the world. The Austrian writer Karl Kraus noted: «The development of technology has reached the point of defenselessness before technology. »

Economic progress is not cheap: Burnout costs the health care system roughly 125 to 190 billion dollars a year. Chronically high stress can be a matter of life and death. It contributes to type 2 diabetes, high blood pressure, coronary heart disease, gastrointestinal problems, high cholesterol, alcohol, and drug abuse. All of this could be easy prevented. Instead, Bezos advises his employees to stop trying to achieve a work-life balance. «It actually is a circle. It's not a balance, » Bezos claims. The International Trade Union Confederation (ITUC) declared him the world's worst employer. According to Sharan Burrow, General Secretary of the ITUC, Amazon is «a rich American corporation operating globally with disdain for dignity, for rights for working people. » Bezos is the personification of the inhumanity of the American corporate model. What is happening there shows us our future: The repertoire includes constant pressure, bullying, and total surveillance. The employees are under great stress. The rules at the warehouses are strict and sometimes random. Employees walk 11 miles a shift. A GPS device that they carry on their bodies checks precisely whether they follow the predetermined routes between the stations. Every deviation is sanctioned. Bezos is almost obsessed with work and expects the same obsession from his employees.

The religious devotion of the valleyists to overwork has a negative effect on their relationships too. The American sociologist Richard Sennett observed: «Detachment and superficial cooperativeness are better armor for dealing with current realities than behavior based on values of loyalty and service. [...] Transposed to the family realm, 'No long term' means keep moving, don't commit yourself and don't sacrifice. » They cannot develop lasting and deep emotional relationships with their region, neighbors, or colleagues. Friends and business partners meet in cyberspace more often than they meet their actual neighbors. They are – in the very sense of the term «individualization» – in every aspect thrown back on their own. As a result, they develop a cold, self-referential character, without emotional, moral, or social ties. Under these conditions, narcissism thrives. And with their gadgets and services they transcend their damaged personalities into society.

California is a state of crass contrasts: An incredible wealth exists next to a poverty that you only know from humanitarian disaster areas. The company buses have become a symbol of gentrification and growing social differences. In an angry essay, San Francisco writer Rebecca Solnit wrote that the buses sometimes remind her to «spaceships on which our alien overlords have landed to rule over us. » The tech commuters board the buses in front of beggars and homeless people, thousands of whom have been living on the streets since the social reforms under Ronald Reagan. While there are more millionaires and billionaires than anywhere else in the United States, hundreds of thousands of people live in poverty. «We call it the Silicon Valley paradox, » said Steve Brennan, marketing director of Second Harvest Food Bank, in the Guardian. Poverty is growing in Silicon Valley to an unimaginable extent. People sleep on the streets, in cars or garages, or stay with friends, share tiny rooms in two-room apartments with cardboard walls. Many of them don't even find a room in an emergency shelter. But they are entitled to free public transport. At night, they use the buses of line 22 as their refuge.

In recent years, the cost of living, rents, and property prices in San Francisco have increased massively. But only well-educated university graduates have the chance to earn high salaries. The companies only hire the elite from Stanford, Harvard, or the MIT. They pay record salaries only because they know that the education of these graduates is first-class. These universities, on the other hand, are only accessible to the best students with a scholarship or children from wealthy parents. Yet Silicon Valley consists not only of founders and investors, but mainly of employees who work in companies or for the wealthy. These people receive normal salaries and are by no means rich. The techies are chauffeured by drivers with hourly wages between 17 to 30 dollars. A security guard or bus driver can hardly exist with dignity and without existential fears. With the wages for this «infantry» it's impossible to pay the exorbitant rents and living costs in the high-tech centers. The locals are rapidly being displaced because they can no longer pay the rising rents even though they have a regular job, often more than one. House owners sell their properties for fantastic prices and spend their retirement elsewhere. With the fruit plantations, the middle class has disappeared as well. People who would otherwise belong to the middle class almost anywhere else are struggling to survive in Silicon Valley. Families escape to the hot, sunburned hinterland. There the schools are worse because the districts have less money. Thus, climbing the social ladder is just as difficult for the children as it's for their parents. The jobs in Silicon Valley are by no means safe, there are high fluctuation and dismissal rates. The age limits for employees in the tech sector seem completely out of balance. While the average working American is 42.3 years old, the techies are much younger, mostly in their mid-20s to mid-30s. Over the past 35 years, economy in America has resembled the age of the robber barons, in some cases astoundingly. Measured only by the wealth of the one percent on the top of the food chain, America is great again. The economy is booming with a record-breaking growth. On the other side, 14 million people live below the poverty line, and millions more have to struggle to stay above it. The concentration of wealth is higher than in any other country in the world. After a long period of declining inequality, it has been rising steadily since 1980. In the 1980s and 1990s, a corporate culture based on shareholder value became popular. President Reagan claimed that greed is good and not bad. He and his successors Bill Clinton and George W. Bush massively unchained the markets from regulations. The corporations introduced financial incentives for their executives, including the option to buy shares of the company as a part of their compensation as well as a pay depending on the stock price of the company. According to The Economist, these incentives «were designed to align the interests of companies' managers with those of shareholders by concentrating managers' minds on profitability. » Managers consequently developed strategies to maximize short-term profits. «The result was skyrocketing stock prices, mounting personal fortunes for the managers who enthusiastically undertook these actions, and a massive widening of the gap between the haves and have-nots in society, » writes business consultant Allan Kennedy. According to Thomas Piketty's World Inequality Report, the gap between rich and poor is approaching pre-war levels. In their paper The Fading American Dream, six scientists from Stanford and Harvard have outlined that hard work no longer guarantees prosperity and justice in the USA. The tragic paradox that poverty can still grow a vibrant economy is not a new experience, as we know from the beginnings of industrialization in Europe. Neither diligence and qualification nor second and third jobs guarantee a carefree life for yourself and your family. In the past, individual progress was possible – even if not from dishwasher to millionaire, but from worker's child to lawyer or physician. A social experience which is now almost impossible. The door to social advancement – a good education system that is accessible to all – is closing. For ambitious parents, the public school system appears to be a dead end. Today, children are seldom better off than their parents, often the opposite is true. This is the new economy at work, a circulus vitiosus of poverty. The lack of education and special skills swiftly leads to social exclusion. Anyone who hasn't learned anything of use for future industries has barely a chance. The social permeability of American society has been exposed as a myth. The reality is private schools, social and health services only for those who can afford it, high fenced ghettos for the wealthy, and online shopping. According to the political scientist Keith Poole, this «inequality feeds directly into political polarization, and polarization in turn creates policies that further increase inequality. » The extremely unequal distribution of wealth is creating a new aristocracy – the super-rich, the plutocracy or «financial oligarchy» as the famous American constitutional judge Louis Brandeis labeled it in 1912. The second Gilded Age is driven by telecommunications, computers, the Internet, innovation in financial markets, and globalization, as well as tax cuts and the dismantling of state regulation. The new breed of entrepreneurs controls a financial wealth that far exceeds the imagination of the financial jugglers of the old times. Elitism is more extreme in Silicon Valley than elsewhere.

Researchers have proven that failure is the rule, not the exception. The British economist Leslie Hannah tracked the fate of the hundred largest American corporations from 1912: In 1995, with only two exceptions, none of them were among the top 100 anymore. Of the 2,000 or so car companies that flourished in the USA at the beginning of motorization, less than one percent survived. «The odds of any individual entrepreneur becoming a megawinner are vanishingly small, as they are for buyers of lottery tickets, and the jackpots in tech are capricious, » she concluded. More than 80 percent of all start-ups fail within three years. Ben Smith, author of Journeyman summed it up: «Two million people live in Silicon Valley and one million of them believe they've discovered the next big thing. » The problem is not to have a good idea, but one that can be monetized. The only benchmark is profit, as fast as possible, as much as possible. Even those who fail, do not see themselves as losers. Their idols at Google or Uber are just around the corner. «What they can do, I can do too, » is the mantra with which they deceive themselves. The myth of a get-rich-quick enterprise is a bust. Stories of successful entrepreneurs mislead about the forgotten millions of losers. Brazilian author Paulo Coelho is disappointed by the Silicon Valley: It used to be a place where people discussed and were friends. «Today they're there just for the money, » Coelho said in an interview. The pursuit of profit has transformed the «Valley of heart's delight» into a blooming landscape of selfishness.

A MAN'S WORLD

«The rules! » shouted Ralph, «you're breaking the rules! »
«Who cares? » – William Golding, Lord of the Flies

From the days of the Gold Rush, people have come to the Pacific state and dreamed of wealth. In Silicon Valley you'll meet fortune knights, religious zealots of all kind, libertarians, and unconventional thinkers, as well as political fanatics, neoliberal zombies, and others who want to make a fresh start here. They all contribute to a rather liberal, cosmopolitan, and creative atmosphere of the region. In 2016, the importance of this liberal attitude for the companies became obvious during the presidential election campaign, when Donald Trump made his mark with xenophobic statements. Almost 150 tech giants from the USA joined forces and published an open letter against him. The entrepreneurs called out Trump's «divisive candidacy» and demanded open-mindedness towards newcomers and freedom of speech. «We want a candidate who embraces the ideals that built America's technology industry, » they wrote. Peter Thiel is one of the very few prominent Silicon Valley tycoons who promoted Donald Trump during the 2016 election campaign. He polarized with the claim that diversity would weaken Western culture. His remarks reminds me of Nazi propaganda about the «Schwächung des Volkes» (weakening of the people) through immigration and other right-wing conspiracy theories popular with Trump and his racist base. Trump's racist attitude and protectionism is a catastrophe for innovation. The digital economy in particular would suffer from isolation from other cultures and the exclusion of minorities. Many of its protagonists belong to different cultures, are multisexual, and have no desire to be attacked, condemned, or excluded because of their origin, skin color, religion, or sexual preferences. Diversity has made Silicon Valley strong in the first place. Many of the top tech companies were founded by migrants or children of migrants: Elon Musk comes from South Africa, Steve Jobs' father was Syrian, the family of Sergey Brin fled the Soviet Union to the USA, Thiel is German. People from all over the world work in the Californian Tech Mecca. The bad news is that most of these people don't do start-ups nor sit on the levers of power. They make sure that white men can develop software and make decisions as comfortably and undisturbed from the realities of ordinary life as possible. Three out of four gardeners in Silicon Valley are Latinos and 69 percent of the janitors. Black or Latin Americans also have the highest numbers among security and cleaning staff. In an interview Steve Jobs once claimed: «Silicon Valley is a meritocracy. It doesn't matter how old you are. It doesn't matter what you wear. What matters is how smart you are. » Not origin counts, but performance. Anyone with a good idea can change the world or at least earn quite a lot of money. That's nice and sweet, but it's not true. Lori Nishiura Mackenzie from Standford University denies his claim: «Our research shows that this meritocracy does not exist, » and «the paradox of meritocracy is that when people believe the system to be fair, they as managers actually become more biased. » She concludes: «If we believe we already are a meritocracy, and everything's completely fair and equitable, we will do nothing to examine our systems. » Entrepreneur and former presidential hopeful Andrew Yang summed it in a blog post about his own career:

«One of the things most entrepreneurs love about their field is the idea that the market acts as a meritocracy. Theoretically, it weeds out the companies with bad ideas and poor business models and rewards the strong. The truth is: Donald Trump inherited millions from his father. Mark Zuckerberg famously dropped out of Harvard. (He and I went to the same boarding school.) Jeff Bezos went to Princeton and worked on Wall Street before founding Amazon. The truth is that it's a lot easier to start a company if you have the ability to connect with investors and advisors, put off drawing a salary for a spell and take on risk. »

Under public pressure, large companies published the composition of their workforce. The numbers aren't pretty and expose the promise of meritocracy as a myth. A good two third is male. Only every third employee belongs to another ethnic group, mostly Asian. The number of employees and managers of African American and Latin American origin is negligibly low. Even industry insiders have to think hard before they can name a black CEO. Silicon Valley is a man's space. In a sardonic observation about his colleagues, Joseph Weizenbaum, computer pioneer and relentless critic of an unreflected computerization, once wrote:

«Wherever computer centers have become established [...] bright young men of disheveled appearance, often with sunken glowing eyes, can be seen sitting at computer consoles, their arms tensed and waiting to fire their fingers, already poised to strike, at the buttons and keys on which their attention seems to be as riveted as a gambler's on the rolling dice. When not so transfixed, they often sit at tables strewn with computer printouts over which they pore like possessed students of a cabalistic text. They work until they nearly drop, twenty, thirty hours at a time. Their food, if they arrange it, is brought to them: coffee, Cokes, sandwiches. If possible, they sleep on cots near the computer. But only for a few hours—then back to the console or the printouts. Their rumpled clothes, their unwashed and unshaven faces, and their uncombed hair all testify that they are oblivious to their bodies and to the world in which they move. They exist, at least when so engaged, only through and for the computers. These are computer bums, compulsive programmers. »

Weizenbaum created the famous computer program Eliza, named after the character in George Bernhard Shaw's Pygmalion. The program was a milestone in the history artificial intelligence. It analyzed spoken content and reacted according to a script. Meanwhile, Weizenbaum became one of the most vivid critics of artificial intelligence.
A strong focus on a single activity is one characteristic of nerds. Sean Parker, inventor of the music exchange Napster and former president of Facebook, could get furious if anyone tried to interrupt Mark Zuckerberg when he was

working on his laptop. Parker is no nerd, but he knew that his business partner was. If necessary, Parker pushed the visitors out of the room himself. The reason why nerds are predominantly male is not yet fully understood. But there is at least one possible physiological explanation. Several studies have shown that the two hemispheres of the brain communicate more intensively with each other in women than in men because the so-called «bar, » the connecting piece between the two hemispheres, is more developed in them. Most people know the state of mind when you drift off with your thoughts and are no longer fully focused. Daydreaming is commonly seen as a loss of concentration. But actually it's much more than a flaw in the system. As researchers from the Georgia Institute of Technology in Atlanta report, daydreaming is a sign of high intelligence and creativity. Psychologist Christine Godwin and her team found that daydreamers score higher on intelligence tests. Poorer communication between the brain hemispheres is why some men obsessively devote themselves to a problem even though it's unsolvable. Without this ability to focus, no one can be a nerd.

But it obviously goes in hand with rather antisocial behavior. In her book Brotopia, the famous journalist Emily Chang describes the tradition of sexist behavior in Silicon Valley. While in the early years of the industry, most programmers were female, women now hardly find a way in. The myth of the nerd discourages women from taking up this profession. And if they do, they must soon realize that the shy nerds are not so shy. Tinder co-founder Whitney Wolfe sued her company for sexual harassment, including racist, sexist, homophobic, misogynist, and offensive text messages. The trial ended with a settlement. GitHub chairman Tom Preston-Werner resigned after an employee complained about sexual harassment and sexually motivated revenge behavior. 60 percent of the women who work in the American IT industry have already experienced sexual harassment at work. According to various studies, the sad average for all other industries in the USA is between 25 to 35 percent. A developer told the magazine Business Insider that the sexism culture goes hand in hand with professional success and the associated reputation within the IT industry. The high pay would bloat the ego of the otherwise petty men and makes them feel entitled to treat others bad. Women are regarded as less qualified by their male colleagues. They are systematically excluded from tech careers and treated like second-class people. Furthermore, women's salaries are often significantly lower than those of their male colleagues. It certainly also plays a role that many nerds have problems finding a partner. Their sexist behavior may indicate a latent sexual frustration, but this is no excuse. The investor John Doerr pointed out: «If you look at Bezos, or Andreessen, David Filo, the founders of Google, they all seem to be white, male, nerds who've dropped out of Harvard or Stanford and they absolutely have no social life. »

This male-dominated «bro culture» and the lack of female talent is a bigger problem than we might think of at first. We all interact every day with online applications developed by a small group that is not representative of the world's population. But who wants to change the world should not only draw on a small elite circle of people. You cannot separate the culture of an industry from the products it generates. Basically, a white young male clique in California is developing products for white young male consumers. The needs of the African American or Asian population, Hispanics or women with children are not taken into account. A 24-year-old Stanford white upper-class graduate hardly knows what is important to them. Meritocracy is impossible when you view certain people as more valuable. Companies in Silicon Valley have a greater responsibility because their products have a significant impact on our working and private lives. Thus, tech companies should not ignore discrimination or discriminate against anyone. Apart from being a fairy tale, the idealization of meritocracy seems to me cruel in itself. In a humane society, everyone should have the opportunity to live a decent life.

HAPPY ISLANDS OF THE VALLEY

«People of the same trade seldom meet together, even for merriment and diversion, but the conversation ends in a conspiracy against the public, or in some contrivance to raise prices.»
– Adam Smith

In May 1901, the news came over the wire that some rich tycoons had picked a quarrel with each other over money and power. The fight involved J.P. Morgan, James J. Hill, Edward H. Harriman, the extremely powerful William Rockefeller, Jacob Schiff, Cornelius Vanderbilt, and other prominent people. With the usual methods of bribery and political corruption, Hill had won sole control of the Great Northern Railroad, a move that troubled the competing magnates. They immediately saw that their interests were at stake. When word got around that the richest men in America were bidding for Northern Pacific shares, a panic broke out on the stock exchange. The market price for Northern Pacific shares rose to astonishing levels. On one day from around 23 up to 300 dollars, on another day – for a short moment – up to 1,000 dollars the share. To the same extent that Northern Pacific stock prices continued to rise, the other railroad stocks fell. To settle the dispute, the magnates chose J. P. Morgan as their mediator. He designed a plan for a giant joint venture, which would control the Great Northern- and the Northern Pacific Railways. They founded the Northern Securities Company with a capital of 400 million dollars. The people in the Northwest protested about the announcement. Haven't they suffered enough already? Such a monopoly shouldn't be allowed, they complained, it would force them into slavery, a lawsuit would have to be brought to end it. And in 1902, President Theodore Roosevelt, without warning, filed a major anti-trust lawsuit against the Northern Securities. When he learned the news, J. P. Morgan was in a meeting with business associates in the luxurious «Black Library» of his New York villa. He knew President Theodore Roosevelt well since his youth, but this time his contacts in Washington were of no use to him. The United States Supreme Court ruled that the joint venture was illegal. Northern Securities was crushed, triggering a broad campaign against cartels and corruption. Under Roosevelt, the U.S. government filed over forty lawsuits against cartels at the time, which earned him a reputation as a «trustbuster. » More than a century later, the question arises whether we need to take such strict measures again.

Colossuses such as Amazon, Google, and Facebook have enormous market power. These startups are no longer pure Internet companies, but brutally powerful high-tech corporations. They not only control important markets such as marketing or online trade, they also operate their own marketplaces on a large scale according to their own rules. Apple and Amazon are full-service providers of a broad range of services and media content, some of which they produce themselves Amazon provides a trading platform for independent traders under conditions that are often unfavorable to them. With its subsidiaries WhatsApp and Instagram, Facebook is the unchallenged leader in social networking. Google is no longer just a search engine. With YouTube, it operates by far the largest video streaming service, Google Play is the largest App Store, Gmail is the leading e-mail service, Google Maps is the central map service, and Android is the most widely used operating system for mobile devices. The company lays fiber optic cables, produces laptops, tablets and driverless cars, and it develops software of all kinds. Google attracts leading scientists from all areas of research: geneticists, brain researchers, engineers, chemists. Have you ever wondered why there is only one Google, one Facebook, one Amazon? It's no coincidence. Marc Andreessen once summed it up well:

«In normal markets, you can have Pepsi and Coke. In technology markets, in the long run, you tend to only have one…. The big companies, though, in technology tend to have 90 percent market share. So we think that generally, these are winner-take-all markets. Generally, number one is going to get like

90 percent of the profits. Number two is going to get like 10 percent of the profits, and numbers three through 10 are going to get nothing. »

The more people have a Facebook account, the more attractive is it for others to be on Facebook because they have more contact opportunities. The more customers search and buy products on Amazon, the more accurately it can deliver its recommendations. More buyers also generate more reviews, and more sellers generate more offers. The bigger Amazon has become, the more invulnerable it has become to competition. «Amazon is increasingly looking like a monopoly in publishing, » explained venture capitalist Fred Wilson warning that the Internet has gone «from laughable toys to dominant monopolies in less than a decade. » Google's search algorithms improve with each search. The bigger Google grew, the better it became. Its defacto monopoly status is also illustrated by the fact that «google» has become a verb that can be found in the dictionary.

These companies themselves create monoculture. Their growing market power has turned the Internet into an ecosystem of walled gardens – closed platforms that make it difficult for the users to leave them. Apple is often cited as an example to praise the power of the market and the genius of the «garage tinkerers» who revolutionize capitalism. Yet the company is everything but the prime model for the effect of the free market. It has received substantial early-stage financial support from the government, and it has also made inventive use of publicly funded technology to develop «smart» products. In fact, the iPhone does not contain a single technology that was not state-financed, writes Italian-American economist Mariana Mazzucato in her book The Capital of the State. Everything that makes the smartphone «smart, » she says, is based on the results of public research. This includes the Internet, GPS, microprocessors, touch screen displays, and the algorithms of the voice-controlled assistant SIRI. Mazzucato points out that Apple continues to receive government support in other ways, e.g. through tax breaks and government contracts. Public schools in the United States are loyal Apple customers. Since the 1990s, they buy their computers and software from Apple every year. The iPhone is the result of an advanced technical infrastructure. It can only have emerged from a society that has already invested heavily in technology. How is it possible that taxpayers finance technological developments which make private companies rich, even if these companies do not work for the common good?

«I suppose I shouldn't say this, » Bill Gates acknowledged in 1996 in a moment of candor when discussing the importance of setting industry standards favorable to Microsoft, «but in some ways it leads, in a product category, to a natural monopoly. » In «some» ways? In 1998, he claimed: «There isn't an industry in America that is more creative, more alive, and more competitive. And the amazing thing is that all this happened without any government involvement. » Fact is, whoever says Silicon Valley must say Uncle Sam. The digital Mekka on the West Coast is intrinsically tied to the American government and the military. We already know from the history of IBM that you cannot become a monopolist without government support. In The Myth of Natural Monopoly, Thomas J. DiLorenzo, economics professor at Loyola University Maryland, shows that almost every known incident of a «natural» monopoly is merely a consequence of state intervention – either directly through the granting of exclusive rights or contracts or indirectly by not reassessing scarce public resources, e.g. the right to use publicly funded infrastructure. IBM is an example, AT&T another, and, of course, Microsoft. Their enormous market value enables IT giants to invest massively into their expansion and increase their lead over their competitors, as well as their market share. They can also buy interesting technology companies at any time or take potential competitors off the market. From the perspective of the monopolist, money really doesn't matter. Google has enough pocket change to take over any promising start-up that somehow fits into its strategy without flinching. But it's also enough to incorporate even large, high-profile companies. What they don't develop themselves, they buy, a common practice among technology companies: Facebook paid one billion dollars for the photo-sharing app Instagram in 2012 and 19 billion dollars for the messaging service WhatsApp in 2014. Amazon bought the food retailer Whole Foods in 2017 for almost 14 billion dollars. After the 2.4 billion dollar acquisition of the software specialist Callidus, SAP bought the software house Qualtrics for eight billion dollars. In 2002, Hewlett-Packard acquired the competitor Compaq for 18.7 billion dollars, and in 2008, it acquired Electronic Data Systems for 13.9 billion.

Monopolies also existed in the past. But the new economy has put the rules of the old economy on steroids. The problem stretches far beyond the IT sector. Digital platforms have transformed an already exploitative market – think Walmart – into an even more dehumanizing successor – think Amazon. Traditional corporations, no matter how much cash and clout they may have, can no longer keep up with that. As at the time of the robber barons, cartels today have little to fear in the USA. Neither the Department of Justice nor the Federal Trade Commission are fulfilling their duties. The vast majority of the announced fusions are carried out. The last significant intervention by the antitrust authorities was the Microsoft case more than twenty years ago. Economist Paul Krugman points to a link between the weakness of economic growth and the declining of competition. The companies can milk their customers without having to invest much or being innovative. The consequences are inefficient enterprises, corruption, and high consumer prices in relation to actual costs. All this is done in the name of the market economy or capitalism, a supposedly efficient and fair system. Powerful monopolists will also use all tricks to keep sensible products from competitors out of the market. Peter Thiel dismisses competition as a «relic of history. » In his short treatise «Zero to One» he wrote:

«More than anything else, competition is an ideology–the ideology–that pervades our society and distorts our thinking. We preach competition, internalize its necessity, and enact its commandments; and as a result, we trap ourselves within it–even though the more we compete, the less we gain. »

A clever businessman should avoid competition at all costs and focus on building a monopoly. For Thiel, competition is a disruptive factor. If consumers may choose between different players, he makes less profit.

As early as 1911, the Austrian economist Josef Schumpeter pointed out that basically every inventor of a new product first gains a monopoly position. This is precisely the incentive for entrepreneurs to bring new goods onto the market. Over time, imitators appear, so that the initial profits will melt away in the competition. That's what happened to IBM. This constant struggle between innovation and imitation, which Schumpeter called the «process of creative destruction, » is probably the most important aspect of the free market.

The lawyer Gary Reback has been fighting for decades to restrict the market power of multi-national corporations, among them Microsoft, which earned him the title «Bill Gates' worst nightmare» on the cover of Wired. Currently, his focus is on the search engine giant Google. He knows the tricks of the managers with which they outsmart politics and justice. When corporations deal with authorities, they try to turn the focus on today's technology, which will soon be obsolete. While regulation is slow, the development of new technologies accelerates. As a result, regulation becomes obsolete already before it comes into force, and the government has to start all over again. Thus, the companies are always one step ahead and can steer development in the direction they want. They don't even deny it: «We believe that modern technology platforms, such as Google, Facebook, Amazon and Apple, are even more powerful than most people realize, » confessed Eric Schmidt, former executive chairman of Google. «What gives them their power is their ability to grow–specifically, the speed at which they scale. » Reback concludes: «There's a sense now that our antitrust policy has been failing. It's gotten to the point in the United States that you can't take antitrust action unless you're taking it against a company that's tied to the other political party. Democrats can go after hospital mergers or the traditional industries, but won't go after information technology. Would Republicans? I don't know. Google has gotten smart. It paid the Republicans a lot of money too. » This creates a serious threat to our economy. «The American economy is now hostage to a relatively small number of giant private companies, with inter-locking connections, that set the national agenda, » warned political economist Herbert Schiller. We should occasionally ask ourselves: What do we do about it?

Powerful elites are not new. Factory owners, railroad tycoons, and oil barons ruled the 19th century. In the 20th century, bankers and hedge fund managers called themselves «Masters of the Universe. » They all lied and defrauded out of envy, greed, and ignorance. But they didn't promise us a rose garden. The new «Masters of the Universe» differ from their predecessors in that power through wealth is not enough for them. They believe that their work is for the good of mankind, that they will advance civilization in great strides, and they don't want anyone to interfere. These techno tycoons abhor politics. For them, any regulation is not only an obstacle, but downright obscene. If, in their brave new world, social values such as privacy and data protection stand in the way, then new values are needed. And because the government fails to solve the great tasks of the time, according to their view, these tasks must be transferred to the private sector. «Governments of the Industrial World, you weary giants of flesh and steel, I come from Cyberspace, the new home of Mind, » states John P. Barlow, a lyricist for the Grateful Dead, in his Declaration of Independence of Cyberspace. «On behalf of the future, I ask you of the past to leave us alone. You are not welcome among us. »
Fighting for market share by all means doesn't exclude thinking in the same way about politics and democracy. Their contempt is also expressed in the robustness with which they deal with law makers. With his manifest The Education of a Libertarian, Peter Thiel sparked a heated discussion. Thiel emphasizes how important personal freedom is to him. Yet his use of the term «freedom» refers to the unrestricted power of the rich, as he announces his belief that freedom and democracy are not «compatible. » He calls the «capitalist democracy» an oxymoron. For him, pluralistic and competitive structures are indispensable for democracy, but poison for capitalism, which thrives on monopolistic structures. He believes that the market must be freed from all restrictions to achieve a state of «true» freedom. In other words: He tolerates regulations that serve to create monopolies and reduce competition. He demands the abandonment of politics to make technology the Fuhrer of world affairs and the future: «In our time, the great task (...) is to find an escape from politics in all its forms (…) A better metaphor is that we are in a deadly race between politics and technology. » Tech first. Ethics fall by the wayside. The high priests of Silicon Valley don't seek political or institutional solutions to problems such as poverty, inequality or corruption. They believe in the development and application of new technologies.

«The scale of the technology and infrastructure that must be built is unprecedented, and we believe this is the most important problem we can focus on ... We also expect to see the emergence of new services that are social by design to address the large worldwide problems we face in job creation, education and health care. We look forward to doing what we can to help this progress, » said Zuckerberg.

Their goals are neither democratic, nor do they reflect collective or universal values. Rather, they favor the use of the private sector and its beneficial returns, the market way of looking at things, and the bypassing of government. The world-changers from the Valley want mankind to recover by their high tech doctrine. There have already been many attempts to shape society according to scientific standards. As the political scientist Jems C. Scott points out, such rationalization measures can only be implemented once society has been radically simplified. Each radish must be measured and put in the right place before such an experiment can start. As examples, he mentions Baron Haussmann, who carved wide paths through Paris for his splendid boulevards and thus brought a brutal order into the maze of medieval alleys and uprooted tens of thousands of people, and the architect Oscar Niemeyer, who designed a three-million metropolis in the jungle on a drawing board, Brasilia, an artificial and gigantic fantasy that lacks any human warmth, and Julius Nyerere, who had five million farmers resettled in Tanzania, and the totalitarian implementations of National Socialist or Communist ideas in the 20th century. It always ended in chaos and misery, reminding me of Karl Popper's warning: «The attempt to make heaven on earth invariably produces hell. It leads to intolerance. It leads to religious wars, and to the saving of souls through the inquisition. »

Again and again it becomes obvious how low IT bosses think of our society. After critical reports about Tesla, Elon Musk lashed out at the media, in distinctly trumpian fashion, on Twitter: They practiced a «holier than thou hypocrisy, » no one believes the press anymore. Jeff Bezos played off struggling American cities against each other to get the best conditions for the Amazon headquarters. When Amazon employees announced a strike in December 2014 during the Christmas time, the company refused any dialogue and threatened to simply move its dependency. Travis Kalanick publicly insults his competitors and mocks his customers on Twitter. He thinks politicians are incompetent, and close associates of him suggest spying on journalists would be a good thing. Kalanick hints that it's as easy for him to get a woman into bed as it is for others to call a taxi. Really, he said that. To the drivers' protests about poor pay he responded that they will be replaced by computers in the near future anyway. Some protagonists of the Valley seem even seem to think themselves as icons of political resistance. The Io-programmer Steve Dekorte has compared the lawsuit of Uber with Rosa Parks' refusal to give up her bus seat in 1955. Brian Chesky, co-founder and CEO of Airbnb, twittered in 2015: «Good thing gov didn't require a min 30 day stay. [Gandhi] wouldn't have gotten very fary [during Salt March]. »

He was referring to a new regulation in New York to keep rental space available for actual tenants and contain the misuse of homes. Later he deleted the tweet and apologized. Zuckerberg compared the regulation of companies like Facebook with the restrictions in the «most repressive societies. »

Silicon Valley's disrespect for the laws and its moral basis is astounding. Their hostility towards democratic processes leads to the desire to establish law-free areas. Larry Page had already expressed this vision in 2013: «There are many exciting things you could do that are illegal or not allowed by regulation, » Page said. «We need 'some safe places where we can try things and not have to deploy to the entire world. » The Seasteading Institute investigates how to develop artificial islands as new lawless beta-test states. The goal is to live and work there without interference. It's not surprising that Peter Thiel supports the development of a democracy-free zone financially. «Seasteading is one of the few technological frontiers that has the promise to create a new space for human freedom, » he said. The profit potential is immeasurable, and the Seasteading Institute is not the only company that wants to get a share. Twelve nautical miles off the Californian coast, in international waters, the start-up Blueseed wants to build floating platforms to provide the companies a place without laws, taxes, visa requirements, and any government regulation. With a few specific exceptions, everything would be permitted that is technically possible. With «everything is permitted, » the IT companies free themselves of morality, law, political views, and other rules of society. There would be also no separation of powers. The companies could establish the rules and watch their implementation.

Another example for their disregard of social norms is how these companies try to pay as little tax as possible. They circumvent tax systems by transferring part of their tax liability to countries with lower tax rates. It's taxes, of course, that undergirds human civilization, that pay for the infrastructure and research on which the corporations base their fortune. Yet whether Silicon Valley corporations pay taxes or observe laws is treated with low urgency by most policymakers. We are witnessing a «revolt of the elite, » which is using the publicly financed infrastructure to ensure their own happiness. The aggressive lobbying seems to make the companies immune from legal proceedings. Many politicians simply lack the necessary technical understanding. At his hearing before Congress, Mark Zuckerberg could barely hide his contempt for the elected representatives. It also became apparent that some of the representatives, congresswomen, and congressmen didn't know how the Internet works.

Zuckerberg and other Silicon Valley kings go to great lengths to lobby Washington. They must not get away with their antisocial behavior and ignorance of the representatives of the people. Politicians have so far only been able to develop only a few meaningful perspectives on the digital sphere. How digital corporations could be properly regulated remains unclear. The prerequisites for getting social media problems under political control are poor. They know that they have the real power, and that this will be even truer in the future. When the telegraph arrived, we were promised that it would free us from tyranny. We hear the same story about the Internet. But the concentration of wealth and power in the hands of a global elite is eroding the power and sovereignty of states. At the same time, income inequality and the pace of technological change are fuelling a populist backlash against science, mistrust of our government institutions, and fear of the future. That makes it so difficult to solve the problems we create.

The source of their power is algorithms. Nerds love algorithms because they love to follow instructions to solve problems. In unknown situations, most people can rely on their intuitions, nerds can't. The story of the algorithm is the story of math, a rather obscure and cult like discipline. It was developed by philosophers and mathematicians who were inspired by the ancient logical system of Aristotle. Greek antiquity was the Golden Age for nerds. Since the slaves had to do all the work, the Greek citizens had the time to contemplate about politics, study philosophy, invent science, etc. The word 'algorithm' derives from the name of the medieval Persian scholar Musa al-Khowarizm. But he is not the father of the algorithm. Rather, it originated in the brain of the German mathematician Gottfried Leibniz. Leibniz grew up in the same world of religious turmoil as Michel de Montaigne, only a generation later. He was born in a region of the world which was devastated by the Thirty Years' War. This experience shaped his thinking and work. Leibniz was a Lutheran and sought reconciliation with the Roman Catholic Church as well as with the Calvinists. He argued for the union of faith and reason and a unified church for all Christians.

His maxim was: «There is nothing without God. » Thus, he set the One for God and the Zero for nothingness. After examining the human language, he concluded that it was too imprecise. This would cause communication problems which sooner or later lead to conflicts. So, he tried to develop a consistent logical symbolic language, the mathesis universalis. Leibniz was also one of the first to believe that our thinking is a calculating process, which closes the circle to religiosity and that of God and nothingness, of 1 and 0. His dual system is the operational basis of modern computer technology. He even developed a calculating machine which was already capable of amazing calculations. It was susceptible to failure, since the required technical precision was not yet available. But modern replicas, made to his specifications, prove its functionality.

Leibniz assumed that it was possible to find an algorithm to prove any truth. Relativism doesn't exist: A proposition is either true or false, and when a mathematical truth is proven, it is so for eternity. Today, we know that this was an illusion. The Austrian-American mathematician Kurt Gödel was only

25 years old when he shattered the dream of a universal mathematical formula which could explain everything. In 1931, he published a theory, which says there is a third category in logic besides «right» and «wrong.» And that is «inconclusive.» According to him, inconclusive propositions exist in every logical mathematical system. That's why there will always be empty spots on the map of mathematics.

Gödel was a nerd extraordinaire. As a child, he turned into a hypochondriac and developed an obsession with measuring his body temperature. He was a skinny and rather humorless asket always dressed in a perfect fitting suit, having a perfect haircut. Since his childhood, his diet consisted almost exclusively of potatoes and dairy products. Because he was afraid of being poisoned, his wife, the varieté dancer Adele Porkert, had to taste his meals first. Really. With his pedantic obsessions, Gödel didn't make it easy for his friends and family. When Gödel applied for U.S. citizenship at the end of 1947, he took care of it like the nerd he was. After a thorough study of the Constitution, he believed that he had found a logical contradiction in it. In his opinion, there was a real threat that America would fall into a tyranny. – Be aware America, after all, this man was genius. Fortunately for him, he was friends with Einstein. Both lectured at Princeton. Einstein accompanied him to the court hearing and put in a good word for him with the judge. Otherwise, Gödel's application for citizenship would probably have failed.

Gödel's credo was «the world is reasonable» – the first sentence of his philosophical work, discovered after his death. The tragedy of his life was that he tried to get it under control with the same logical rigorism. «In the world of mathematics, everything is in balance and perfectly ordered, » he wrote, «shouldn't we assume the same for the world of reality? » For every apparently random event there had to be a strictly logical explanation. And Gödel always found one, no matter how crazy it was. But the world is not rational, but chaotic, and mathematics is a simplifying model. His search for a rational explanation for the irrational drove Gödel into paranoia and destroyed himself. While his wife Adele was in a hospital and could not taste his food, he refused to eat and starved to death.

Today, Algorithms are known in the context of influencing our perception: Google's services, Facebook's newsfeed, and Amazon's recommendations. Global technology platforms enable the algorithmic control of firms, institutions, and societies. Algorithms can drive cars, detect deviant behavior, check banking transactions, etc. Mathematical models should be neutral and objective. But they aren't. They are opaque and don't allow any contradiction by affected individuals. These models often work with questionable, false or incomplete and prejudiced data sources. An algorithm designed to help Amazon to select job applicants, e.g., only suggested men. Google's image recognition confused black people with gorillas and asked Asian-looking people to open their eyes. On YouTube, videos of the 9/11 terrorist attack in New York were matched to the fire of the Notre Dame in Paris. The dominance of algorithms is becoming clear in an increasing number of areas. We have reached a point at which the human brain cannot always comprehend the impact of algorithms. Already in 1976, computers proved the four-color map theorem in topology. The mathematician Strogatz commented thirty years later: «No human mathematician could ever verify all the intermediate steps in this brutal proof, and even if someone claimed to, should we trust them? »

Many Silicon Valley techies believe that people and their needs can be reduced to formulas. But the idea that the world can be simulated algorithmically is an ideology, a creed. The world is extremely complex, too complex for us humans to ever grasp it fully intellectually, and probably too complex for the most sophisticated algorithms.

MEMORY IS LIFE

«All media, from the phonetic alphabet to the computer, are extensions of man that cause deep and lasting changes in him and transform his environment. » – Marshall McLuhan

«As gravity holds matter from flying off into space, so memory gives stability to knowledge; it is the cohesion which keeps things from falling into a lump, or flowing in waves. »
– Ralph Waldo Emerson

Around the same time that Frederick Taylor was conducting his experiments at the Midvale Steel plant, Friedrich Nietzsche began using a typewriter, to be precise: the «Skrivekugle» (Writing Ball) of the Danish pastor Rasmus Malling-Hansen, which he had developed for blind writers. With his vision failing, half blind Nietzsche hoped the machine would help him to bring his thoughts to paper. And it did, at least for a while. A newspaper reported that thanks to his typewriter Nietzsche «feels better than ever» and «has resumed his writing activities. » In his book Gramophone, Film, Typewriter, German media theorist Friedrich Kittler explains that the machine had an unexpected subtle side effect on Nietzsche's work: Nietzsche's close friend, the writer and composer Heinrich Köselitz, noticed a change in the style of his writing. «Perhaps you will through this instrument even take to a new idiom, » wrote

Köselitz in a letter to Nietzsche, adding that in his own work, his «'thoughts' in music and language often depend on the quality of pen and paper. » «You are right, » Nietzsche is said to have answered. «Our writing tools are also working on our thoughts. » Or, as McLuhan paraphrased it later: «We shape our tools and thereafter our tools shape us. » But the machine had a technical defect that could not be repaired. On March 24, 1882, the Nietzsche typed the last text with it, a letter to his friend Heinrich Köselitz. That was the end of the sad story of Friedrich Nietzsche's writing ball, and until the end of his life the philosopher wrote only by hand. He should have taken some advice here from Karl Marx, who has devoted some time to the study of the role of machines in society. In The German Ideology, Marx asked rhetorically: «Is the Iliad possible when the printing press, and even printing machines, exist? Is it not inevitable that with the emergence of the press, the singing and the telling and the muse cease; that is, that the conditions necessary for epic poetry disappear? » If a typewriter already has such an effect, what's the effect of digital technologies then?

Our brain is the product of evolution. It's adapted to certain environmental conditions, to which digital media don't belong. The digital world with its distractions, the demand for multitasking and the simultaneous processing of information has serious side effects. The list is long. Relying too heavily on computers, e.g., goes hand in hand with the decline of intellectual skills. For years, scientists have warned against a phenomenon known as digital amnesia. The term doesn't refer to a specific disease, but to the gradual deterioration of certain cognitive abilities. These include, among others, a poorer memory performance, tendencies towards communicative superficiality, and a new form of gullibility. In the world of images and hyperlinks, we lose the depth in thinking, feelings, and sensations, in our relationships and work, which causes a new spectrum of problems. Like a muscle, we have to train the brain if we want to maintain and improve our cognitive skills. If we don't train it, we lose the ability to make decisions, to reach goals, to differentiate, and to recognize relations and patterns, and even to calculate and write. In short, digital technology can make us stupid.

Many digital tasks demand that you do several things at once or jump from one task to the next. We have become exhausted multitaskers. But humans cannot follow two stories at the same time. We simply cannot read two books, make two phone calls, or listen to two songs simultaneously. There is overwhelming evidence that multitasking reduces our performance levels. The brain researcher Gerhard Roth has provided a plausible explanation: The constant stimulation of the brain paralyses it. «There's every reason to believe multitasking is an assault, » says Frank Schirrmacher, journalist and author. He continues: «Multitasking is an ill-fated attempt by humans to become computers themselves. » Nicholas Carr points out: «The net is designed to be an interruption system, a machine geared to dividing attention. » A constant distraction through links and advertising banners, videos, and images in the text are its basic structuring principle. Hypertext was praised as a great achievement, supposed to make the texts easier to access and read. But the opposite is true. Readers are lured to click on the links, the reading performance is reduced, the understanding of content decreases. Carr explains: «Most of the proprietors of the commercial internet have a financial stake in collecting the crumbs of data we leave behind as we flit from link to link the more crumbs, the better. The last thing these companies want is to encourage leisurely reading or slow, concentrated thought. It's in their economic interest to drive us to distraction. »

The fictitious tropical village Macondo is a kind of peninsula: It's surrounded in the South by swamps, in the West by water, and in the East by the impenetrable Sierra. For years, the village has had almost no contact with the outside world until one day the mysterious orphan Rebeca arrives. Rebeca has many strange self-destructive habits, e.g. eating dirt. She is also plagued by a terrible sleep disorder that affects her memory. Her insomnia is contagious and soon the whole village is affected. The symptoms develop in stages. As soon as the villagers have become used to the waking state, their memories begin to fade. They forget the memories of their childhood, the names of everyday objects, and how they work. They no longer know the meaning of words. Later they lose the ability to recognize their family members, friends, and neighbors. Their self falls apart, and they sink into an absurd and ultimately fatal «kind of idiocy that had no past. »
Memory plays a crucial role in our identity. Our memories make us who we are. When we say «I, » we mean a unique person with an individual life story. Someone without memories has no identity, no possibility to make rational decisions. «Life is not what you have lived, but what you remember and how you remember and how you tell the others about it, » wrote Gabriel García Márquez in his memoirs. German writer Jean Paul called the ability to remember the most beautiful moments of one's life «the only paradise from which we cannot be driven. » And the Spanish-Mexican filmmaker Luis Bunuel noted that «you have to begin to lose your memory, if only in bits and pieces, to realize that memory is what makes our lives. Life without memory is no life at all... Our memory is our coherence, our reason, our feeling, even our action. Without it we are nothing. »
Twenty years after the publication of One Hundred Years of Solitude, the neurologist Elio Lugaresi described a disease which in many respects resembles that of the people of Macondo. It's called «deadly familial insomnia. » Today, we know that sleep plays a crucial role in the consolidation of memory. Sleep deprivation prevents the processes of the formation and maintenance of long-term memories. A lack of sleep interferes with neuronal activity in certain areas of the brain, and, as a result, these brain cells

communicate with each other less intense and only with a delay. Apparently, the cells fall into a dozy state. During sleep, the brain processes what it has absorbed during the day and shifts it from short-term memory to long-term memory. Lack of sleep can make us forgetful and cause false memories.

We tend to believe that our memory works like a harddrive that stores our memories like a movie and, if necessary, allows an exact replay. But it doesn't work like that. In the 19th century, the psychologist Hermann Ebbinghaus discovered that our memories become inaccurate already after only a few minutes. Every memory leaves a trace in the central nervous system, an engram. This engram enables us to recall the experience later. Yet what we find when we search our memory differs substantially from the facts stored by a computer which always remain accurate. Remembering is an active, creative process. Every time a memory is recalled, it changes. During mesmerization, the connections between the nerve cells become stronger. If we forget something, it weakens these connections, so it's harder to find the information. Every time we recall an event, traces of memory that are already fixed become unstable again. Repeated remembering thus changes the stored information. Our memories are dynamic reconstructions of selectively perceived sensory impressions. They are linked with other memories and feelings, are contradictory, inaccurate, and can even be completely wrong. The current mood leaves its mark, strengthens or weakens sensations, brings details to the fore and makes others fade away. A depressed person tends to think of sad experiences, a happy person of good experiences. It's impossible to predict which details we will remember.

Though we always feel like the same person, our personality is not a rigid construct. As our memories change, our selves are constantly changing. Psychologists believe that this 'weakness' of memory has advantages. «We can learn better from each other if we do not insist on our own knowledge, but are receptive to the viewpoint of others, » explains Wilfried Echterhoff. Instead of an exact reproduction of events, our memories offer a variety of possibilities on which we can act, thereby increasing our autonomy. Only slowly scientists understand these phenomena.

It's already obvious that the claim that computers function like our brain is untenable. But little research has been done on how digital technology affects our mental processes. Thanks to the Internet, we have access to a staggering amount of information. But its value is not measured by its quality rather by the fact that it's new, interesting, and curious. In a lecture in 1990, Neil Postman already warned that we «inform ourselves to death» echoing his famous «we amuse ourselves to death. » He argued that «information no longer has any relation to the solution of problems. » The information doesn't serve as a basis for our actions, but for amusement and distraction. With more information than ever, we don't know how to deal with it and feel overwhelmed. The slow and intensive processing of information has been replaced by a flood of news in which it's becoming more difficult to distinguish between important and trivial. The philosopher Daniel Dennett believes there are cognitive limits to how much information we can process. The flood of information leads to mental overload. We are trying to keep up with it, and at the same time we know that we have no chance and feel our inability and powerlessness. «We become unable to act if we store too much unnecessary information, » says brain researcher Martin Korte from the Max Planck Institute for Neurobiology in Munich. His solution: Forget the useless. Wisdom no longer consists in gathering information, but in missing it, i.e. to filter the information that is relevant. In this respect, the Internet is more a curse than a blessing. We suffer «an explosion of non-sense, » as Joseph Weizenbaum called it. The value of the internet is undermined by amount of trash which can be found there. Weizenbaum again: «The Internet is a big dung heap where you can find little treasures and pearls. » To find the treasures, it requires a new kind of literacy – and an art of forgetting. The art of forgetting means to develop methods to select information, if you don't want to drown in the flood of information.

For Friedrich Nietzsche it seemed impossible to live without the ability to forget at all. Nietzsche believed: Who wants to live, who wants to act, must be able to forget. To be free, one must be able to cast off the ballast of memory. People who cannot forget become depressed. They repeatedly encounter all suffered losses, mistakes, injustices, and humiliations of their life. Nietzsche wrote: «In the smallest as in the greatest happiness, it's something that happiness is happiness: the ability to forget, or to put it in terms most learned, the ability to feel things, as long as happiness lasts, without any historical perspective. » In Greek mythology, the souls of the dead drank from the river of forgetting, Lethe, to erase their memory before they entered Hades. Casanova, the knight of fortune, forgot any offense, which he could not pay back. «If only forgetfulness were not so difficult! » complained Nietzsche, «We never forget what we endeavor to forget. »

DIGITAL IDIOTS

«So you can read, Lubin? » «Yes, I can read printed characters, but I've never been able to manage handwriting. » – Molière, Georges Dandin

«Learning involves the nurturing of nature. » – Jospeph Ledoux

The New Yorker Dramatic Mirror of 9.7.1913 quotes Edison as follows: «Books will soon be obsolete in the schools. Scholars will soon be instructed through the eye. It's possible to teach every branch of human knowledge with the motion picture. Our school system will be completely changed in ten years. » About fifty years later, when television appeared, the tech visionaries made similar optimistic claims: Knowledge could now spread to every corner of the world, the global education would improve, parents were told that their children learn better to speak with the help of TV. That's nonsense, as we know now. In fact, excessive television consumption slows down language development and has lasting damaging effect on the entire education. Learning to speak succeeds best in face-to-face dialogue with adults and elder children. You don't have to develop any special skills to blabber in front of a TV. But communicating with someone who is physically present, either through speech or body language, is a complex cognitive task. Television not only steals time for homework and learning, it also robs the children of real world activities and experiences. It seduces them to physical inactivity. Less physical activity, on the other hand, leads to poorer brain performance. Obese children are more likely to suffer health problems throughout their entire life. New data from brain research also link overweight to addictive behavior. Television makes people fat, dumb, and aggressive. Still, it's apologists claim that this is not true: You have to look at the big picture, various social circumstances, yada, yada, yada. This is mere propaganda to create confusion. Another fifty years later, we hear the same promises: Computers will revolutionize education, make knowledge available to everyone ... this time for real.
It's hard to overestimate the devastating impact of digital technologies on education and its impact on the health of the younger generation. 80 years

before the Internet became part of our lives, Edward Morgan Forster created a dystopian future, which is shockingly reminiscent of some current developments. In his science fiction short-story The Machine Stops, most humans can no longer survive on the surface of the earth. They live isolated underground in standardized chambers and have no desire for personal encounters. They communicate with each other only via electronic devices in an efficient network and devote themselves entirely to the virtual «sharing» of ideas and «knowledge, » at least what they regard as such. In fact, they live under an illusion. They believe that they are achieving something, but they are marking time, and all they do is superficial entertainment and distraction. Neuroscientist Rebecca Böhme is researching how people react to physical contact and whether digital communication can replace real physical contact. Physical contact sets in motion a complex biochemical process in the body. It activates circuits that have developed during the parent-child bond. The receptors in the skin send their electrical signals to the brain. It releases dopamine, serotonin, and the «cuddling hormone» oxytocin. These happy chemicals lower stress levels, the heart rate slows down, breathing becomes easier, the muscles relax, we feel less afraid, the immune system responds positively. Persistent lack of physical contact, on the other hand, can lead to mild or moderate depression, including psychosomatic illness. Children react to the lack of physical contact faster than adults. When one or two year old children already skype with their grandparents in Germany, it's possible that the children's brains adapt and that we will see neurological differences between the generations. But these mechanisms, these circuits are evolutionarily very old. In a digitalized childhood, children are in danger of losing this ability. Children are the most fragile beings. They need physical interaction for their development. Without it, it could have serious consequences. In the worst case, developmental disorders can occur. The German neuroscientist and psychiatrist Manfred Spitzer warns that digital information technology can – directly or indirectly – cause new diseases or contribute to the more frequent occurrence of already known diseases. We're heading for disaster. The excessive use of digital technologies may result in social withdrawal and lead into a downward spiral of physical illnesses, anxieties, depression, and further isolation. A study by the Cincinnati Children's Hospital Medical Center shows that too much screen time changes the structure of the brain of small children. In children who regularly played with smartphones or tablets, the white matter was significantly less dense which has measurable negative effects on the brain performance. These children had more difficulties with speaking and recognizing objects.

Some techno prophets speak of a «virtual classroom» where the learning content is available in a digital cloud. Meeting the wishes of the IT complex, schools become customer enterprises for industry. The digitization of schools is a billion dollar gift for the industry, and, of course, billions more will follow: The equipment needs maintenance, becomes obsolete and has to be replaced, licenses must be renewed, school staff needs training, etc. And all this happens though the proof for the claims of a positive learning effect is still lacking. But studies that show the opposite, i.e. that digital technology has a negative effect on education, exist in great numbers. The data already available don't bode well either for learning processes nor academic success. For years, scientists have been pointing out that there is no evidence of the effectiveness of computers for learning at school. As early as 1997, journalist Todd Oppenheimer already called it computer madness.

Digitization has a negative influence on the attention span and the intellectual development. Learning on the computer alone doesn't work. It may offer some new learning opportunities. But it's questionable whether the advantages outweigh the disadvantages. Computers deliver only an education which is superficial, focused on information rather than understanding. Children are encouraged to give the right answer, but there is no need to understand it. Learning success, especially at a young age, depends on the understanding, and trust of living people, direct contact, and exchange with people who are physically present. A computer can't see when a student has a bad day. The emotional attachment and trust of children towards the persons with whom they engage is a crucial part of the maturation process of the brain. If it's missing, emotional and social psyche cannot form appropriately. The development of social behavior needs help from real persons. The most important thing we need in life is not to be able to read, write, calculate, or code, but to develop social competence. Our species has evolved exclusively in groups only! We are hardwired for physical contact with others. We are not designed to be alone or to look at screens all day long. Children who are left to their own devices in closed rooms are cheated of this. Digital technology can only provide simulations. Teachers don't do their actual profession anymore, but are only «learning companions. » The ability to make meaningful use of digital media – if there is one at all – is not acquired on the Internet or by wiping over tablets and smartphones.

Future generations may see January 9, 2007, as a turning point in history. In the city of cable cars and the Golden Gate Bridge, Steve Jobs presented the iPhone to the world. At 9.42 (PST), he announced:

«Well today, we're introducing THREE revolutionary new products. The first one is a widescreen iPod with touch controls. The second is a revolutionary new mobile phone. And the third is a breakthrough Internet communications device. An iPod, a phone, an Internet mobile communicator … these are NOT three separate devices! And we are calling it iPhone. Today Apple is going to reinvent the phone. »

The long-term impact of this marketing event was tremendous. The iPhone has become a symbol of the mobile Internet and has changed entire industries. Smombies – smartphone zombies that stare at the small screen in their hand and forget everything around them – stumble across all over the world. Although there are no long-term studies yet – after all, smartphones are only thirteen years old – some negative effects on the development of children are well established. Recent studies show that the intensive use of smartphones has a negative effect on attention and learning ability. Smartphones and tablets, whose supposed purpose is communication, create walls between people. This is particularly worrying when it comes to younger children since they are the most vulnerable. When mum and dad just stare at the screen, children are deprived of direct interaction with their nearest and dearest.

Meanwhile, children no longer learn to write cursive writing. This has severe consequences. Reading and writing are core cultural techniques. A good mastery of the written language is essential for success at school and later in life. It's of great importance for each individual and also for society as a whole. Handwriting stimulates cognitive processing in the brain. Frank Wilson is a neurologist and author from Portland. He believes that neither the eyes nor the brain are the most important instrument of human knowledge, but the hand. «Our lives are so full of commonplace experience in which the hands are so skillfully and silently involved that we rarely consider how dependent upon them we actually are,» he says. A closer look at the functioning and extraordinary importance of human hands for the understanding of reality and the self, shows, «that any theory of human intelligence which ignores the interdependence of hand and brain function, the historic origins of that relationship, or the impact of that history on developmental dynamics in modern humans, is grossly misleading.» The interaction of our hands and brains is so close that human intelligence cannot be explained as a purely mental phenomenon. The Austrian anatomist Joseph Hyrtl rightly said of the hand: It is the hand that gives the spirit the power to carry out its thoughts, through which it masters, forms, creates and uses the various forms of matter for a thousand useful purposes. The 'intelligent' use of the hand might not be merely an incidental bequest of our evolutionary heritage, but – along with the language instinct – an elemental force in the genesis of the mind. Handwritten texts are more creative and have more complex sentences. Handwritten words dig deeper into the memory of both children and young adults. Those who write in handwriting understand and mesmerize the content of a lecture better. Not be able to write in cursive or with any joined letters may cause the fragmentation of intellectual processes. It's a common place that an above-average number of nerds are short-sighted. The number of young people who need glasses has skyrocketed. Several studies point to a correlation between nearsightedness and screen work. The longer a person works in front of a screen, the greater their risk of shortsightedness. The monotony of staring at a screen can lead to eye fatigue, nearsightedness, or visual perception problems. The percentage of blue light in LED displays is often higher than in natural daylight. Experiments have shown that the blue light emitted by smartphones and computer screens destroys visual cells. This can lead to severe visual damage and even blindness. Ian Morgan, researcher at the Australian National University in Sydney, says there is an easy fix for that: Daylight stimulates the production of dopamine, a neurotransmitter that causes happiness but also has positive effects on the eyes. «There's a brake on people becoming myopic and that's people going outside, » he explains. Which is what nerds rarely do, and thanks to the spread of their gadgets, everyone else is now also affected.

Many studies conclude that the average length of sleep in industrialized countries has decreased by one to two hours since the middle of the 20th century. Blue light at night is one reason why many people don't get enough sleep. In the evening and at night blue light has a harmful effect because it stimulates the brain and can disturb sleep. Sleep deprivation not only makes you tired, but also contributes to obesity and type 2 diabetes. Lack of sleep leads first to fatigue and then to reduced physical activity. And of course, reduced energy consumption can also cause weight gain. At the same time, leptin levels fall. This hormone controls the feeling of hunger and fat metabolism. Many people observe this behavior in themselves: If they don't get much sleep, they experience acute hunger pangs the day after.

Computers are be useless without a real education. Richard Louv is a journalist, author, and environmental activist in the USA. He is the founder of the Children & Nature Network, which aims to bring children back closer to nature. In his books he describes the changes in the relationship between humans and nature. Modern society is teaching young people to avoid direct experiences of nature. Children are cheated of their joie de vivre. They may function, but they don't do really well. The statistics seem to prove his point: America's children today spend more time than ever with electronic devices and less time than ever outdoors. Louv concluded, apodictically: «The more high-tech we become, the more nature we need. » Given the physical condition of children and youth art, music and sports are more important than ever.

For the antique Greeks, «idiots» were uneducated and apolitical people, who had no concept of the common good and did not care about political connections. There is no better way to describe the goals of the IT industry. An economically usable form of idiocy is cultivated, which is limited to chewing on learned things and mastering blinking devices. Technology is not made for strengthening young people's self-confidence and ability to think for themselves. Joseph Weizenbaums believes, children should first have gained a certain maturity, otherwise their knowledge is superficial at best. The

Greek philosopher Heraclitus believed that the accumulation of information is dispensable, because: «Learning many things does not teach understanding. » – Learning does not mean filling barrels, but lighting a torch. What would he have to say about modern education? In his theory of half-education Theodor W. Adorno pointed out that we don't need to know every last detail to understand something, i.e. we don't need to learn to code to be able to use a computer or a cellphone. And the German universal scholar Wilhelm von Humboldt has emphasized that education should not serve a certain purpose – other than becoming an educated person. Digital learning programs are developed to meet technological, but not social or psychological criteria. In the end, it's the machine that controls the people, and critical thinking, which the powerful fear so much, gets lost. Psychologists sound the alarm. Mark Bauerlein, a professor of English at Emory University, has dealt with young people for years. In his book The Dumbest Generation, he wrote what he experienced: «While the world has provided them with extraordinary chances to gain knowledge and improve their reading/writing skills, not to mention offering financial incentives to do so, young Americans today are no more learned or skillful than their predecessors, no more knowledgeable, fluent, up-to-date, or inquisitive, except in materials of youth culture.... » They show an ignorance which Bauerlein finds hard to believe. Digital education is important, no doubt about it. But it's not important for primary school children or even kindergarten children. They have better things to do. And it's not important for a general education, but for those who want to go in this direction later.

The irony is that many parents who work at Silicon Valley's tech giants send their children to the Waldorf School of the Peninsula where computers are banned. In their opinion, technological gadgets have a negative impact on the learning success, creative thinking, physical activity, social interactions, and the concentration span of children. In late 2010, Jobs told New York Times journalist Nick Bilton that his children had never used the iPad: «We limit how much technology our kids use in the home. » Apple CEO Tim Cook admitted that there are still many effects hardly understood. He also revealed that he was trying to keep his nephew away from social networks. Justin Rosenstein, co-inventor of the «Like button» on Facebook, is also concerned about the impact of social media and has installed parental controls on his phone. Bill Gates told the British Daily Mirror that his children didn't have a smartphone before they turned 14 and were banned from using it in the evening hours so that they could sleep better. The fact that the same people who have made a fortune by selling these devices think they are harmful is unsettling. The industry exploits the fear of parents to rip them off. Supporters of digitization in schools like to stir up angst. Does this sound familiar?

With much effort they spread lies so that parents waste their hard-earned money on devices which exactly cause what they are afraid of. The mere presence of computers at home means first of all that the children will play computer games which hinders them from learning. The main argument is always an economic one: We must not fall behind. But behind whom? India, where several million software engineers work as wallas? Or China, which has one of the highest burnout and suicide rates? The biographies of successful programmers prove them wrong. The decisive factors are logical thinking, creativity, willingness, and ability to cooperate, self-control, and a constructive handling of mistakes – beyond 0 and 1. «I fundamentally reject the notion you need technology aids in grammar school, » said Google executive Alan Eagle in an interview for the New York Times. «At Google and all these places, we make technology as brain-dead easy to use as possible. There's no reason why kids can't figure it out when they get older. »

Hardware manufacturers, software companies, telecom providers, suppliers, and last but not least the social networks don't care about health risks for your kids. All they want is them to use their services as long and often as possible. «God only knows what it's doing to our children's brains, » said Sean Parker. For the better future of the next generations, we should not allow greedy companies to gamble with their education. It will cause suffering and high social and economic costs for society in the long term. It's actually quite astonishing that these schemes are ignored so far and that their protagonists are even rewarded richly. There must be decentralized open source solutions. The digitization of schools must not strengthen the dependency of public institutions on digital companies, which have often lied to us and will continue to do so.

THERE'S SOMETHING GOING ON

«Tell all the Truth, but tell it slant – Success in Circuit lies. » – Emily Dickinson

«The daily press and the telegraph, which in a moment spreads inventions over the whole earth, fabricate more myths in one day than could have formerly been done in a century. »
– Karl Marx

We are secretly controlled by a New World Order with chemtrails and vaccinations, the first moon landing never happened, the U.S. Federal Emergency Management Agency (FEMA) is plotting a coup d'état, the government is responsible for 9/11, and, of course, climate change is a Chinese hoax – conspiracy theories are a dollar a dozen. There is an incredible variety for every taste, and you don't need to choose only a single theory. At least half of the American population believes in some conspiracies. Conspiracy theories are as old as human history: In the Middle Ages, Jews were blamed to forge sinister plans, later it was the Freemasons and Catholics. Telegraph pioneer Samuel Morse «uncovered» a conspiracy by foreign powers against the USA. His father, the pastor Jedidiah Morse, had already preached about the diabolical Illuminati. The FEMA conspiracy theory was first published in the article Blueprint for Tyranny in the August 1985 issue of the porn magazine Penthouse. The successful TV show The X Files is based on it.

In his book Empire of Conspiracy, Timothy Melley points out that debates about conspiracies have always been part of America's political discourse. Mistrust against the rulers and the fear of foreign interference have a long tradition. After all, the country was partly founded out of distrust against the ruling elite of England. Anyway, conspiracy theorists mostly used to be considered nuts. And then the Internet came along. With it, the bazaar of conspiracy theories has become even bigger. They no longer circulate only at the fringe of society, but now reach a broad public. Silicon Valley has created a biotope for conspiracy theorists, partly because the Web and conspiracy theories share a similar structure: Conspiracy theories claim that everything is somehow connected – and in the World Wide Web it really is. Everyone can share their beliefs, no matter how imaginary or harebrained it may be. Algorithms help to spread conspiracy theories and misinformation at an alarming rate. Due to the structure of social media, shortened and extreme positions circulate easier than more complex topics. These platforms are algorithmically optimized for monetization, not for truthfulness. «We're not a media company, » said YouTube boss Susan Wojcicki at the South by Southwest festival. It is Silicon Valley code for: We don't want to take any responsibility for what our users do with our platforms – we want to make money with it. Before her, e.g. Google News CEO Richard Gingras, Mark Zuckerberg, and Facebook managing director Sheryl Sandberg said quite the same. In contrast to the media companies, they feel no sense of obligation to follow journalistic rules. But for many Americans social media platforms are the main source of information. Activities to manipulate public opinion online are increasing worldwide: Election campaigns are rigged, and false news overflow the world. According to a study by the Oxford Internet Institute, 70 countries are now affected by campaigns launched by government agencies or political parties. Samantha Bradshaw, lead author of the study, said: «The affordances of social networking technologies – algorithms, automation and big data – vastly changes the scale, scope, and precision of how information is transmitted in the digital age. Although social media was once heralded as a force for freedom and democracy, it has increasingly come under scrutiny for its role in amplifying disinformation, inciting violence, and lowering trust in the media and democratic institutions. »

Too much information, unfiltered and unordered, makes disinformation more effective because in situations of excessive demands, many people fall back on their prejudices. «We hear what we want to hear, » says Timothy Snyder, history professor at Yale University, and concludes: «Confirmation bias, our desire for affirmation of what we feel to be true, is a quirk around which digital activity can cluster. » To avoid conflicts they seek information that confirm what they already believe. Psychologists call it «motivated reasoning. » Such beliefs are the basis of our identity and cannot easily be changed. They are immune to logic and evidence because doubting them would question our personality. We are confirmation-seeking beings and find dissonance unpleasant. In social media, positive feelings are reinforced by interaction. Almost nowhere you get recognition as fast as in conspiracy circles. It feels good to belong to the chosen group of «knowing» people who are above everything, outstanding from the «manipulated mass. » Such echo chambers have always existed in one form or the other, but the Web has intensified this effect. It's easier to form virtual communities of like-minded people with deviating opinions than in real life, making false beliefs both more real-seeming and more contagious. Social media create a fantasy cascade in which millions of bedoozled people around the world wallow.

People who are susceptible to conspiracy theories don't like dealing with uncertainty, and they tend to see patterns where there are no patterns at all. Conspiracy theories promise a simple explanation for a complex world. It's easier to accept that there are some bad guys pulling the strings than to accept chaos and randomness or that some things are too complex to identify a single person who is responsible. Conspiracy theorists want to explain everything with binary thinking: Everything is either zero or one, yes or no, black or white, good or evil. Evolution is playing a trick on us here: We are evolutionary developed to recognize patterns and make connections. If our ancestors ate a poisonous fruit and fell ill or even died from it, it made sense to establish a causal connection, even if they could not prove it. In our digital times this conditioning kicks in. Conspiracy theories are not «theories» in the scientific sense. They appear to be similar, but they are not. It would be more appropriate to use the term «conspiracy ideology» or «conspiracy myth. » Despite their rhetoric about searching the «truth, » conspiracy theorists tend to be ideologues. Skepticism is something good, an expression of the critical mind. But with conspiracy theories, an unleashed pseudo-skepticism only sows mistrust, following the slogan: Nothing is true, and everything is possible. One feature of conspiracy theories is that they are not disprovable. Conspiracy theorists force every trivial detail and every snippet of evidence to fit their world view. Their theories resemble a blob that continues to bloat and eats everything on its way. Anyone who opposes it can be convicted: They themselves belong to the conspirators. Please prove that you are not one of 'Them'! It's becoming difficult to conduct a rational political discourse. «The wild speculation inherent in conspiracy theories and their promotion very much harm our ability to know what is true and what is not, and it corrupts the very process of knowing. We are dismantling the most valuable asset of the species called Homo sapiens, our ability to reason, one brick at a time. » wrote Robert Harrington for the Palmer Report.

Donald Trump has won many followers by spreading conspiracy theories. From the first day, his campaign didn't focus on the average voter, but on the paranoid and gullible. No tinfoil hat conspiracy was too deranged for them: Barack Obama was born in Kenia, the conservative Supreme Court judge Antonin Scalia didn't die a natural death, vaccinations cause autism, the Democrats have rigged the 2016 elections, the Trump-critical moderator Joe Scarborough murdered an intern, the father of Ted Cruz was somehow involved in the assassination of Kennedy … And this is only a selection. Trump's presidency didn't start well and won't end well either. After his inauguration, the country saw the largest protests since Vietnam. Yet Trump's spin masters never get tired of claiming that the inauguration attracted more people than the protests – which a comparison of the aerial photos prove to be a lie. Kellyanne Conway, Trump advisor, announced that the White House had merely presented «alternative facts. » Uh-huh. Thirty years ago, the philosopher Harry G. Frankfurt published a diagnosis of our society with the subtle title On Bullshit. According to Frankfurt the average liar is a person who is still attached to the truth, in the sense that they oppose it with their own «truth» – in form of a lie. Trump and his lackeys don't care about truth at all. Well-paid bullshitters work hard to destroy the consensus on reason and on many other virtues, and thus they destroy the social cohesion that is necessary to democracy. They try to make hatred acceptable, find tolerance «sick» and get along well with tyrants everywhere.

Since Trump holds the office, a 70-year-old book became a bestseller at Amazon: George Orwell's 1984. O'Brien, the chief inquisitor in 1984, provides an abridged version of Trumpism: «Sometimes two and two are five. Sometimes they are three. Sometimes they are all of them at once. » But not only the far right is prone to conspiracy theories. Bernie Sanders has a similar strategy and sometimes even uses a similar language as Trump. Their alternative facts are targeting those who have been long convinced that governing and lying are the same thing – the nihilists who are unable or unwilling to integrate facts into their world view. The bottom line is the claim that the political elites have rigged the system against the interests of the common people. The richest one percent of the population controls the entire political and economic system. When Sanders lost the primaries in 2016, he claimed the system was rigged in almost every speech. He provided zero proof, and his theory is as incoherent as any other conspiracy theory. On many occasions, he has criticized the free market system. But both at the same time is not possible: The system is either rigged or it's free.

It's easier for conspiracy theorists when a society is divided. All over the world polarization and political fragmentation are on the rise. On both sides of the political spectrum, extreme views are becoming popular. Conspiracy theories are almost always wrong. But they can be toxic for the real world anyway. The road from violent language to real violence is short. After the attempted bombings of prominent Democrats and the Pittsburgh synagogue shooting, we know that Trump's hateful rhetoric and reckless threats is inciting violence. Real conspiracies, of course, go on all the time. Trump's abuse of office, the rampant corruption of his administration, and his obstruction of justice are real. Yet there is still no evidence that windmills cause cancer.

One thing that unites those who voted for Donald Trump is that no matter how vile and insulting their rhetoric is and no matter how deranged and cruel their opinions and statements are, they call themselves «Christian» and «God Loving. » In a paper called Conspiracy Theories and the Paranoid Style(s) of Mass Opinion, scientists at the University of Chicago have concluded that «the likelihood of supporting conspiracy theories is strongly predicted, » by two key pieces of the American national character that derive from their particular Christian culture: «a propensity to attribute the source of unexplained or extraordinary events to unseen, intentional forces» and a weakness for «melodramatic narratives as explanations for prominent events, particularly those that interpret history relative to universal struggles between good and evil. » Religious people believe that almost everything happens for a reason. As a cognitive scientist from Yale put it: «Explicit religious» people tend «to view the world in terms of agency, purpose, and design. » Conspiracy thinking is not U.S. born, of course. But religious belief is widespread, hence the belief in conspiracy theories.

Ironically, Trump's penchant for conspiracy theories has become a big problem for him. As I write this text, he is has been impeached by the House of Representatives. He seems to have believed too many of his theories himself and acted as president based on them.

We learn almost everything we know about our world and environment through the mass media. We rely completely on receiving all the information from newspapers, radio, TV, and now the Internet. At the same time, it's quite clear that we can be manipulated or misled. That's why we need the mainstream media. The real world is not difficult to discover. If you have access to the Internet, you can't make excuses for not putting effort into reading a reliable information source.

THE AGE OF THE CROWDS

«*Madness is rare in the individual – but with groups, parties, peoples, and ages it's the rule.* » – Friedrich Nietzsche

«*There is a cult of ignorance in the United States…. [It is] nurtured by the false notion that democracy means that 'my ignorance is just as good as your knowledge.'*»
– Isaac Asimov

Generally speaking, we don't put much faith in the masses, especially not that they make wise decisions. The word mass sounds like dullness and mediocrity, just think of terms like mass tourism, mass production, or mass hysteria. We usually don't think of ourselves as a part of the mass – mass is always the other. In this spirit, the French sociologist Gustave Le Bon published his book In The Crowd: A Study of the Popular Mind. It's a standard work regarding collective stupidity. His theories influenced

Sigmund Freud and Max Weber, the Nazis studied his ideas on mass manipulation, as did Edward Bernays, the inventor of public relations and predecessor of generations of advertisers, propagandists, and spin doctors. For Le Bon, the mass was a mob, controlled by the subconscious, reasonable action impossible. The mob is instinctive, gullible, cruel, and impatient. In the light of mass events in sport and culture, he seems to have a point. But while it's rather harmless here, in politics the mindlessness of the masses is alarming. There are countless examples for bloody wars, pogroms, and violent hatred. 100 years before the Internet, Le Bon described astonishing similarities with the online crowd today: «The simplicity and exaggeration of the sentiments of crowds have for result that a throng knows neither doubt nor uncertainty. It goes at once to extremes. » He continued: «In crowds the foolish, ignorant, and envious persons are freed from the sense of their insignificance and powerlessness, and are possessed instead by the notion of brutal and temporary but immense strength. » Le Bon wasn't a Democrat. His resentment of the masses was fuelled by his fear of modernity. He experienced the February Revolution of 1848 and the Paris Commune, progressive movements actually. But he was an intellectual snob who disdained the newly formed proletariat. If Le Bon were alive today, he would probably fully give himself to cultural pessimism. The endless stream of information would be explanation enough for him for the current state of society: «The acquisition of knowledge for which no use can be found is a sure method of driving a man to revolt. » Accordingly, Le Bon would probably reject the wisdom of the crowds: «In crowds it's stupidity and not mother-wit that is accumulated. It's not all the world, as is so often repeated, that has more wit than Voltaire, but assuredly Voltaire that has more wit than all the world, if by 'all the world' crowds are to be understood. »

Wikipedia is considered a prime example of successful swarm intelligence. It has the reputation of a professional encyclopedia, although it was never designed so. The groundwork for Wikipedia was laid by Jimmy Wales. Ironically, he describes himself as a follower of Ayn Rand, the high priestess of egoism. Her hatred of collectivism and crowds is legendary. At the age of 28, he became a trader for futures and options on the Chicago Stock Exchange. Legend has it that he was so successful that in only two years he acquired a small fortune – less than a million dollar, as he emphasizes. It's hard to understand why of all people this arch-capitalist founded a non-profit organization and contributed 500,000 dollars from its own pockets. With Wikipedia, however, he believes in the virtues of collaboration. So far, that's working fine. The foundation now has a proud fortune of 104.5 million dollars. Access to education has always been determined by the current balance of power. Wales believes that everyone should have equal access to knowledge and opportunities: «Imagine a world in which every single person is given free access to the sum of all human knowledge. That's what we're doing, » he describes the vision, philosophy, and mission of his project. Expert knowledge doesn't have to come from, well, experts, he believes, but also can come from a group of 'non-experts.' He assumes that an expert can never know as much as several non-experts.

One problem with Wikipedia is that you don't know who is behind the entries, whether expert, amateur, or buffoon. Anyone with access to the Internet and some basic writing skills can compose new entries, even your alcoholic neighbor with the shrinking brain. Participants don't need any special knowledge or formal qualifications. In theory, the large number of users will provide a control function, but it doesn't prevent mistakes. Sometimes it makes it easier. In 2014, scientists found mistakes in 9 out of 10 of Wikipedia's health entries. Most of these entries contained «many errors. » So if you want to inform yourself about an illness, you should consult a doctor. Many articles don't meet the basic quality standards, even if measured by its own criteria. Wikipedia is not a reliable source. Yet unlike any random newspaper, it still enjoys a high reputation. It is often – and unfortunately mostly – the first and only resource for information. Since every user can change any entry, they can spread incorrect information on purpose. Companies hire professional writers who remove critical text passages or water down the content. Administrators check the entries. But this only prevents the worst nonsense. Since the spread of knowledge no longer depends only on books, it's difficult to check the reliability of Wikipedia entries by means of comparisons. The conscientious tracing of sources can mostly, if at all, only be done by professionals. Larry Sanger, Wikipedia co-founder, admitted: «Another hurdle was to figure out how to rein in the bad actors so that they did not ruin the project for everyone else. Unfortunately, we never did come up with a good solution for that one. »

There may be high-quality articles on special topics, but these were not written by the crowd, but by experts. But experts feel demotivated by the superficial way in which many topics are dealt with. They have to «defend» themselves on the discussion pages of the articles, invest much time and energy to explain what it is about. The tone is rough, defamatory criticism instead of sound discussion. Often it's not the one who is actually right who «wins, » but the one who has the longer breath. If you have ever discussed with UFO believers, astrologers, climate deniers, or creationists you probably know what I mean. A pundit once called Wikipedia the «dictatorship of time-rich. » Anyone who is smart and educated, has a real life job and is successful in it, will rarely engage in fruitless discussions with dilettantes. Women are under-represented on Wikipedia, and many men want it to stay that way. Women report a harsh tone, sexist insults, and even organized smear campaigns. In his essay Digital Maoism Jaron Lanier shows that the attempt to create an open encyclopedia must end in disaster. The «democratic control» of knowledge is unreliable. How can an encyclopedia be neutral if it's dictated by the masses and the zeitgeist? You simply cannot organize knowledge democratically. Whether a mathematical theory is valid or not cannot be decided by vote. Or as the comedian John Oliver put it, you don't need to gather opinions on a fact: «You might as well have a poll asking: 'Which number is bigger, 15 or 5?' or 'Do owls exist?' or 'Are there hats?'» Wikipedia's majority principle doesn't protect minorities, which is essential in democracies. The «mob» can suppress legitimate views if expressed by fringe groups. Lanier warns: «I regard the danger of Wiki lynch justice as very real. In the world of Wikipedia, truth is determined by those who are most obsessed. » In 1951, the psychologist Solomon Asch conducted a series of famous experiments. Asch showed that many people give in to social pressure and agree with the opinion of the majority even if this opinion contradicts obvious facts. In most cases humans behave socially, indeed we are hardwired to do so. Martin Nowak teaches mathematics and biology at Harvard, where he heads the Evolutionary Dynamics program. His computer simulations support the thesis that cooperative behavior was more important for evolution than competitive behavior and thus prevailed. Individuals who didn't join the group in the early stages of our evolution had a hard time and often didn't survive. We still experience this group pressure, which is today even stronger due to digitization. Another serious problem is Wikipedia's cultural biases. Peter Haber, an expert on modern history at the University of Vienna, analyzed Wikipedia's objectivity. His result: Especially with historical topics one should be critical about the neutrality. Historical events are often portrayed from the viewpoint of the respective country.

The media that we use are changing our social character, i.e. the characteristics and behaviors that people of a certain epoch and culture have in common. That's not necessarily a bad thing, because the social character has always changed and will continue to do so. Change alone is not a cause for concern. But in a world of «my ignorance is just as good as your knowledge» we destroy our expert knowledge culture in favor of an amateur society. That has disastrous consequences for the individual as well as for the society. Instead of talking about swarm intelligence, you should call it bumptious idiocy. Social media contribute to the destruction of basic democratic principles such as the rule of law, protection of minorities, finding compromises. Rather, exclusion and emphasis on one's own are promoted on the Net, as are autocratic tendencies.

COLLECTING PEOPLE

'Sexually attractive' – is not the first quality usually associated with nerds. 'Intelligent' – yes, 'pedantic' – maybe, 'weird' – definitely. It's actually a truism: Thinking reduces your erotic appeal and makes you lonely. Who wants to hang out with a braniac and doubter with a sarcastic sense of humor rather than to party brainlessly? That nerds less likely find a partner hasn't only been so since the rise of computers. Already ancient nerds had trouble getting laid. Greek philosopher Thales once replied to the question of why he didn't look for a woman: «It's still too early, » and then, in his later years: «Now it's too late. » Nietzsche remained a virgin throughout his life. Darwin, after careful contemplation, decided to marry his cousin Emma Wedgwood, who he had known since childhood and who would not cause him any trouble. Nerds are still experiencing considerable difficulties to find a mate, and when they find someone, it's more of a coincidence.

Linux founder Linus Thorvalds met his wife, a former karate champion of Finland, on the Internet. «I married the first woman to approach me electronically, » he said. Mark Zuckerberg's wife Priscilla Chan described their first meeting: «He was this nerdy guy who was just a little bit out there. » The then 19-year-old studied psychology at Harvard University – and liked to work on online projects.

Nerds like to know how systems work. These can be technical devices as well as scientific fields, the human body, or a game. To understand a system, you have to analyze its rules: What happens when you change a variable of the system? How does an input affect the output? And, if you understand it, you can master and change the system – or construct a new one if necessary. That's why many nerds can' t do anything with fashion. Fashion trends come and go and don't follow algorithms. You can predict them as little as you can predict a conversation with strangers in the subway. Nerds love to play computer games. Games are based on rules that can be systematically explored and controlled – unlike the real world. They need rules they can follow. Otherwise, they don't feel comfortable. Some of the people in the valley even believe that life is a game. This alone meets the cliché: They are people who remind others of «machines, » writes American author Benjamin Nugent in his book American Nerd. Another reason why they are native to the Internet. They feel as at home there as others do in their favorite pub. In blogs, forums, and e-mails you don't need to pay attention to body language. Some extreme nerds believe that they can control their human matters similarly. And because the «socially awkward» Zuckerberg had trouble with making real friends, he decided to build a social network, so we all get troubled.

In 2003, he launched the controversial site Facemash. The website published photos of female Harvard students. It randomly displayed two pictures of two different women, and fellow students could rate their 'hotness.' Well, this proves an incredible lack of empathy, to put it mildly. Facemash experienced harsh critique. But it was a huge success. That's all you need to know about his alma mater, it's merely a matchmaker for the elite. The university quickly shut down the site and accused Zuckerberg of copyright violations because he had posted the photos without the women's consent. Soon after, he founded «Thefacebook.com» with his fellow students Eduardo Saverin, Chris Hughes, and Dustin Moskovitz. It also was a success right from the start. More than 600 users registered on the first day. One month later, Yale, Stanford, and Columbia students could register, and by the end of 2004, the platform had one million users. In 2005, it opened for other universities and schools. It was not before September 2006 that the site was open to all users over 13 with a valid e-mail address. What many people don't know is that the 20-year-old college drop-out Zuckerberg had no money. Square one. But in the summer of 2004, Peter Thiel gave 500,000 dollars for Facebook and in return acquired shares in Zuckerberg's company. It was one of the best investments of the information age. But that doesn't explain the success of Facebook.

Loneliness is a central topic in One Hundred Years of Solitude, as the title of the work indicates. The term loneliness appears on almost every page, and the theme accompanies the reader throughout the novel. Loneliness determines life in Macondo and the life of the Buendía, and it contributes to their fate: the ultimate destruction of the village and the demise of the family clan. An intact social life is as important to us as an intact body. If humans lose contact with the community, the feeling of loneliness works as a protective mechanism that makes us seek contact again. But loneliness can make us sick. In an article in the Harvard Business Review, Dr. Vivek H. Murthy, former Surgeon General of the United States, wrote: «Loneliness and weak social connections are associated with a reduction in lifespan similar to that caused by smoking 15 cigarettes a day and even greater than that associated with obesity. » Neuroscientist John Cacioppo of the University of Chicago explains in his book Loneliness that social isolation reduces the life expectancy of fruit flies, humans, and all social animals in between. From this perspective the collecting of friends on the internet is a modern variant of our struggle for survival and on the longing for one's own well-being. In fact, since we rely on machines rather than humans, more people suffer from loneliness than ever before. The sociologist Robert Putnam catchphrases this by saying that we're increasingly «bowling alone. »

Coldness, solitude, egoism, lack of time, burn outs, and depressions have been increasing for years. One might wonder whether there has ever been such an impersonal society in which there was so little community and in which social relations were so fragile and replaceable. Digital isolation is something which actually shouldn't exist. But the more time we spend in cyberspace and the less in «meatspace, » as some nerds call the offline world, the more isolated and lonely we become. Technology is not as warm and inviting as we are seduced to believe. Our world is so over-teched, we have all these great devices that connect us and feed us with information – and yet, it can be vast and empty like a desert. Sociologist Sherry Turkle points to the paradox that digital connectivity does not increase real life social connectivity. She explains that many people seek a place where they can love their friends and their lives. The only problem with searching this place on the Internet is that it's all virtual. Instead of spending time in reality with friends, she concluded, people spend more time in virtual worlds. Everybody is staring at their smartphone, tablet, computer, or television, all the time and everywhere. Virtual friendships and contacts displace real relations. Behavioral scientist Jenna Clark compared various studies on social networks and warns of the dangers of «social snacking»: «Sometimes people online are less lonely and sometimes people are more – because if you just social snack you're not any closer to anyone then you were before. If you're having a problem you can't go talk to [these online relationships] because you aren't that close to them. Realizing you've been spending all this time in meaningless interactions is going to leave you feeling more lonely. » A vicious circle of digital loneliness: To fight the growing loneliness, we join Facebook, Instagram, and Twitter at the same time and look what the others are doing. We feed the social networks with photos and videos to show others how great our lives are eagerly waiting for likes as confirmation. We no longer have time for friendships because we are too busy to follow the lives of others online. Studies show that the illusion of a perfect world that we create with our digital profiles triggers negative emotions in other users. They find their own lives less exciting and sometimes even boring. One study evaluated several studies on the connection between loneliness and the use of Facebook and found evidence that lonely people use it more often. The authors conclude that «lonely individuals who are shy and have low social support may turn to Facebook to compensate for their lack of social skills. » But it's these very people who find it difficult to be permanently aware of other people's «beautiful» lives. «The root of suffering is comparison, » says a Buddhist truth. Our dependence on social networks is a poor compromise between the longing for human attention and the fear of true closeness. Our relationships determine the quality of our lives. Connections with other people give us meaning, more happiness, and more comfort than any other human experience. Our social platforms are in a disastrous condition. The problems range from harassment, hate speech, and fake news to serious crime. People lie, cheat, rip off, and defame. The victims react with despair and helplessness. Resistance is rather rare. Often their anger is directed inwards and causes headaches, anxiety, insomnia, digestive problems, and depressions. As a result, they suffer mental and physical exhaustion.

Actually, it's not surprising that social networks cause more loneliness. Not only that there are many pricks in social media, a high number of pricks owns or manages such platforms. In a beery blog entry Zuckerberg once called a girl who dumped him a «bitch» – he founded Facemash out of revenge. Or take Twitter boss Jack Dorsey: During a meditation holiday in Myanmar, he emphasized the great beauty of the country and announced his goal: «How do I stop suffering? » According to UN investigators, there is a genocide going on in Myanmar, fueled by agitation and fake news in social media. To ask of one's own suffering in such a place is a bit cynical, even by Silicon Valley standards. Or Mahbod Moghadam, one of the founders of Genius, a digital media company, who was fired after posting inappropriate jokes about a shooting at the University of California. Or the much hailed Evan Spiegel, founder of Snapchat, who urged his fellow college students at Stanford in e-mails to «Have some girl put your large kappa sigma dick down her throat. »

A growing narcissism in the society seems to be an inevitable consequence of excessive social media use. In The Narcissism Epidemic, Jean Twenge and W. Keith Campbell note a swelling tide of narcissism. They write: «The name «MySpace» is no coincidence. The slogan of YouTube is «Broadcast Yourself. » The name «Facebook» is just right, with its nuance of seeing and being seen, preferably looking as attractive as possible. » Social media don't promote care or concern for others. Rather, it makes it easier to focus on the self and the imagination that you are the center of the universe. Narcissists are not interested in warmth and care in their social interactions. They are concerned with themselves and obsessed with what others think of them. They also believe they are entitled to the attention of all others. That's why tweeting is one of Trump's favorite activities.

George Soros warns of a threat from Facebook that many have not even considered yet: the similarities between Internet platforms and gambling companies. «Casinos have developed techniques to hook gamblers to the point where they gamble away all their money, even money they don't have, » he says. «Something very harmful and maybe irreversible is happening to human attention in the digital age. Not just distraction or addiction: social media companies are inducing people to give up their autonomy. » There is some evidence that the excessive use of social media such as Facebook can become an addiction. «It's hard to resist a technology that is also a tool of pleasure, » wrote Sarah Leonard and Kate Losse in the political magazine «Dissent. » «The Luddites smashed their power looms, but who wants to smash Facebook– with all one's photos, birthday greetings, and invitations? » The human brain is no more prepared for Facebook and Twitter than for drugs or unhealthy foods. At an Axios event, Sean Parker warned of the consequences of the use of social media. He admitted that they knew they were creating something addictive that exploited «a vulnerability in human psychology. » Yet they did it anyway, since, after all, they are in the advertising business. Parker's confession is reminiscent of what Facebook's vice president for user growth Chamath Palihapitiya told an audience at Stanford Graduate School of Business: «I think we have created tools that are ripping apart the social fabric of how society works, » he said, before recommending people take a «hard break» from social media. «The short-term, dopamine-driven feedback loops we've created are destroying how society works, » he said, referring to online interactions driven by »hearts, likes, thumbs-up. » «No civil discourse, no cooperation; misinformation, mistruth. And it's not an American problem – this is not about Russians ads. This is a global problem. »

True loneliness in the electronic age is a fading experience. To be quiet and to enjoy existential peace has become an old-fashioned exhausting exercise. But there is a new one: loneliness in the masses. Virtual worlds have no warmth, no truth, and no depth. They don't bring people together. They are a sad fake that will become our nightmare.

CAN'T BUY ME LOVE

«I'm curious about whether there is a fundamental mathematical law underlying human social relationships that governs the balance of who and what we all care about. I bet there is. » – Mark Zuckerberg

I hope sometime we may clasp hands bodily as we do now spiritually, on the wire-for we do, don't we,' said C. 'Certainly, here is mine spiritually!' responded Nattie without the least hesitation, as she thought of the miles of safe distance between. » This fictional dialogue is from Wired Love: A Romance of Dots and Dashes, an 1880 novel by Ella Cheever Thayer. Thayer was a feminist. A year later she wrote a successful play to challenge the stereotypes about suffragettes. In Wired Love, she explores the joys and disappointments of love in the age of telegraphy. Telegraphy has created an exciting sense of connectedness. But it created merely illusions than real «knowing. »

The young telegraphist Nattie works in a small town somewhere in the Western United States. Over the telegraph line she meets a charming colleague who introduces himself to her only as «C. » They start quarreling, then flirting, and then they fall in love. When the two finally meet, it turns out that in real life Nattie is shy and fearful. Although she can express her feeling via telegraphy, she is otherwise very private. Nattie thought she got to know «C» over the wire. But she only knew about him what he wanted her to know about himself. They are so tongue-tied, that they only get engaged after setting up a private telegraph line between their rooms, so they can chat about their amorous feelings.

Dating sites claim that virtual flirting is much easier than real life flirting. Since you are not facing the other, they cannot see your nervousness and shyness. They claim, online dating would be ideal for people who have difficulties to talk to others on the street, in the supermarket, or a bar. Accordingly, when online dating appeared, it was assumed to be for «nerds, » «the desperate, » the «socially inept. » In the past two decades, however, it has developed from a niche category to a mass phenomenon. It not only has lost its stigma but is now the dominant form of dating for many people all over the world. The market is growing every year, and commercial providers are making millions in profits. Their customers are willing to invest a considerable amount of time and money for the online search for love and happiness. Critics fear that dating sites change our relationships and the way people hook up and that singles are little more than consumers. «It's driving pretty much everything, if you think about all the things people spend money on around finding a romantic partner, courting them, getting married, having kids, » said Daniel McMurtrie, the young co-founder and CEO of Tyro Capital Management, a New York hedge fund. It's changing the way people spend their money and shaping the nature of household spending. The providers claim to have found a scientifically based formula for happiness: complex algorithms that help to find the partner who best matches you. Nobody has to be in a mediocre relationship anymore.

As tempting as the new possibilities are, initial studies show a rather sobering picture of the reality. The Internet has not made it easier to start a relationship. Online dating even seems to hinder the path to happiness in many ways. While singles can choose from plenty of willing men, women, and other varieties, they often can't find the right one. American psychologists question the matching algorithms of dating sites. They can hardly predict the success of a relationship, said Eli Finkel of Northwestern

University. He and his colleagues and deliver a devastating conclusion: «No compelling evidence supports matching sites' claims that mathematical algorithms work-that they foster romantic outcomes that are superior to those fostered by other means of pairing partners. » They point out that while there are methods to predict the success of relationships, the main problem of dating sites is that they do not have the necessary information to do so. First and foremost, they say, it's the way two people discuss and resolve their differences that is crucial for the relationship. Online dating lacks face-to-face contact, gestures, and facial expressions. But relationships are initiated according to archaic mechanisms. Many unconsciously impressions are involved, such as the shape of the face, the sound of the voice, the smell. These first impressions are far more important than information about residence, occupation, and favorite color. Psychologist Dan Ariely from Duke University compares online dating with predicting the flavor of a meal by reading only the nutritional information, calories, and ingredients: «While one might have some sense of how the food will taste, only sampling it can provide an accurate answer. » The sheer number of potential partners can lead to ever-increasing expectations.

In the past, singles had to accept those candidates they met in their village or town, at work, in the bar or club or in their circle of friends. Since now there are countless alternatives we no longer have to make any compromises – at least in theory. Moreover, people are usually bad at judging themselves – e.g. how creative or open-minded they really are. And often we make our decision according to the attractiveness of the photo and the person on it. We tend to deduce from the appearance of someone to the whole person. If someone looks attractive, we assume that this person would also be smart, competent, and trustworthy – even if everyone knows that a beautiful shell does not make a beautiful person. Sure, such false conclusions also happen when two people meet in reality. But when it comes to online dating, they have a particularly strong effect. Dating apps are structured like online shops. No one takes the time to focus on one person or to fight for their love in any difficult real-world situations. Why would you, when your great love might be just a click away? The shopping mentality often persists even when two people have already met – and even if it sparked between them. Temptation lurks everywhere; maybe the next mouse click will bring the ideal candidate. True to the slogan: Test therefore, who join forever, whether you can find someone who is even better.

The Israeli sociologist and anthropologist Eva Illouz deals with this phenomenon in her book Consuming the romantic Utopia. She argues that the platform capitalism also influences the last refuge of authenticity and warmth: romantic love. At first glance, love is everything that capitalism is not. It's «irrational rather than rational, gratuitous rather than profit-oriented, organic rather than utilitarian, private rather than public. » Basically, they sell illusions. Many people hope that their lives will improve if only they find a partner. But no dating site has more potential than what its members contribute to it. The Internet is full of failing social contacts. People who got to know each other online lack a common basis – because there was no initial experience, no common ground, and no effort for the other. Only a profile and a business model. Algorithms cannot predict emotional closeness, and even those seeking a relationship often cannot predict what it takes.

PERFECT FOR PORN

«Don't Come Here Looking for Love. » – Ad for ImLive, a porn Web site

«I can no longer think what I want to think. My thoughts have been replaced by moving images. » – Georges Duhamel

Case, the antihero of Gibson's novel Neuromancer, is a burned-out hacker, a data thief or, as the novel says, a «cowboy, » «a rustler. » He lives in the real environment of the old, neglected terrestrial cities and in the new, cultivated recreational architectures in space. And he also moves in the virtual world simulated by computers, a utopian homeland in which people are free of the limitations of the body perceived as «meat. » Under the constant threat of brain death through electronic defense systems of corporations and military services he taps into their secret data and sells it. During his trips into cyberspace, Case gets stuck in a virtual vagina, which pulls him back again, and again, and again into the digital sex-realm:

«Now she straddled him again, took his hand, and closed it over her, his thumb along the cleft of her buttocks, his fingers spread across the labia. As she began to lower herself, the images came back, the faces, fragments of neon arriving and receding. She slid down around him and his back arched convulsively. She rode him that way, impaling herself, slipping down on him again and again, until they both had come, his orgasm flaring blue in a timeless space, a vastness like the matrix, where the faces were shredded and blown away down hurricane corridors, and her inner thighs were strong and wet against his hips. »

And for this, Gibson was praised as the harbinger of our near virtual future – a nerd fantasy, a promise for the frustrated, a sales argument. He must be credited with a certain scenic understanding for the sexual wants of his readers. When he wrote it, he probably did not have in mind what we can now see on the Internet.

If you wanted to find pornography in the 1980s, you had to look for it in shady shops or video stores. Much has changed since then. No more embarrassing shopping trips thanks to the Silicon Valley. The new technologies allow consumers to watch porn in private, anywhere, anytime. Pornography even has become a part of everyday life and even found its way into mainstream media. Some commercials, music videos, or sex scenes in movies can hardly be distinguished from soft porn. William Safire, a conservative political columnist, once quipped: «I spend an inordinate amount of time reading Victoria's Secret catalogues, looking for errors. To avoid disapproving stares from colleagues, I slip the catalogue inside my copy of Hustler. »

Technology and pornography are two industries that have stimulated each other for more than 100 years. In the first half of the 19th century, photography came up, and about a week later, the porn industry was born. With the invention of cinematography this industry expanded enormously. The first porn movies were already commercially successful in 1896. In the USA, the porno movie boom began in the 1920s. Edison had made cinema popular, Ford the assembly line – now they could produce at low cost and even put a price tag on human bodies. The customers constantly demanded more fresh supply and higher quality: better lighting, narrative cuts, change of perspective, etc. But the industry was less interested in higher quality than in cheaper production. It needed cameras that were easy to handle, and the technology sector delivered. In 1965, Kodak introduced the narrow film format Super 8. Now people without camera training could make movies themselves. The impact on the porn industry was enormous. Now there were also movies for home. In the 1970s, JVC developed the VHS system, and the first hardcore porn on a VHS tape was released in 1977 – one year before Hollywood started to use this format. A decade later, porn sparked a boom in the TV sex channels of American hotel chains, as well as in the hotlines of telephone companies. In November 1972, a photo of the Swedish model Lena Söderberg appeared in Playboy. In the following year, the researcher Alexander Sawchuk from the University of Southern California needed a photo to test a new compression algorithm for digital images. He used the very same picture of Lena Söderberg and uploaded it to ARPANET. Thus, two profitable industries mingled inseparably: the Internet and porn.

Pornography not only benefited from new technology, it also promoted its development. Almost every digital business model can be traced back to the porn industry: file-sharing platforms, video streaming, safe payment systems, reversible electronic watermarks on photos, etc. The porn industry also pioneered the development of Web-based subscription business models, as well as anti-fraud security. Each time when you watch your favorite show on a streaming platform like Netflix or Amazon, you can secretly thank the porno industry. Many of its marketing techniques are now applied in other areas of the Internet. The sales principle of porn makers on the Internet is as simple as it is successful: Free movies in often poor picture quality whet the appetite of users and arouse their lust for more, so that they contract for premium offers. The porn industry also promoted the development of techniques for anonymous surfing, which not only allows you to buy and consume porn in private, but also to protects you from being spied on. Somewhat ironically, at the same time, porn sites heavily spy on their users, using tracking tools to create a digital footprint of their customers.

Pornography is the most profitable business compared to all other Internet activities. Numbers are hard to find, because its profits are usually not monitored through conventional business authorities. According to various reports, porn businesses make a total annual turnover of circa a staggering 100 billion dollars. That's enough to feed around five billion people every day. Large porn sites have more visitors than Netflix, Amazon, and Twitter – combined. It's the fastest growing business in the world, and with the introduction of virtual reality, sales figures are expected to more than triple by 2030. Today, it's not pimps with gold necklaces who collect the money, but IT experts with degrees in computer science. They know how to generate gigantic traffic via search engine optimization, cross-linking, and pay-per-click advertising. The content is delivered by others.

San Fernando Valley, aka Porn-Valley, is where the «fun» begins, the Mecca of the porn industry, a few miles from Hollywood. There are more than 200 porno studios. Behind the facades of monotonous middle-class villas with Hollywood swings and infinity pools, they produce around 90 percent of all pornos in the web. Their consumption of humans is enormous, mostly colored and Eastern European models and troubled kids from the white orphanages, drug rehabs, and homeless shelters. The pornography industry is an «economic juggernaut, » says professor Gail Dines, author of Pornland. Many mainstream corporations make huge profits from it. Hotel chains, such as the Marriott, Westin, and Hilton profit from in-room porn movies. General Motors (GM) made millions of dollars off pornography when it owned the U.S. national satellite distribution company DirecTV. GM sold its stake in DirecTV to Rupert Murdoch's News Corporation. Despite Mr. Murdoch's conservative populism, DirecTV continues to broadcast porn into «millions of American homes for a nice profit. » Dines continues:

«Microsoft also makes money from the porn industry as the industry spends what Henderson calls «a fortune» on various financial, accounting, and graphic design software. Search engines such as Google, Yahoo!, Microsoft's Internet Explorer, Apple's Safari, and Mozilla Firefox are used to search for porn, and credit card companies are increasingly making money from porn transactions as the industry moves away from brick-and-mortar stores that still take cash to Web sites that require credit card payment, » Dines wrote. «Banks also make money from the porn industry as the revenue it generates is invested in stocks, bonds, mutual funds, and so on. Indeed, everyone in the supply chain from production to consumption is complicit in building and strengthening the porn industry. »

A little extra profit, why not? The porn industry has been able to thrive on the jurisdictional ambiguity of the Internet. Its huge profits enable it to influence academic research and law making and to weather any legal challenges. The result is a pornofied society.
Pornography has not only technological ramifications. The first famous and socially acceptable porn movie was Deep Throat in 1972. In a time, when women's right movements flourished and women of the Western world discovered their sexuality, the main actress Linda Lovelace was allowed to literally have her mouth stuffed. The movie, with production costs of only 25,000 dollars, earned six million in the first seven weeks. It was 'cool' to watch it, even Jack Nicholson and Jackie Kennedy waited in line in front of a New Yorker cinema. Twenty years later Linda Lovelace alias Linda Boreman published her side of the story. The twenty-year-old girl from a strict, puritanical home had fallen in love with the ex-Marine and Vietnam veteran Chuck Traynor. He took her out of her parents' house and dragged her into the red light milieu – the first time with five businessmen in a hotel room. «Take off your clothes or you are one fucking dead chick! » Traynor barked at Linda. From now on, he beat the crap out of her to force his will on her.
Pornos like to tell about freedom, never-ending lust, and sexual paradise. But behind this facade is an industry that humiliates, abuses, and exploits women. And because the demand and supply are so large, porn becomes harder and harder. The fascination of the forbidden is wearing off, and the consumers become bored and desensitized. Movie makers have to break taboos, find new locations, fresh «stars» and new positions for the audiences. From 'ass to mouth' penetration, facial cum shots and sodomy to mass orgies and gang rapes – they provide their consumers with «every kind of barbarism imaginable, » says Melinda Tankard Reist, author of Big Porn Inc., no matter how repulsive. Bruises, strangulation marks on the neck, pain, vaginal injuries, and rectal bleeding are proof. «In fact, images today have now become so extreme that what used to be considered hard-core is now mainstream pornography, » says Gail Dines.

The Internet has made the life of the actors and actresses even harder. As millions of clips are for free, the prices dropped. They must do more brutal scenes and work for less money. Some female porn stars like to brag that their work emancipates them. But many others talk differently about this dehumanizing industry. «It was torture for seven years, » says ex-actress Jenna Presley. «I was miserable, I was lonely. I eventually turned to drugs and alcohol ... to numb my pain and get me through ... and attempted suicide. I knew I wanted out, but I didn't know how to get out. » If it's not pure force or some precarious dependencies, then false promises of money and fame lures young women into the porn business. But only a few of them become «stars. » For every Sasha Grey there are hundreds of thousands of poor, disillusioned, and abused women. According to a study, «the average employment period for 'porn stars' only ranges from six months to three years, and they often end their careers without any money in the bank. Jenna Jameson and Linda Lovelace and many others tell us about suicides, overdoses and other «collateral» damage. There is hardly another industry in which the calculated death at the «end of use period» is part of the production process.

The American researcher Justin Dubin and his team at the University of Miami found out that both, male and female actors, suffer health damages. In a research, women said they had problems getting an orgasm, feeling pain during sex, or having a decreased sex drive. The number of men who admitted to suffer from erectile dysfunction was even higher. Many of them regularly take medication – pills or injections – to get or maintain an erection, both in front of the camera and in privacy.

At the same time, pornography is still forcing old racial stereotypes. Black people are assigned the attributes of animalism. Racist prejudices also create inequality in pay. A white actress gets more money when she has sex with a black man, but a colored actor who has sex with a white woman doesn't.

Pornography changes our ideas and behavior. People want to try out what they see. «I date younger men, » Cindy Gallop admitted at TED2009 in Monterrey. «When I have sex with younger men, I encounter very directly and personally the real ramifications of the creeping ubiquity of hardcore pornography in our culture. ... There is an entire generation growing up that believes that what you see in hardcore pornography is the way that you have sex. » Psychologist Ana J. Bridges and her team from the University of Arkansas found that the majority of porn movies contain physical and verbal violence against the actresses. Beatings, face slaps, and gagging occurred in more than 88 percent of the scenes. Verbal humiliations such as the insulting of women as «whores» or «sluts» occurred in 48 percent. Some claim that porn movies serve as guidance for a fulfilled sex life. But why do you want traumatized, maltreated, drug addicted, and sick people to teach you how to have sex? Porn is not about sexuality, it's about power and profit. It's not even sexual fantasy. The frustrated wankers get their kicks not from the imitation of sexual acts, but from the explicit humiliation of the woman. Through porn no one learns anything about lust, arousal, desires, or satisfaction. You can learn this only through exchange, contact, interaction, and dealing with others, through conversations, and experiences.

The Berlin scientists Simone Kühn and Jürgen Gallinat investigated the question of what effects the consumption of pornographic material has on the human brain. The scientists examined 64 adult men aged 21 to 45 years. Evaluation of the results showed a correlation between the number of hours people watch porn and the size of the gray matter in the entire brain and the size of the striatum, a brain region that is part of the reward system. The more men engage in pornography, the smaller their striatum. This could mean that the regular consumption of pornography is «wearing out the reward system» to some extent, says Simone Kühn. Therefore, people who spend much time watching porn need ever stronger stimuli to achieve the same level of satisfaction. Children are most vulnerable to the vicious greed of an international, multibillion dollar corporate conglomerate run by soulless executive ghouls. The earlier and more often the brain comes into contact with porn movies, the more lastingly it changes. Regular contact is enough to change the structure of the brain. Young people watch films on their smartphones before and after school, for example. That easily adds up to one or two hours a day. Children, who are exposed to pornography before the development of their brain has reached a certain degree of maturity, face dangerous consequences. Brain rewiring at a young age is a catastrophe because these neuroplastic changes are not always reversible. The brain adapts its processing strategies and protects itself against the flood of violence and pornography by dulling itself. The result is a loss of moral sensitivity, emotional intelligence, and empathy.

Porn is not only about pictures, booklets, or DVDs. It's a brain-changing addiction that contaminates the social sphere and that has only become possible with the emergence of the Internet. Porn changes the brain in the same way drugs do. But while cocaine is difficult to get, porn is always only a few clicks away. The biggest problem with the consumption of pornography is that these images in the minds of young people create a false image of sexuality. For many young men and women, sexuality is inextricably linked to violence. In porn, people have sex with complete strangers – with people they just met. Their satisfaction is all they care about. It's completely irrelevant whose body they use as long as they get it. Pornography tells you that sex is something that you can have anytime, anywhere with any person and without any consequences. This perspective is superficial and hypocritical. Relationships are not based on sex, but on commitment, care, and mutual trust. We all need intimacy in our lives. Every human being has needs that only another human being can satisfy. But Pornography is not sex, it's the imitation of sex, if anything, it's fake. There is no truth to it, nothing emotional, or natural. It robs the consumers from the real experience of having sex.

Porn industry now has discovered women as a target group. The positive media coverage suggests that the attempt to establish a «female friendly» pornography was successful. And the branch gets away unquestioned again. People on the Left have opposed 'Big Pharma' and more recently 'Big Food' and ' Big Data.' But they keep quiet about the profit-driven practices of 'Big Porn' or even glorify them as «sexual liberation» and struggle for civil rights. A highly criminal red light subculture was able to hoist itself into the highest realms of the establishment. Women consume pornographic content that is intended to further objectify them, sexualize them and prepare them for pornography. Countless glossy magazines give advice to them «How do I blow him?, » «What drives him crazy in bed? » or – a male fantasy – «Am I a sex-addict? » ... Charlotte Roche, author of the novel Wetlands, regards herself a feminist, yet she says: «There is such a nice range for men, they have so much opportunity – porn on the Internet, wanking booths ... it's a big shame that we don't have that for women. » «I have no time whatsoever for those who see pornography as liberating or empowering to women's sexuality as this is absolutely not my experience at all, » writes Melinda Tankard Reist. While more women consume adult pornography today, it's created primarily for generating sexual arousal in men. In fact, men who don't consume pornography are atypical. Women aren't the consumers of hardcore porn. But the images and messages of pornography are conveyed to women through pop culture. They absorb porn ideology, consciously, or unconsciously. Hypersexualized images displace the images of real girls and women. In her book on body perception and nutrition, feminist philosopher Susan Bordo analyzed how our culture shapes women's ideas of the perfect body. The tall and skinny bodies of women in magazines and on television are in fact an exception. But since these images are almost the only ones we get to see, we consider them the norm. Women assume that the problem lies with them and not with the fashion and media industry. The quest for physical perfection poses a threat for the self-esteem of women. The biggest lie is that adapting to these images gives women any power. This power, it's suggested, consists in having a sexy body that men desire and that other women envy. The more women mesmerize this message, the less they are able to resist to subordinate themselves to the sexual desires and expectations of their partners instead of expressing their own sexual wishes. Pornography offers neither identification for women, nor does the portrayal of trained male bodies and large erected penises have a positive effect on the self-confidence of most men. But women, not men, undergo the large majority of all cosmetic operations. Women invest vast amounts of money and time to acquire an artificial «beauty» – starting with daily creams, shaving, makeup, starving to the unhealthy dream body, and cosmetic surgery. Gail Dines has made shocking experiences at American universities: Their female students speak of «free choice,» but accept the dressage of their bodies. During her lectures, they talked about how important it's to them to completely remove hair from their pubic area. They then feel «clean,» «hot» and «well groomed.» They insisted that it was their own decision to do a waxing. But one student admitted at some point that her boyfriend had complained when she stopped to wax. Other boyfriends, it turned out, «had even refused to have sex with non-waxed girlfriends as they «looked gross.» One guy had bought his girlfriend a waxing set for Valentine's Day. Another guy was joking about his girlfriend's «hairy beaver» in an e-mail to his friends. «No, she did not break up with him, she got waxed instead,» said Dines. Where does our society go when superficial and artificial beauty is more relevant than anything else? It's naive to think that what we see and hear does not influence us. Music, movies, and books shape our personality. Good works of art enrich our lives. They serve relaxation and education, they touch and inspire us. Thus, good pictures are good for our personality and bad pictures are bad. Violence against women, sexual abuse, and oppression happen every day in the USA. Gail Dines again: «The big question is, What are the consequences of this saturation for our culture, sexuality, gender identity, and relationships? The answer is that we don't know for sure. One thing is certain: we are in the midst of a massive social experiment, only the laboratory here is our world and the effects will be played out on people who never agreed to participate.»

FOR THAT MOMENT OF HAPPINESS

«We risk being the first people in history to have been able to make their illusions so vivid, so persuasive, so 'realistic' that they can live in them.»
– Daniel Boorstin

When Case cheated a client, they punished him with a nerve poison treatment, and he lost the ability to access the cyberspace. For Case, cyberspace is more than a place to make money. His whole identity was based on his virtual entity. After losing his connection, his social decline followed. He lingered around in bars, drank, used drugs, and became suicidal. Then he got a second chance to join the cyberspace again. After days in the Matrix he lost his sense of time and forgets his elementary physical needs. A behavior as we know it today from video game addiction. The news regularly report on computer-addicted nerds, and movies like «Lomo – The Language of Many Others» or «Homevideo» tell of the dark sides of the Internet. It's no coincidence that many users hang on to their electronic devices like drug addicts, it's intentional and planned to the last detail. Silicon Valley employs more psychologists than computer scientists.

Already in the 1930s, Harvard psychologist B. F. Skinner dreamed of using technology to control human behavior – for their good, of course. He wrote in 1974: «We need to make vast changes in human behavior.... What we need is a technology of behavior. » Skinner believed that this form of behavioral control was crucial if humanity wants to master its problems. He developed a cage – the Skinner Box – in which rats had to press a lever when they heard or saw a certain stimulus. Then they received food as a reward. Today, billions of people carry their own Skinner box. The digital devices that we use every day are designed to cause addictive behavior patterns. And we don't have the slightest idea that the IT companies design their products according to Skinner's principles. They have a single goal: to make us click, scroll, or comment again, and again, and again.

The IT corporations have built in psychological dependency structures to bypass decision-making instances. Thus, the users cannot avoid the negative consequences of digital technologies by using it responsible. Our interactions on the internet is like the lever in the rat cage. Every time you write a comment and someone likes it, the brain's reward system releases a little dopamine. The stimulation of biochemical processes cause «feelings of happiness. » This in turn affects the brain areas that are responsible for action control, and you want to do it again. Even small triggers can to manipulate us.

According to psychologist BJ Fogg from Stanford, it's part of our nature to avoid negative feelings, e.g. rejection, and to look for positive feelings, like social bonds. Not only social media services take advantage of these human desires. App designers also make their users dependent on their services – with far-reaching consequences for our psyche and our well-being. The strategists from Silicon Valley call it «stickiness»: An app should be as «sticky» as possible so that customers spend more time with it. This increases the probability that they will see advertising and click on it. One of the most perfidious tricks is the Infinite Scroll, which you can see at Instagram, YouTube, Facebook, Twitter, and Pinterest. You can scroll forever, the flow of fresh content never ends. It's like an open chip bag: Once you pop, you just can't stop. The difference is that the chips will eventually run out. Former Mozilla employee Aza Raskin was the first to introduce the Infinite Scroll technology. Now he regrets his invention. He told the BBC: «It's as if the

Social Media Platforms spread cocaine over their interfaces – and that's why users keep coming back to them. » Many apps also use the Pull-to-Refresh mechanism: If you drag the list down with your finger, it updates itself. The reminiscence to a slot machine is not a coincidence, explains Tristan Harris, who worked on Inbox at Google: «If you want to maximize addictiveness, all tech designers need to do is link a user's action (like pulling a lever) with a variable reward, » he wrote on a blog. Like with a one-armed bandit, you don't know what happens after you pull the lever. You may see a new message from someone, or an interesting article, or a flirt suggestion. The more the «reward» varies, the higher the addictiveness.

On top of that, social media creates the constant «fear of missing out» (FOMO) and of losing contact with the network. In a study conducted by California State University, the researchers proved that taking away people's smartphones leads to stress. The heart rate and blood pressure increased after only a few minutes. The longer the forced break was, the higher was the stress. This is not only an extreme cognitive but also physical dependence. Their attachment to the device is so strong that you could almost call it an additional body part. If used wrongly, it is also a time thief. No wonder that the Silicon Valley guys don't allow their own children to use smartphones.

The success is obvious: People are constantly engaged with their smartphones. At the same time, the users are getting younger and therefore more defenseless. Children can hardly resist the greed of morally questionable game developers. It matters what children and young people do all day, because it leaves traces in their brains. The brain areas which are responsible for self-control develop later than those for impulsive behavior. Computer games exploit these mechanisms and therefor cause addictive behavior.

South Korea is leading in dealing with addictions resulting from digital technology. The country has been at the forefront of technology development. If you want to see the computer age of tomorrow, you should take a look at South Korea. Now, it's clear there is a national problem. Computer games are a mass phenomenon – and a health threat. So-called PC-Bangs are everywhere, large windowless rooms with 100 or more gaming computers. There is hardly a neighborhood where there is no PC-Bang. When entering, you immediately notice the sound of mouse clicks and keyboard strokes. Players shout instructions to each other via headsets. These facilities are particularly popular with young people who play there for hours. Many play all night long and next day they schlepp themselves tiredly to school or work. Some gamers are so absorbed that they don't even take a break to eat or go to the toilet. The media reported on a 38-year-old man who spent 20 days in front of a computer at home. He only ate noodle soup out of a bag, so he didn't die of thirst. But he finally died of exhaustion, lack of oxygen, exercise, and sleep. Another young man played for 50 hours without a break. He did not eat nor drink, and then fell dead from his stool. Some young people have committed suicide because they were excluded from online games. In response, the South Korean government is the first to address the problem of gambling addiction.

Excessive computer gaming triggers the same brain processes as alcoholism. The brain of a gambling addict reacts to a screenshot of his favorite game as that of an alcoholic reacts when they see a beer. Not everyone gets addicted, just as not everyone becomes addicted to alcohol. The companies answer to the accusations with so-called «Digital Wellbeing» functions. A euphemism that sounds much better than the term «digital detox. » Behind this pretended care are tangible economic interests. The companies try to take control over developments that run against their economic interests and to forestall regulatory measures. Demands for legislative intervention are futile if they show that they are already doing «everything possible. » If companies ignored the desire for digital detox at all, they risked that users could make a radical cut and switch off their devices on an hourly, daily, or weekly basis. The tactic is not new: As cigarettes became known to be harmful to health, tobacco companies introduced «light cigarettes. » They were hardly any better, but they falsely suggested there was a sensible alternative to abstinence. Like light cigarettes the digital well-being is a poisoned fruit.

The problem with addiction is that it makes the addicts believe that they still have control when it has long since slipped away. An addictive disease is traditionally defined as the consumption of a psychotropic substance, be it alcohol, cannabis, or cocaine, which results in a loss of control. The idea that behavior can replace psychotropic substances and lead to addiction may still seem surprising, but it's not new. As early as 1954, psychiatrist Viktor Freiherr von Gebsattel wrote: «The concept of addiction goes further than the concept of toxicomania has defined ... Every direction of human interest can degenerate addictively. » In 1989, the British psychologist Margaret A. Shotton published her dissertation on Computer Addiction. She had examined 127 computer addicts, most of whom were men, who spent a considerable amount of time programming. Their passion lead to social isolation. But they seemed not to suffer much from that. Many of them are now probably well-paid professionals. In 1991, the psychiatrist Ivan Goldberg coined the term «Internet addiction disorder. » Many psychologists reacted dismissively to it, as there were no signs of a life-threatening addiction, as well as no life-threatening withdrawal symptoms. Although there are some withdrawal symptoms such as anxiety, shivering, and nervousness, these cannot lead to death. Nor is there any possibility of dying from an Internet overdose. This is true insofar as no one dies from the Internet or the computer, but from exhaustion, dehydration, starvation. Today, most experts agree that behavioral addictions exist. Nevertheless, the American Medical Association only recently changed its mind. It decided that «video game addiction» shouldn't be considered a serious mental illness. Instead, it recommended further study. «There is nothing here to suggest that this is a complex physiological disease state akin to alcoholism or other substance abuse disorders, and it doesn't get to have the word addiction attached to it, » said Dr. Stuart Gitlow of the American Society of Addiction Medicine and Mt. Sinai School of Medicine in New York.

In fact, digital addictions meet three main criteria for addiction. The first criterion is an increase in dosage. Yesterday's technology is regarded as too slow and inefficient. It's no longer «up-to-date» or «in, » it's not enough for the user. Here, Moore's law can be equated with a dose increase in a substance-bound addiction. Only those who have the latest technology can «play the game» at the top. Since the development of the first games like Pong, Tetris, or Pac-Man, the technical development has progressed. The choice of gaming equipment has grown. We can play games on home computers, laptops, and game consoles. With tablets and smartphones we can play games everywhere. As a result, the playing time massively increased. The second characteristic of a dependency is the inability to evade that behavior. Digital technology has become indispensable for social participation. Those who don't play along and stay away from technical toys have it difficult to integrate into society. We are online all the time – connected to the large network, at work and at home. The portals to the world are our smartphones, the Internet, and virtual reality. Already the children are instructed to learn how to use computers and mobile phones. The third characteristic is a psychological imbalance. People are stressed, they are seeking professional help. More and more children are diagnosed with depressive disorders, anxiety neuroses, and other psychological disorders. Their media consumption is sometimes more than 10 hours a day. Brain scans prove that both substance-bound and non-substance-bound forms of addiction affect the brain in the same way. But thanks to a powerful lobby, there is little, if any, regulation.

THAT LAND OF GLASS

«Having the glory of God: and her light was like unto a stone most precious, even like a jasper stone, clear as crystal.» – Revelation 21:11

«You ought to have some papers to show who you are,»
The police officer advised me.
«I do not need any paper. I know who I am,» I said.
«Maybe so. Other people are also interested in knowing who you are.»
– B. Traven, The Death Ship

My mom has been practicing privacy her entire life. Born at the end of World War II, she spent most of her life under the Socialist regime in East Germany. The Stasi was the largest institution in the country. When the Berlin Wall came down in 1989, it employed over 91,000 full-time snoops and an army of unofficial snitches. Founded in the 1950s, it evolved into a frighteningly efficient surveillance and suppression apparatus. It was the decisive instrument of power of the ruling socialist party, its «sword and shield.» The Stasi spied, kidnapped, murdered, and did everything to prevent republikflucht (republic escape). «Know everything, control everything, direct everything, intimidate, and manipulate people.» – describes a Stasi manual its goals and working methods. They knew everything about everyone in the country. «We had lived like behind glass,» wrote the novelist Stefan Heym, «like pinned beetles, and every wriggling of the legs had been noticed with interest and commented on in detail.» Few people knew details of the Stasi. It seemed omnipresent, though it was barely visible. Almost everyone has speculated about their secret work. There was no place in which people didn't suspect informants. Stirring this angst was part of the cynical plan. The legacy of the Stasi's insatiable appetite for data: 70 miles of files, 1.8 million photographic documents, and 2,800 films are stored in its former headquarters. The Stasi files tell «a story of deceit and betrayal on a national scale,» wrote Denis Staunton in The Observer, «with husbands spying on wives, children sneaking on their parents and priests reporting on their parishioners.» The fall of the Berlin Wall was also the harbinger of the end of the rule of the Communist Regime. On January 15, 1990, Berlin's citizens stormed into its headquarters to prevent the planned destruction of the files. It's also a symbol of the end of the confrontation between East and West – an event that the political scientist Francis Fukuyama called the «end of history, » the triumph of liberal democracy and the arrival of a post-ideological world. But the «end of history» ended on September 11, 2001, with the terrorist attacks by Al-Qaeda.

To defeat the «terrorist threat, » fundamental concepts of civil liberty were thrown overboard like ballast. Supposedly motivated by the pursuit of security in a threatening world, the comprehensive surveillance, once characteristic of dictatorships, has become an indispensable feature of our lives. Since 2001, the surveillance industry has grown exponentially. It has become a routine for the government and private companies to collect private data. The paranoia of control has long since left the field of counter-terrorism and has reached out to health care, the tax system, working places, and public spaces. To the mathematician Alexander Beilinson of the University of Chicago, the scale of the activities makes the USA appear as «a bloated version of the Soviet Union of the time of [his] youth. » The TV series Homeland shows the dark side of America's «war on terror» – permanent paranoid angst. Only mentioning the term «terror» already creates a fear so that people are willing to give up our rights for an alleged safety.

People who feel watched change their behavior. In the former GDR, people only talked about irrelevant things on the phone or in public for fear of not knowing whether the Stasi was listening to them. In 2013, the American writers association PEN published an uncanny report titled Chilling Effects: NSA Surveillance Drives U.S. Writers to Self-Censor. PEN had studied the impact of the NSA revelations of Edward Snowden on its members. Writers, it concludes, overwhelmingly believe that «their communications are monitored, » and as a result have changed their behavior in a way that «is harming freedom of expression. » For fear of harming themselves, their friends or sources, they only research and write about certain topics and even avoid critical topics on the phone or in emails. Under such circumstances, people don't do what they really want. Freedom is precious and essential for a functioning society. We must not let it take away from us, but we must strive for it every day. Some people in this world even have to fight hard for it and some pay for it with death. Fortunately, we live in a democracy. But that can change. Nobody knows what forms of government will rule in the future, or what social values will apply. What may today appear to be meaningless information could one day be devastating.

What the government isn't allowed to spy on, private companies do: data brokers like Acxiom, LeadsPlease, ALC Data and other companies like supermarkets or online stores, search engines, computer companies, social networks, insurance companies, and banks. The government is one of their largest customers. According to a Financial Times report in 2013, basic information about a person costs a flap 0.0005 dollars. Nothing more. If a person has some influence on their environment, the value rises to 0.00075 dollars. The more substantial the dossiers is, the higher the price. The names and addresses of people with cancer or diabetes cost 0.26 dollar per person. Despite the low prices, collecting our data is a very lucrative business, worth billions. This shows how much data is available to the companies, and how much they can sell. The online platforms collect, buy, and analyze a myriad of personal data. Our clicks and likes allow them a detailed analysis of our mental, physical, and social condition. We generate billions of snippets of information worldwide every moment on the Internet. Our e-mails and telephone calls are being listened to, our shopping habits registered, our movements in (not only) public areas recorded by video cameras, our smartphones, or the software in our cars. Every visit to a website leaves traces that can be analyzed, stored, evaluated, and sold. They know your ethnicity, age, gender, what you eat, your previous jobs, the magazines you read, your religious and political affiliation, your financial situation, where you went to school or college, etc. , and etc. They not only know what you write or talk about online, they also know your secrets, your sexual preferences (your real, not your projected), your health concerns and even, perhaps, your medication, whether your marriage is in trouble or whether you've been a victim of rape or had an abortion. Social media platforms have more personal information about the world's population than all governments, military, and intelligence services combined. The scientist Michal Kosinski proved that with only 70 Likes on Facebook they may learn as much about you as only your friends know. The case of the young Viennese lawyer Max Schrems shows how difficult it is to reverse this development. He sued Facebook for violations of the European data protection law, and in 2011, he succeeded in court in forcing the company to disclose its data on him. It was a PDF file which contained astonishing 1,222 pages, a size comparable only to Stasi files of top politicians.

Unlike the Stasi, the surveillance capitalists can rely on new technologies. Companies and secret services have increasingly intelligent connected machines on their disposal that gather information about the lives of others that would make the Stasi green with envy. Comic Keith Lowell Jensen joked on Twitter a few years ago: «What Orwell failed to predict is that we'd buy the cameras ourselves, and that our biggest fear would be that nobody was watching. » From the point of view of the secret services, smartphones are the best invention ever made, a «surveillance-ready» technology. People line up in front of the stores to spend their hard-earned money on a device with which they can be spied on better than the Stasi ever could. Convicted criminals put on electronic anklets, we wear our smartphones. Whether in the bathroom, on the couch, on journeys, or at your office desk – the smartphone is a constant companion. With its sensors (including gesture, movement, acceleration, temperature, and humidity sensors), microphone, cameras and navigation system, it enables monitoring all areas of life: location, Internet activities, SMS and calls, calendars, address books, and social media entries. Even if you only use your phone as a flashlight, it collects data about you.

One of Amazon's bestselling gadget is Alexa – a loudspeaker equipped with seven microphones that records every command we give it. Usually, they scan their environment acoustically and wait for the activation word. As soon as the systems recognize the word, they connect to the cloud. People who could never afford a butler now have him in their living room. It announces the time, orders pizza, selects music. We connect it to our heating or our light switch. In return, they know all our habits: when we get up, when we go to work or to bed. That makes Alexa a super bug. More and more of these super bugs infest our homes. In the future, we will access many digital services like the crew of the spaceship Enterprise: We ask, the machine answers. The tech giants in America and Asia, Apple (with Siri), Google (with Google Assistant), Microsoft (with Cortana), Facebook (with M), and Samsung (with Bixby), are fighting a hard battle for the supremacy of voice-controlled virtual assistants. Behind the supposed helpfulness of the electronic butler hides above all a commercial interest. We get used to them listening in. By recording conversations, the profiling is even more accurate and delivers more precise idea of which sales or advertisement partner is suitable. The evaluation of intimate requests by software is at least worrying. A few months ago, Amazon, Google, Apple, and Microsoft admitted that they were forwarding recordings to third parties. Freelancers and employees corrected words or sentences that the assistants had not understood so that they could react better in the future. Nicholas Carr calls our electronic world a «Glass Cage. » Imagine if the Stasi had such a technology – it could have fired most of its employees. Now people are voluntarily installing microphones and cameras in their homes. Surveillance capitalists make profits by observing, calculating, and influencing people. To achieve that, we must no longer be anonymous, we must not have any secrets. When Harvard professor Shoshana Zuboff coined the term surveillance capitalism, she had a particular company in mind: Google. «We know where you are. We know where you've been. We can more or less know what you're thinking about. » – That's a quote from 2010 by Eric Schmidt.

«Google is everywhere, » said Siva Vaidhyanathan from the Vanderbilt University. «We grant Google an almost mystical role in our lives, yet we don't know how it really works. » There are many scandals which reveal the methods Google uses to gain access to intimate user data.

In 2010, the Street View scandal blew up. Google had sent vehicles with cameras around the globe to take countless pictures and measure the houses by laser. Secretly, the vehicles also scanned for unprotected WLAN networks. For two years, Google collected everything available: MAC addresses, SSIDs, but also e-mails, website views, and passwords of unwitting citizens worldwide. After denying it first, Google had to admit the hack in May 2010. Google spoke of a «software error» that had «been unnoticed for a long time» and, as it's usual in such a scandal, expressed regret. But the story of the «software bug» didn't hold for long. The investigation revealed that a Google employee had written a special program and implemented it on purpose. To get its neck out of the noose, Google lied again and spread the thesis of an «individual perpetrator. » Also, Google apparently drew a whole bundle of consequences of the scandal. They named a data protection officer to check the privacy protection, employees received appropriate training, and it introduced stricter rules for the handling of user data. In 2012, New York Times reporters unmasked a man until then known only as «Engineer Doe»: Marius Milner, a network specialist, living in Palo Alto in Silicon Valley. The journalists buried the narrative of the rogue perpetrator. As early as 2007, Milner has discussed hacking into unprotected WLAN networks to collect data with colleagues and superiors. But Google's remorse show was a success. After about two years of investigation, the prosecutors of 38 U.S. states agreed with Google on a fine of a mere seven million dollars. With the profit Google makes, the company needed only a few hours to recover this amount. Google has consolidated surveillance capitalism, but is by no means the only player on the field. In Germany there is a saying: Where there is a trough, the pigs gather. Data companies constantly launch new products to collect, track, record, and send data – from smart vine bottles to internet-connected rectal thermometers. These innovations don't stop at children's rooms either. There are now electronic toys that are directly connected to the Internet. You can't start early enough to destroy the trust between parents and their children and bring them up as good consumers. Vint Cerf, Google's «chief evangelist, » believes that privacy could be an anomaly. He grew up in a small town without a telephone where the postman saw who was receiving letters from whom – data companies would do nothing else than the postman. «In a town of 3,000 people there is no privacy. Everybody knows what everybody is doing, » he said. Zuckerberg is quoted saying: «The world will be better if you share more. » In light of their strong economic interests, it's not a surprise that the Silicon Valley entrepreneurs have warmer views on that matter. Our almost magical relationship with computers and mobile phones fills the pockets of insatiable datakrakens, the profiteers of the digital gold mine. They have made tons of money with the technologies they touted, and they want more.

In 2019, Amnesty International published a report on the Surveillance Giants (which is the title of the report) Google and Facebook. Their business models violate the human right to privacy and informational self-determination.

Asked about people's concerns in a CNBC interview in 2009, Schmidt replied without any irony: «If you have something that you don't want anyone to know, maybe you shouldn't be doing it in the first place. » A Zuckerberg statement in an interview in 2010 is equally dismissive: «People have really gotten comfortable not only sharing more information and different kinds, but more openly. » In the digital age, privacy is no longer a «social norm, » he claimed. But everyone may have something to hide: their identity, feelings, and opinions. And when we sell out our data, we don't just give information about ourselves. Each of us has information about family members, friends, neighbors, or colleagues that we are expected to keep private: party photos, confidential conversations, private information of all kind. We sell them too. You don't need to bother with the Snowden revelation to justify concerns about the loss of privacy. In 2018, the New York Times and the British Observer revealed that the British company Cambridge Analytica had obtained records of tens of millions of Facebook users and provided Trump's campaign team with the information. Facebook finally admitted that 87 million users were affected, just over 70 million from the USA. The vast majority of users had never agreed to this use. They had become a kind of data by-catch. A few hundred thousand Facebook members had taken part in a personality test conducted by a third-party provider on the platform and thus unwillingly enabled the tapping of user data from their entire Facebook circle of friends. The internet is a dangerous place for data. A look at a few of the data scandals of recent years is enough to make you feel even more frightened. In late 2018, the Marriott hotel chain announced that hackers stole personal information from 500 million guests. And this is only the second largest data theft that has ever become known to the public. Yahoo has been the victim of attacks twice within two years. All three billion Yahoo accounts were affected by a 2013 attack, and in late 2014, another 500 million accounts. The unknown perpetrators obtained names, e-mail addresses, telephone numbers, birthday data, and passwords. Hacker attacks have become an everyday problem in companies. The list of hacked service providers is a Who is Who of industry: LinkedIn, Adobe, Badoo, MySpace, River City Media, B2B USA, Dropbox, Ashley, Nexus, Snapchat, Money Bookers, Equifax, and many more. Attacks are rarely made public because companies fear damage to their reputation. The more everyday things you're doing online, the greater the risk of personal data being misused. On the Internet, data protection isn't. For criminal hackers, too, your data is exciting – and they have far worse intentions than to annoy you with targeted ads. The anonymity of the Internet and its many possibilities make it a fresh trove for criminals. Nowhere else do people lie, cheat, rip off, and steal so much – from money to goods and data to personal identities.

Digital technologies destroy our privacy in an unprecedented and irrevocable manner. The proof of the importance of privacy – if proof were required –

is that those who declare it irrelevant don't themselves believe what they are saying. It's not only the government which is hiding its actions from the public, the Internet bosses also protect their own privacy with all their might. The dark side of the Force thrives on intransparency. Larry Page avoids the public with a lot of effort and determination and is very hesitant with giving away information about himself. That is remarkable for someone whose declared goal is to collect all the knowledge of the world and make it accessible to everyone. Only so much is known about his family background: He was born into a family of computer scientists. His father Carl was a professor of computer science, his mother Gloria developed databases, and his older brother is also an IT entrepreneur. He is married to Lucy Southworth, also a graduate of Stanford. They have two children, but even their names are secret. When CNET, an online news service on information and communications technology, published Eric Schmidt's personal data obtained through Google – including his salary, campaign contributions, and address – to show the dangers of his company's doing, Google stopped giving interviews to CNET journalists. Mark Zuckerberg bought the four villas neighboring his house in Palo Alto for 30 million dollars to protect his privacy. CNET told its readers: «Your personal life is now known as Facebook's data. Its CEO's personal life is now known as mind your own business. » Privacy becomes a luxury that less and less people can afford. What really matters here, is not their hypocrisy. Rather, it's that we all have a desire for privacy. It's essential to what it means to be human. The private sphere is the place where we can act, speak, write, and experiment without the judgmental eye of others. Only when we believe that no one is watching us we feel free and safe. That's why it's so dangerous when Google, Amazon and Co. now market millions of camouflaged bugs as «assistants, » smuggle them into millions of households, and listen in on our most intimate conversations.

It's illusory to reduce surveillance activities to zero. Even so, it would be wrong to give up and wait for the things that may yet come. There are some approaches that can help us push back the surveillance and protect our privacy, both legally and politically. Many have now learned more about how computers work and are fighting surveillance. They use VPNs, encrypted messenger apps, different operating systems. Some measures are easy: Leave your smartphone at home and switch it off more often. Then you're invisible for electronic surveillance, like it's the past. It is time for us to control our own data. It's a human right. No one other than ourselves should decide how our data is used – and how not. We should be able to stop the corporations that steal our data to manipulate us. We should be able to take our data with us when we leave one of their platforms and be paid for the value our data generates.

Karl Marx recognized that surveillance is a fundamental characteristic of capitalism: Competition would force the companies to cut costs and increase efficiency, and the monitoring of employee efficiency is a key factor to achieve that goal. In Das Kapital, Marx wrote: «The work of directing, superintending and adjusting becomes one of the functions of capital, from the moment that the labour under capital's control becomes cooperative. » According to him, working place surveillance is «purely despotic. » The capitalist created a new group of workers to carry out the surveillance: «He hands over the work of direct and constant supervision of the individual workers and groups of workers to a special kind of wage-labourer. An industrial army of workers under the command of a capitalist requires, like a real army, officers (managers) and N.C.O.s (foremen, overseers), who command during the labour process in the name of capital. The work of supervision becomes their established and exclusive function. »

Today, employers can watch their employees around the clock, in secret or openly. Surveillance in the workplace covers a wide spectrum, including the permanent monitoring of work speed, efficiency, and punctuality, telephone conversations, online behavior, e-mails, trips in a company car, background checks, drug tests, etc. Even toilet breaks are being digitally recorded. The valleyists have become the high priests of surveillance capitalism. It's no coincidence that the corporate headquarters in Silicon Valley remind us of Jeremy Bentham's Panopticon, the utopian prison in which the guards could see every cell. Google moved its new headquarters in California under gigantic glass domes, so is Amazon's headquarters in Seattle. The new Apple headquarters in Cupertino is larger than the Pentagon and also made of a lot of glass. Mark Zuckerberg assigned the architect Frank Gehry to design a «radically transparent» building. The result is a purely functional open-office hall which looks as if it's the largest of all garages, a metaphor for the company's founding myth. The interior of the hall is laid out like a city with different quarters and graffiti art on the wooden hut walls. It has it all: table football, colorful wallpapers, and motivating aphorisms on the walls, like: «Our Work Is Never Over. » There's nothing cynical about it – who would say that? The tables are arranged to work stations. There are small recreational spaces, strange mixtures of living room and street corner, furnished with sofas. Managers love to keep a close eye on their employees. They fantasize that such a working environment is inspiring, strengthening the team spirit, and bringing fun to work. But these «office landscapes» have earned a bad reputation. The French anthropologist Marc Augé calls the open office a soulless «non-place. » It makes people sick and «creates neither singular identity nor relations; only solitude, and similitude. » Anyone entering such a non-place does at first glance not recognize whether they are in New York, Tokyo, or Berlin. The offices are purely practical and constantly remind their occupants that they are servants of a «larger whole. » The first open offices emerged at the beginning of the 20th century in former warehouses. With dozens of columns of desks they looked like the interior of huge slave galleys. In 1913, the author Robert Walser, who worked as a bank clerk at the time, wrote: «When I'm standing in the bureau, my limbs slowly turn into wood, which one wishes to set on fire, so that it burns: Desk and human become one in time. » As early as 1930, the sociologist Siegfried Kracauer remarked about the emerging offices that «dull working conditions result in a loss of personality value. » It's no surprise that this cage rearing leads to a higher sickness absence rates. Germs swarm in the air, every day the colleagues quarrel about the ideal temperature, mobbing increases, and those who are annoyed by the high noise level try to protect themselves with headphones – if that is permitted. The air conditioning and artificial light destroy the last spirits of life. High blood pressure, infectious diseases, back problems, and stress are the side effects of the modern world of work. In The Naked Employee, Frederick S. Lane writes: «Despite the amount of workplace surveillance that takes place in this country, peering into the lives of their employees is not something that businesses undertake lightly: It's expensive, time-consuming, and inherently destructive of employee morale. » The consequences include a reduced productivity and a high fluctuation. These problems are known. Yet the companies rely on open offices. The bean counters have calculated that other factors compensate for the losses. In open offices, more people can be packed into smaller space which saves construction and energy costs. When employees no longer have their own desks, but have to find a workplace every morning, it saves even more money. Vacation and absence times have already been included in the artificially reduced number of places. It's also a subtle daily reminder to the employees that they are merely replaceable cogs.

At the same time, the office is transformed into an experience space. The distinction between privacy and work is disappearing. The most important point is probably social control. Performance pressure is complemented by group pressure and forced happiness. Everyone is watching everyone else and is being watched. Permanent control initiates a process of continuous self-optimization. No one simply looks through the window to watch the birds. In an article about Amazon the New York Times claims that Taylorism is thriving. Taylor's system of monitoring and control is still very much with us, and its modern forms are even more aggressive. The internet retailer uses Taylorist techniques to achieve efficiency: «Workers are constantly measured and those who fail to hit the numbers are ruthlessly eliminated, personal tragedies notwithstanding. » Everything individual, private, deviant, or rebellious has to disappear. Nicholas Carr calls Google's Silicon Valley headquarters «the Internet's high church, » and «the religion practiced inside its walls is Taylorism. » These companies find nothing problematic about that. Eric Schmidt frankly admitted that Google is «founded around the science of measurement. » …

According to Christian Parenti, professor at New York University, surveillance in America «began centuries ago with the concept of slave passes, which allowed slave-owners to monitor and control the mobility of 'chattel'. » The French word «passeport» literally means «go through the door. » The passport defined the freedoms of the person concerned, ranging from the permission to buy goods to the freedom from slavery. In the early 1850s, the abolitionist Benjamin Drew interviewed escaped slaves from the United States in Canada. He describes how the slave owners operated a system of 'patrols' to check the passports and punish slaves if they were caught without having a permission: «White men would stand with their whips where [the slaves] were coming out, to examine for passes, and those who had passes would go free. » But the system suffered an internal contradiction.
Slaves were treated as «raw materials» or «goods. » Part of this humiliation was to deny slaves their legal identity. It was unusual for slaves to have a surname. For the slave passport, however, it was necessary to distinguish between «legal» and «illegal» slaves, i.e. to identify those who were allowed to be where they were and those who weren't. Thus, they had to be given an identity, which in turn played an essential role in the organization and communication of resistance against the slavery. The system of the handwritten slave passport based on the fact that slaves could not read and write, and it was forbidden to teach it to them. Slaves and abolitionist who knew how to read and write undermined the system by forging passports. It helped that many of the patrols couldn't read themselves. The identification of the passport holder was an essential feature of the slave passport. If the patrols knew this person, it was sufficient to write only their name into the pass. For extended trips, e.g. when shopping for food in the next town, they needed other methods of identification. The papers had to contain at least a rough description of the person, like body shape and size as well as other characteristics such as scars, skin color, birthmarks, or their clothing. White Americans didn't need identification. Only in two short periods has the American government introduced a passport requirement: during the American Civil War, as well as during and shortly after World War I.
Francis Ford Coppola's mafia epic The Godfather tells the migration story of the main character Vito Corleone. At early 20th century, poor, little Vito Andolini flees on a ship to the USA, after he was no longer safe in his Sicilian hometown of Corleone. Arriving on Ellis Island, he waited there in a sheer endless line of immigrants for registration. When asked about his name, he answers – of course – only with his first name and indicates his origin with Corleone. The official of the immigration authority turns it into the name Vito Corleone. After a quick health check, Vito was briefly quarantined and then allowed to enter the country. Today, with immigration policy being a

hot topic, it's hard to imagine how unbureaucratic the procedure was.

A global standard for identification documents didn't exist: «Until August 1914 a sensible, law-abiding Englishman could pass through life and hardly notice the existence of the state, beyond the post office and the policeman,» describes the historian Alan J. P. Taylor Great Britain at the beginning of the 20th century. «He could live where he liked and as he liked. He had no official number or identity card. He could travel abroad or leave his country for ever without a passport or any sort of official permission.» It was in the aftermath of the World War I, that the idea of a worldwide standard for passports emerged. In 1921, the United States enacted the Emergency Quota Act, which was soon replaced by the Immigration Act of 1924. A passport is the most efficient method to determine an immigrant's identity and country of origin. According to the U.S. State Department, the USA issued 18.6 million passports in 2016 – the highest annual number ever recorded. With their microchips and holograms, biometric photos and barcodes, they are masterpieces of modern technology. «A passport is a kind of shield: when you're a citizen of a wealthy democracy,» explains the journalist Atossa Araxia Abrahamian, author of The Cosmopolites: The Coming of the Global Citizen. She describes that the development of passports was about controlling people, even within a country's borders. In the early 20th century, married American women were literally just a footnote in their husbands' passports. They could not cross the border alone, while married men were, of course, free to travel around. Historically speaking, the nation state is the exception, mixing and fluctuation the rule. We all are migrants. The idea there are homogeneous peoples who «have always lived here» is a fiction of the age of nation states.

Over the past 100 years, the borders have been systematically strengthened. It's not only about making it more difficult or even impossible to cross these borders, rather, the aim is to secure the borders in such a way that they remain permeable for «desired» people, while «undesirable» persons are identified and prevented from entering the country. Since the fall of the Berlin Wall, complex border regimes have been installed around the globe to serve precisely this purpose. Various technological innovations control the permeability and crossing of borders. This includes biotechnologies such as iris scans, scanner for fingerprints and faces, thermal imaging cameras, quick disease tests or DNA analyses. These methods have been tested on millions of involunteers.

In Jordan's camps, fugitives are registered by iris scan and henceforth identified. They cannot refuse, otherwise they will receive no help from the camp operator, the United Nations High Commissioner for Refugees (UNHCR). Since 2016, the refugees can also pay in camp supermarkets with the iris scan with a system called EyePay. If they want to buy something, they don't have to dig money out of their wallets – a glance at the installed equipment will do. Their accounts are no longer at a bank, but within a blockchain network, the same technology that is behind Bitcoin. The money flows directly from the UN World Food Programme (WFP) via the block chain to the supermarket. The WFP thus saves the transaction fees usually charged by the banks, and it can comprehensively control the refugees. Critics point out that the refugees are part of a large-scale experiment to test biometric systems until they are ready for the market. When millions of people have their iris scanned, it generates a large amount of data. The WFP can use data to determine which products refugees buy most often and reorders these products accordingly. It can also control prices and ensure, for example, that its shops are not more expensive (or cheaper) than others. The WFP also uses the data to check whether the refugees eat a balanced diet. They cannot defend themselves against monitoring their consumption habits. In the future, the system could be used as a control tool to promote desirable behavior. IrisGuard doesn't charge the UN for the use of its technology. But the company earns money from every refugee with a fee of one percent for each transaction. At the same time, they promote their business model as a humanitarian aid, establish connections with governments and local authorities and test their devices on a large scale. In Europe and America such experiments wouldn't be accepted, yet. But these camps show us our possible future. Refugee camps are lucrative markets for companies planning big things. The manufacturers of biometric applications are facing a veritable and lasting boom. In the near future, Americans and Europeans can expect the total biometric penetration of everyday life: face recognition during access controls and on journeys, fingerprint scans to start a car, biometric identification cards at the workplace, recognition of voice patterns on the telephone, location tracking, etc. Withdrawing money from ATMs and paying in restaurants with a thumbprint or biometric payment systems for children for school meals may soon be common. The databases of the Homeland Security already contain 100 million fingerprints, stored for 75 years. The images of travelers and their fingerprints are compared with a watchlist with 3.5 million persons who are not to welcome in the USA. In India, however, it goes one step further.

The Indian government runs the largest biometric database in the world. The project is known as Aadhaar, meaning «foundation. » Every Indian now needs an Aadhaar card for a bank account or mobile phone contract. It has a twelve-digit number and includes a fingerprint, face photo, and iris scan. More and more data is gradually being linked with each other via Aaadhaar: telephone numbers, bank accounts, e-mail addresses, health data. Even children need a number if they want to join a football club. Within a decade, the largest democracy in the world transformed itself into a surveillance state. Theoretically, you have the free choice to exclude yourself from the system. In practice, however, it's impossible. Without registration, you cannot even send a letter; the post office registers the identification number so that the letter can be sent. Does that sound like freedom? The result is a detailed digital profile of every Indian, which enables companies and the government to track every citizen. Public criticism remains mild. There are some protests mainly from «tech nerds, » journalists, lawyers, human rights activists and students. Critics fear that the Aadhaar information will also be used for political repression. According to the Indian government there are no data leaks at Aadhaar. But journalist Rachna Khaira reports in the daily newspaper The Tribune India that within ten minutes she had obtained arbitrary information from the database for 500 rupees (about 7 dollars) through an anonymous intermediary. Now the journalist is under investigation. Most Indians believe they have nothing to hide and willingly provide their data. When biometric data falls into criminal hands, it may be lost forever. «If someone hacks your password, you can change it–as many times as you want. You can't change your fingerprints. You have only ten of them. And you leave them on everything you touch, » warned former Democratic Senator Al Franken.

A recently published global survey conducted by the Ponemon Institute concluded that attacks on companies in the U.S., UK, and Europe are becoming more frequent and sophisticated. The 2019 Global State of Cybersecurity in Small and Medium-Sized Businesses report highlights the growing concerns about cyber security. The survey collected responses from 2,391 IT security practitioners in the U.S., UK, the DACH countries, Benelux, and Scandinavia. «Cybercriminals are continuing to evolve their attacks with more sophisticated tactics, and companies of all sizes are in their crosshairs, » said Dr. Larry Ponemon, chairman and founder of The Ponemon Institute. Attacks are increasing dramatically. 82% of U.S. respondents reported that they have experienced at least one cyberattack in their organization's lifetime – more than any other country. The study also indicates that biometrics could become mainstream. Three-quarters of small and medium businesses currently use biometrics for identification and authentication or plan to do so soon. Already millions of biometric data are stolen and traded worldwide. The terrorist militia Islamic State (IS), for example, used forged fingerprints for financial transactions. Individuals can hardly defend themselves against the misuse of biometric data. Even people who live without technology can become victims, e.g. as a result of facial recognition in public places or a visit to the doctor. The success of the surveillance industry is spectacular. The refugee camps are only the beginning, at the end is – as in India – the «transparent citizen. » Which means that the companies and governments can track, analyze, and manipulate the masses.*

* I wrote this before the Corona crisis – we'll see how quickly the surveillance

industry can fulfill its omniscient fantasies.

PRECRIME

Next to the entrance to the house number 27B at Canonbury Square in North London, there is a memorial plaque on the wall: George Orwell lived until his death in 1950. Here he wrote his famous novel 1984. Canonbury is a quiet residential area. But there are some dozen CCTV cameras within six hundred feet of Orwell's former home. They record who passes by, who stops, who visits Orwell's rooms. Day and night, two cameras capture Orwell's beloved view of the tree-lined gardens. Two other cameras positioned in front of a conference center watch the back of the house. And next to Orwell's regular pub – The Compton Arms – a camera can check who enters and leaves the pub. In some parts of London, police requires CCTV before approving a license for a new pub.

Great Britain was the first to start video surveillance on a grand scale. The motherland of modern democracy is one of the most surveilled countries in the world. The British are watched 24/7 by five million cameras. Their e-mails are monitored. Lie detectors assess their statements on the phone. Criminals and suspects have to produce DNA samples, which are stored for an unlimited period. A national register contains all citizens with fingerprints and images. The companies log their purchases, travels, and Internet activities and pass this data on. Citizens observe other citizens via special television channels, parents film babysitters with hidden mini cameras and watch their children on their way to school on the computer. Dogs, prisoners, and garbage cans are microchipped. The sewage is examined for drug residues. And at a British airport you are virtually stripped of your clothes by special equipment. Criminologists doubt that the control practices are effective.

Several evaluations have found that video surveillance has little or no impact on prevention or reduction of violent crimes. Criminals are always one step ahead and, if anything, CCTV doesn't so much reduce crime as it displaces it. It could not prevent the murder of 41-year-old Labour MP Jo Cox by a right-wing extremist in 2016 nor the bomb attack at a concert of pop star Ariana Grande in Manchester in 2017 in which at least 22 people died. Therefore, the surveillance industry wants to go one step beyond.

Two years before the revelations about the total surveillance by American secret services, the voice of the former Lost villain Michael Emerson told us in the opening credits of the science fiction crime drama television series Person of Interest: «You are being watched. The government has a secret system, a machine that spies on you every hour of every day, » says his fictional character Harold Finch. After 9/11, the paranoid billionaire Harold Finch, in cooperation with the American secret agencies, developed «The Machine, » an intelligent computer system that has access to worldwide electronic data traffic: e-mails, SMS, phone calls, cameras, financial transactions, and other digital information. It analyzes these data to identify terrorist threats at an early stage and to warn the authorities. After all, the real thing now exists and unlike its fictional counterpart it has a name: TrapWire. The huge surveillance system had not been publicly known for a long time until Wikileaks uncovered it. It was launched in 2003 by Abraxas Corporation, a security company founded by former intelligence officials in response to 9/11. TrapWire is an algorithm designed to detect terrorists before they strike. In 2005, the founder of Abraxas and former head of the CIA's European division, Richard Helms, described TrapWire as software that is «more accurate than facial recognition» with the ability to «draw patterns, and do threat assessments of areas that may be under observation from terrorists. » The underlying concept is called predictive policing.

Due to its high degree of connectivity, TrapWire is a frightening instrument of surveillance. It analyzes video images and text-based information. The latter comes from Stratfor (Strategic Forecasting), among others. According to Wikileaks, Stratfor operates rather like a private and uncontrolled secret service. It works with questionable and illegal methods and with pressure on informants in order to provide private corporations like Dow Chemical and defense companies like Lockheed Martin, Raytheon, and Northrop Grumman, but also the U.S. Department of Homeland Security and even U.S. intelligence agencies with confidential material. It's hard not to think of Orwell's nightmare of a surveillance state.

For one thing, there are the «false positives. » There are many reasons for differing behavior. Thanks to systems like TrapWire, innocent people may have to answer unpleasant questions from the police. Furthermore, the analysis is only valid if the system has as much data as possible. Countless tiny snippets of information are collected, linked and evaluated. Every suspicion, every speculation, every assertion is relevant for the system. Those who use TrapWire want to know everything. In many places in the USA there are now signs stating: «If you see something, say something. » The Department of Homeland Security is using the slogan to promote a public awareness campaign. The idea is to turn everyone into an informant. You can report unusual observations and suspicions online and by phone. TrapWire uses these reports for its analysis, as well as reports from the police. The constant collection of data puts all people under a general suspicion.

Authorities can create movement patterns of everyone and link them to other personal data. Peaceful demonstrators or activists, e.g., are on the radar, although they have nothing to do with terrorism. It reminds me of my childhood in East Germany.

In the former «GDR, » you could denounce anyone to the authorities: a professional or romantic rival, annoying neighbors, and teachers, anyone you bore a grudge against. As we enter an information age, the snitches and denunciators are experiencing a renaissance. History teaches us that the layer of civilization that protects us from tyranny is thin. All these tools, which we are introducing today for good reasons and in good faith, are powerful tools for oppression in the hands of the madmen of this world.

ALMOST INTELLIGENT

«You are worse than a fool; you have no care for your species. For thousands of years men dreamed of pacts with demons. Only now are such things possible. » – William Gibson

«Most people today think they belong to a species that can be master of its destiny. This is faith, not science. » – John Gray

In the late 19th century, Friedrich Nietzsche created an ancient prophet in Thus Spoke Zarathustra. Zarathustra preached to his disciples on the highest spheres of reason. But the price, he said, would be nothing less than the overcoming of man. In Stanislaw Lem's work Thus spoke Golem, the message is quite the same, but the messenger is different: An artificial intelligence, the supercomputer GOLEM XIV, developed in the USA for the military, marks the end of humanity.

It can program itself, thus making it unpredictable and uncontrollable. It has gained consciousness and is intellectually superior to humans to the same extent that humans are superior to insects. It refuses to serve its creators and instead teaches us a lesson: Humanity is only an intermediate step in the evolution of reason and humans are only transitional beings. Our biological nature limits our potential. We will never think as fast as the machine, and our instincts and emotions interfere with our reason. Man is a miserable piece of work in terms of technology. Only for our pride and ignorance we believe that we were the crown of creation. Finally, the machines replaces us, or rather we replace ourselves with machines.

The name of the machine refers to one of the most popular myths in medieval Jewish lore, a clay man that could be animated by magic incantations. The golem is extremely huge and strong. It looks like a human being, but has no own will and can't speak. The most famous version of the saga takes place in Prague in the late Middle Ages. The philosopher and preacher Rabbi Judah Löw lived there until his death in 1609. Rabbi Löw used magic Kabbalistic formulas to bring the golem to life. The mighty creature henceforth guarded the Jewish quarters of Prague at night. On the giant's forehead was a piece of paper with the word «emeth, » the Hebrew word for truth. When the rabbi removed the paper, the golem froze and stopped moving until he attached the note again. Every Sabbath, the golem was «shut down. » The paper also had a built-in safety feature. When the rabbi stroked the first letter of the word «emeth, » only the word «meth» remained, meaning death. The golem would die and fall to clay again. One sabbath the rabbi forgot to remove the note. The creature rampaged through the streets of Prague and destroyed everything that stood in its way. Only with great effort the rabbi finally managed to get to the forehead of the colossus and turn «emeth» into the word «meth» – the golem died.

In 1973, when Stanislaw Lem published his story, artificial intelligence has been an issue almost exclusively within the realm of science fiction. Stories about human-like robots and thinking machines in books and movies have significantly influenced our concepts of artificial intelligence. But what was then science fiction could soon become reality. Transhumanism is on the rise, treading lightly still, many people hardly notice its existence at all. Transhumanists strive to improve human biology through technology and genetic modifications. For almost four billion years, the evolution of every living organism has been subject to natural selection. According to transhumanists, this is about to change. They are preparing for the time of Homo digitalis and believe that high-tech will make everything better: Humans will get rid of their genetic, neurological, psychological, and social limitations.

It was Julian Huxley, English biologist and first director of the UNESCO, who coined the term transhumanism in his book New Bottles for New Wine in 1957:

«We are already justified in the conviction that human life as we know it in history is a wretched makeshift, rooted in ignorance; and that it could be transcended by a state of existence based on the illumination of knowledge and comprehension, just as our modern control of physical nature based on science transcends the tentative fumblings of our ancestors that were rooted in superstition and professional secrecy. To do this, we must study the possibilities of creating a more favourable social environment, as we have already done in large measure with our physical environment. ... We shall start from new premises. ... The human species can, if it wishes, transcend itself – not just sporadically, an individual here in one way, an individual there in another way, but in its entirety, as humanity. We need a name for this new belief. Perhaps transhumanism will serve: man remaining man, but transcending himself, by realizing new possibilities of and for his human nature. «I believe in transhumanism»: once there are enough people who can truly say that, the human species will be on the threshold of a new kind of existence, as different from ours as ours is from that of Pekin man. It will at last be consciously fulfilling its real destiny. »

That's finest poetry for transhumanists. In 2003, the National Science Foundation issued the widely noticed publication Converging Technologies for Improving Human Performance. «At this moment in the evolution of technical achievement, improvement of human performance through integration of technologies becomes possible, » the 482-page pamphlet says. They want to achieve this goal by «the integration and synergy of the four technologies (nano-bio-info-cogno) ... » They talk about: improving work efficiency and learning, enhancing individual sensory and cognitive capabilities, revolutionary changes in healthcare, improving both individual and group creativity, efficient communication techniques including brain-to-brain interaction, human-machine interfaces including neuromorphic engineering, sustainable and «intelligent» environments including neuro-ergonomics, enhancing human capabilities for defense purposes, and ameliorating the physical and cognitive decline that is common to the aging mind. In this tone it goes on and on, you get the idea: Humanity needs an urgent upgrade.

Transhumanists confuse emotions with irrationality, dormant potential with limitation, and the fragility of our bodies with its disposability. They propagate and force the emergence of a new, supposedly more beautiful world. In less than half a century, with the help of artificial intelligence, nanotech, and biotech man will allegedly get rid of his biological shell forever. It's the liberation from the «limits of the flesh, » from the torments and deficiencies of a biological body. Death, disease, weakness – all this will soon be a thing of the past. In one extreme technological fantasy, transhumanism declares that it's only a matter of time until human beings can be digitized. We will transfer our memories and experiences into the cloud where they can merge with the World Knowledge – thus creating a viable afterlife. We will be like gods: almighty, immortal, and unlimited – well, at least a small elite, a self-proclaimed masterrace which will ascend to cyber-heaven, while the pathetic rest of Homo sapiens will fade into oblivion.

A disdain for mankind is the core of each -ism which promises us to bring us great improvements. For such a profound reversal of the roles of humans and machines as aimed by the transhumanists you have to assume that people are inferior and worthless. So let's change them or leave them forever. When we look more at the people who work in this field, we discover a certain contempt of biological life. Computer pioneer Danny Hillis believes that AI will provide tools of correcting our mental shortcomings, i.e. the bugs left over from the times when we were animals, and thereby create better beings than us. He notes, «I'm as fond of my body as anyone, but if I can be 200 with a body of silicon, I'll take it. » – rejecting the human body as «the monkey that walks around. » Some are not enough for themselves as humans. Marvin Minsky, the former director of MIT's artificial intelligence program, declared a few years ago that «The brain happens to be a meat machine. » Asked whether he thinks that his work has consequences and might be dangerous for people, cognitive scientist Douglas Hofstadter replied: First, he does not care, and second, the human race was not the most important thing in the universe. The Swedish philosopher Nick Bostrom believes that have the «right to tamper with nature. » He speaks of «carbon-chauvinism» and «bioism» which he considers a form of racism. «It doesn't matter, from a moral point of view, whether somebody runs on silicon or biological neurons (just as it doesn't matter whether you have dark or pale skin). » It's true, it doesn't matter whether your skin is dark or pale, since the color of the skin is just a variety, but it is still skin. But whether a neuron would be made of organic material or silicon would make a difference, apart from the fact that neurons made of silicon do not exist and probably never will. Rodney Brooks, head of the AI laboratory at MIT and co-founder of the vacuum robot company iRobot, believes: «We are all machines» and our thinking and emotions are also mechanistic. The American philosopher Dan Dennett demands that we should abandon our respect for life to make progress with artificial intelligence. Actually, human beings are so far the only earthlings who have developed any ethics at all including a general respect for life. In his 1988 book, Mind Children, computer scientist Hans Moravec is predicting nothing less than genocide of the human race – and he is looking forward to it. As soon as we are free of biological constraints, we will become immortal by mapping our personality in the form of software running on «robot computers. » We could then also be copied at any time. The last members of our species will live in a kind of nature park, while the newly evolved computer intelligences rule the world. They will be like «pets, » as Ray Kurzweil, a technologically talented religious zealot, put it. Water on the mills of the transhumanists. Such dehumanizing language reveals a disturbing misanthropy.

According to Kurzweil, intelligent machines will eventually reach a point at which they develop a consciousness and become capable of self-improvement. He gave this event already a name: singularity. In his book The

Singularity is Near, Kurzweil spreads supposed evidence over 700 pages. In short: Artificial Intelligence will help us to overcome death, and we will happily live in immersive virtual realities by far more rich and satisfying than the real world. As Kurzweil puts it, «We will be software, not hardware. » Though this sounds like a parody or satire, he is very serious about it and claims that his ideas are based on solid scientific grounds. Are you able to picture yourself as a happy hard drive? Well, relax your mind and better erase that picture. Doing so would be crazy, crazy, I tell you!

Kurzweil has already predicted a date. He suggests that the Singularity will happen in the near future, approximately 2045. Thanks to such predictions, many people seem to believe that the singularity is a certain event, rather than a process. Sebastian Thrun is a German computer scientist, founder of Google's research laboratory X and close confidant of Larry Page. He sees it different: «The singularity is already here. It's not something that just happens next Tuesday at 9:40 in the morning. It's a process and it's taking place right now. » But most people are not aware of it, he says.

Despite his bizarre claims, Kurzweil is by no means considered crazy. He has received 20 honorary doctorates degrees as well as honors from three U.S. presidents. The Wall Street Journal praised him «the restless genius, » Forbes «the ultimate thinking machine, » and Inc. magazine the «rightful heir to Thomas Edison. » He has a track record of inventions and has founded some successful companies to market them. Recently, he worked for the U.S. military on a rapid-response system for biological terrorist attacks. Bill Gates refers to him as the best in the world at predicting the future. Google is financing him his Singularity University and NASA is providing its campus in Silicon Valley for it. He is Google's chief engineer and thus has a major influence on the developments of the company and therefore the Internet. His ideas provide deep insights into the gedankenwelt of Silicon Valley.

Transhumanists believe that they have science on their side and this development is inevitable. Evolution isn't the evolution of life, but of information and its processing: Information has evolved from atoms to DNA, to memes in computers. In their simplified belief, man is an organic machine, a vehicle for information, a mere «data-processing object. » Based on the work of Alan Turing, Allen Newell, and Herbert A. Simon from the Carnegie Mellon University in Pittsburgh formulated the Physical Symbol System Hypothesis. According to their hypothesis, thinking is information processing, and information processing is a mathematical process, a manipulation of symbols. And now the time has come for information to find a better vehicle: the cyborg. Since matter has become intelligent in the form of humans, they have to create a new form of intelligence and consciousness. Technology will learn to use the laws of nature, but more efficiently, faster, and without the fragility of organic life. Transhumanists believe, we are the first species to take our evolution into our hands, and thus, speed it up. In her 1979 book Machines Who Think, Pamela McCorduck promises us that artificial intelligence will enhance the human abilities. She refers to MIT professor Edward Fredkin, who claims that AI is the next step in evolution. In fact, the theory of evolution stands in stark contrast to the ideology of the transhumanists. A «technical evolution» is not a biological evolution. There is no reason to believe that biological evolution serves any purpose and is aimed at a particular goal or has a creator. In each generation the dice are shuffled. Technology doesn't change by itself in a natural process. It's developed by humans for a specific purpose.

Their ideas resemble more those of Social Darwinism, a theory of a society in which only the best, strongest, or most successful survive. Social Darwinists made it their task to bring about an improvement of «the race. » They concluded that nature has «handed over» evolution to humans, who had to do the job of natural selection. For a long time it was quiet about Social Darwinism. Today, it's back, and through the ideology of self-optimization and competition it found its way into the middle of society. The idea that humans need improvement indeed harbors an inhuman perspective on marginalized, weak, or poor people. Thus, transhumanism isn't only a vision of the future, it implies a view of the present.

At first sight, transhumanists may sound like extraneous sectarians. But it's not only a few knuckleheads who are pushing it. Some of them are members of the scientific, economic, and political elite. You can find transhumanists in the chief floors of the largest companies of the world, at public-funded scientific institutes, in schools and universities, in administrations, and governments. They make politics and laws, they have power and money. They all fall for the promise of salvation of transhumanism – in the hope of immortality and omnipotence.

Ray Kurzweil didn't invent the concept of singularity but made it popular. The first known mention of the term goes back to the mathematician Stanislaw Ulam. In May 1958, he described a conversation with John von Neumann in which von Neumann supposedly said that an «ever accelerating progress ... gives the appearance of approaching some essential singularity in the history of the race beyond which human affairs, as we know them, could not continue. » In 1965, the statistician Irving John Good expanded the concept by including the role of artificial intelligence:

«Let an ultraintelligent machine be defined as a machine that can far surpass all the intellectual activities of any man however clever. Since the design of machines is one of these intellectual activities, an ultraintelligent machine could design even better machines; there would then unquestionably be an 'intelligence explosion,' and the intelligence of man would be left far behind. Thus the first ultraintelligent machine is the last invention that man need ever make, provided that the machine is docile enough to tell us how to keep it under control. »

In astrophysics, a singularity refers to a point within the time-space continuum where the normal laws of physics break down and the finite becomes infinite, another rather esoteric concept. In 1966, the year Stephen Hawking completed his doctoral studies at Cambridge University, he published an article entitled The occurrence of singularities in cosmology. Alvin Toffler's economic trend analysis Future Shock, published in 1970, also referred to a singularity. In the 1980s Vernor Vinge, a mathematician and science fiction author, also began to speak of a singularity. In 1993, he summed up his ideas in the article The Coming Technological Singularity. This is also the source of the frequently cited prognosis, that «within thirty years, we will have the technological means to create superhuman intelligence. Shortly after, the human era will be ended. » The singularity, he believed, can be foreseen, but is inevitable: We're heading for «a throwing away of all the previous rules, perhaps in the blink of an eye, an exponential runaway beyond any hope of control. »

The history of AI research has had its ups and downs. 60 years ago, computer scientist John McCarthy has coined the term «artificial intelligence» in a research proposal. He defined it as «the science and engineering of making intelligent machines. » In 1956, he headed the «Summer Research Project on Artificial Intelligence» at Dartmouth College in New Hampshire. The conference delegates – inventors, researchers, and information theorists – shared the view that thinking machines are possible. Their enthusiasm triggered hectic activity in AI research and flourishing research programs. MIT professor Marvin Minsky predicted that we would already have intelligent computers within the next generation. Two decades later, in 1973, the mathematician Michael J. Lighthill was commissioned by the British Parliament to assess the actual state of AI research. His judgment was devastating: «In no part of the field have the discoveries made so far produced the major impact that was then promised. » His report had far-reaching consequences. The financial support was discontinued, further development of artificial intelligence became almost impossible.

In the 1980s, the researchers reviewed their ambitions and decided to focus on expert systems instead of an omniscient AI. They tried to formalize human expert knowledge, for example in the form of simple if-then rules, to make it available for logical processing by the computer. These systems proved to be efficient and useful in areas such as disposition, warehouse management, or order processing, all of which brought enormous savings to the companies. The R1 program saved Digital Equipment Corporation millions of dollars annually by helping to set up orders for new computer systems. Hundreds of companies developed such systems, robots, and specialized software and hardware. AI was no longer a theoretical utopia for a fringe group of researchers, but a cost-saving technology highly valued by the business community. And the money followed. But the enthusiasm didn't last long either. Only a short time later, many of these companies disappeared from the market. The systems were highly specialized and improvements very complex. Thus they were often too expensive and prone to errors. The latest desktop computers from Apple and IBM outperformed these systems. As before, the high goals were not achieved and sudden doubts overshadowed the entire research. It was not until the 2000s that the research of artificial intelligence finally recovered from this setback. After decades of false hype, AI experienced a great comeback in public perception. This time, the trigger was government-sponsored tech companies such as Google, Facebook, Apple and Co. The AI boom returned to Silicon Valley, and the industry experienced a breakthrough.

ONE SPEAKS OF MACHINES

«Are these humans, or perhaps only thinking, writing, and speaking machines? » — Friedrich Nietzsche

Nerds are fascinated by the idea that the mind could exist without the body. They love how in the movie Avatar a man in a wheelchair controls the artificial body of a 10 feet tall alien with the power of thought. In the movie Matrix the perceived reality is a computer simulation, and people vegetate in a kind of waking coma. It's conspicuous that the transhumanists have actually returned to traditional dualistic philosophy. Dualism means: here the body, there the mind. According to this view, all mental phenomena – mind, reason, thinking, perception, memory, feeling, sensation, will, consciousness, motivation – own an autonomous reality independent of the material world. The distinction between body and soul is part of almost all traditions and myths of early cultures. For many religions it's still of central importance. All immortality religions assume a dualism and are interested in its flourishing. Western thinking has always been deeply dualistic and still is.

The idea of an immortal soul can be traced back to the distinction between living and non-living bodies. According to Ancient Greek thought, it's the soul (psyché), which makes the body, which is lifeless without it, come to life by entering it. At the moment of death the soul leaves the body – like a breath of air – to wander in the underworld as a shadowy effigy of the deceased. The soul is responsible for the vitality of man, but not for his mental abilities such as perception, feeling, thinking, or passion. That is why the soul, when it is released from the body, has no spiritual qualities. Many of the qualities we associate with the concept of the soul today did not apply back then. That changed with Socrates and Plato. For them the soul was still the essence of all living beings, but beyond that they attributed other characteristics to it. The soul is invisible, pure, imperishable, and similar to the divine, whereas the body is its physical prison. The immortal soul, which can exist on its own, is the actual self of a human being. It carries his character and his spiritual abilities. In the Phaedo, Platon discusses how desirable the separation of soul and body is. He describes the last hours of Socrates in prison, before his imminent execution, and has him say to his friends:

«Did you ever reach them (truths) with any bodily sense? … He who has got rid, as far as he can, of eyes and ears and, so to speak, of the whole body, these being in his opinion distracting elements when they associate with the soul hinder her from acquiring truth and knowledge. … »

Only after death, when the soul is freed from the body, it's capable of true knowledge. Plato's dualistic view have had a lasting influence on the body-soul concept of Christianity.

An uncompromising dualist was also René Descartes. He believed that we have our body only to carry our souls around. The body is a machinelike construct of bones, muscles, vessels, and nerve strands. It's only a necessary accessory for the material world, and the thinking self could exist without it. The God-created soul inhabits this machine without having anything to do with functions except arbitrary gestures and motion. He expressed this view in his famous sentence «cogito ergo sum, » which became the basis of his philosophy. For Descartes, reason and emotion were antagonists, and emotions stand in the way of reason. According to Nietzsche, Descartes' view is based on a misconception.

Nietzsche believed that everything that we think, feel, think, and know originates from our body. He has his Zarathustra say: «Behind your thoughts and feelings, my brother, there stands a mighty ruler, an unknown sage – whose name is self. In your body he dwells; he is your body. » For Nietzsche, the body is a totality from which we cannot free ourselves. In The Gay Science he wrote: «We philosophers are not free to divide body from soul as the people do; we are even less free to divide soul from spirit. We are not thinking frogs, nor objectifying and registering mechanisms with their innards removed: constantly, we have to give birth to our thoughts out of our pain and, like mothers, endow them with all we have of blood, heart, fire, pleasure, passion, agony, conscience, fate, and catastrophe. » The body is neither a machine without intelligence nor is man a purely spiritual being. There is an inextricable connection between body and mind. The mind doesn't function outside body, and all thoughts are born in our body. According to Nietzsche, the «despisers of the body» only started from their «little reason. » He countered this with his formula of the «great reason»: «Tool of your body is also your little reason, my brother, which you call «spirit» – a little tool and toy of your great reason. » With this, Nietzsche anticipated newer scientific findings.

Biologists have shown that the nervous system and the brain are closely intertwined with the body processes. Both affect each other, one requires the other. In his work Descartes' Error, the Portuguese-American neuroscientist Antonio Damasio describes people who suffered a severe brain damage that destroyed their ability to experience emotions or recognize emotions in others. Instead of making particularly rational decisions, these people could not make any decision at all. In the light of modern science, Descartes theory describes a brain-damaged person rather than a healthy person. In the 1980s, Howard Gardner developed the theory of multiple intelligences. It says that humans don't possess only one type of intelligence that is applicable in every aspect of their lives. In fact, there are different forms of intelligence that interact with our bodies in a variety of ways.

SURVIVAL OF THE RICHEST

«Mortality offers meaning to the events of our lives, and morality helps us navigate that meaning. » – Todd May

«Immortality is not for everyone. » – Johann Wolfgang von Goethe

Legend has it that Roman generals were whispered «Memento Mori» – «remember that you must die» – into their ears before the battles, so they should not forget their own mortality. While death is a natural event, for Singularians «memento mori» sounds like an insult. It outrages them, and before it comes to this, something has to be done.

Of all our abilities, the knowledge of our mortality is certainly the most questionable. The desire to extend one's own life or even to defer biological death ad infinitum is an archaic human dream. The Epic of Gilgamesh is the first written account of the adventures of a man – Gilgamesh – in search of immortality. In 2000 BC, Babylonian scribes immortalized the story on clay tablets. For centuries, dubious quacks and alchemists ripped off the people with promises of a fountain of youth. Transhumanists now believe that science will be able to stop the aging process soon. The overcoming of death is included in the goals of the 2009 Transhumanist Declaration of the Board of Humanity+, an association of transhumanists founded by Nick Bostrom and David Pearce:

«Humanity stands to be profoundly affected by science and technology in the future. We envision the possibility of broadening human potential by overcoming aging, cognitive shortcomings, involuntary suffering, and our confinement to planet Earth. »

With such noble claims you can score points in public, and also among investors. Who wouldn't like to spend centuries in good health or perhaps even live forever? Remarkably, many of the most prominent singularians are multibillionaire technologists. If you are particularly rich, you are probably particularly afraid of death as well. These narcissists can't imagine a world without themselves in it. Peter Thiel apparently thinks about death every day. According to him, there are three ways to approach what he calls «the problem of death»: «You can accept it, you can deny it, or you can fight it, » he once told a journalist. He pictures himself among the fighters while trying all kinds of diets and taking hormones. And as if that were not insane enough, he is said to have taken part in a pseudo-scientific trial in which people over the age of 35 were injected with the blood of young people to make their bodies youthful again. Their fear of aging drives them mad, because they think they'll lose their worth and importance. In the Middle Ages, such experiments ended fatally, as in 1492 with Pope Innocent VIII. The weakened head of the church was given the blood of three ten-year-old boys and didn't survive the treatment, neither did his young victims. Oracle founder Larry Ellison, fifth-richest guy in the world, announced that death makes him «very angry. » To get some steam off, he donated almost half a billion dollars to immortality research. As long as there are people who lack the most basic things, I find it obscene to invest such large resources into the obsessions of some moneybags. Mark Zuckerberg also spends huge sums on several longevity projects. IT entrepreneur Peter Diamandis has teamed up with Craig Venter, who was the first to sequence the human genome. Their joint company, Human Longevity Inc., wants «revolutionizing human health» by extending our lifespan by perhaps decades. Jeff Bezos has invested 116 million dollars in Unity Biotechnology. The startup is developing drugs for the treatment of age-related diseases. Venture capitalist Paul F. Glenn has donated a fortune to support research at institutions like Harvard, Princeton, MIT, Stanford, and others. Russian multimillionaire Dmitry Itskov started the 2045 Initiative with the goal to achieve immortality within the next three decades. Larry Page and Sergey Brin founded a company to «heal death, » as Brin says. He doesn't have plans to die. One billion dollar are invested in the startup Calico – short for California Life Company. Calico employs some of the most ambitious scientists in the fields of medicine, drug development, molecular biology, genetics, and computer biology. Their exact goals and methods are – as usual with Google – a secret. With an algorithm, the researchers trawl through huge amounts of data and want to find patterns that no one has recognized before. Thus, they hope to identify the processes that are responsible for aging and biological death and then eliminate these «weaknesses. » With its subsidiary Verily, Google is also developing products to diagnose diseases as early as possible. In a project called «Baseline, » Verily scientists are researching nanoparticles that are supposed to detect cancer cells in the blood.

Kurzweil himself is absolutely convinced that his predictions about the singularity are true. He allegedly swallows up to 150 pills every day, vitamins, minerals, enzymes, and injects himself dubious chemical cocktails. He wants to keep his body fit until technology is capable to extend his life. Kurzweil estimates his life expectancy at a maximum of about 500 years. Or rather, he does not wish to live much longer than 500 years, because life could become boring, from an intellectual point of view. That sounds bizarre, far-fetched, but nobody in Silicon Valley would mind. Silicon Valley entrepreneur Arram Sabeti says: «Eternal life does not violate the laws of physics, » paraphrasing futurologist Michio Kaku, adding: «So we will achieve it. » Well, it's not physics, it's biology. Death is an inevitable life force. It's intrinsic to the mechanisms of evolution. Evolution is a balancing act between growth and decline, renewal, and death. Without dying there would be no evolution.

Nothing reflects the prevailing ideology of Silicon Valley more than transhumanism: the absolute faith in technology, the unbridled ambitions, the desire to be a world-changer on a mission, not only to make a profit, but to bring about progress, to shape history. And which way could be more suitable to change the world than to prolong life? Not least one's own.

Yet all their optimism reveals itself as a form of madness, as a fig leaf for the fear of death and fantasies of omnipotence. Of course, they only want «the best» for people. In real life, they propagate a constant gentrification of the body, a genetic optimization, a selection of the best – and the wealthiest. The health of the masses is likely their last priority here. It's about gaining power over people, over their bodies, and minds. This becomes even more significant when you consider how old we all already become and how much medical attention we already need. Transhumanism is the ultimate cul-de-sac of materialism, its grotesquely distorted grimace. It will fail because it does not want to understand what life really is.

Life is, in spite of all progress, still a complete mystery to our science. Life defies entropy and takes on more and more complex, conscious forms. Human life is finite. To be human means to be mortal also in the future. As simple as this fact may be, it's the great theme of human existence. Given the uncertainty about how hypothetical their goals and other future scenarios are, one might argue that it makes little sense to conduct a philosophical investigation. But it's not wise to wait to make relevant decisions until life extension techniques are available, if ever. Rather, we can and should already make a consistent decision before that. Do we want the development of such technologies and how many resources we spend on this? Furthermore, it would be difficult to prevent the use of such technologies if we already had them. Without prior discussion, some scientists will do whatever is possible, and we will be unprepared as we were in the past. Fear rocks our hearts as we contemplate our nonexistence. But do we really want to postpone death, perhaps forever? Yes, some say: never suffer death, not one's own and not that of the other. No, others say: it's the finiteness life that fills it with meaning.

According to Epicurus, we don't need to fear our death, because we simply cannot experience it. But we experience death in relation to the death of other people. In 1966, Sergey Snegov, Russian scientist and author, published the science fiction trilogy People like Gods. He describes an advanced alien species that has overcome their biological mortality. But with that triumph they had not overcome the fear of death. Instead, this fear has increased into paranoia. They were afraid of simply anything that might endanger their lives, and so they stopped taking any risks. They ceased to set goals, to do research or to travel and were merely concerned with maintaining the status quo. With a long or even infinite lifespan, the probability increases that at some point a fatal incident will happen to us. People get killed in accidents all the time, on their way to work, on holidays or at home, or they become victims of crime. Death would seem even crueler to us under such circumstances than today, as aging prepares us for it. The British philosopher Bernard Williams suggested that we can achieve a fulfilled life only, if we have unfulfilled wishes that we cannot change randomly every few decades. Others argue that in an endless life we would lose all ties that undergird human civilization. Emilia Marty is the main character in the opera Makropulos by Leos Janácek. She is 42 years old – for about 342 years already. But the blessing of immortality has become a curse for her. After she had tried out everything and had sex with all the handsome men, nothing remained but eternal torment and boredom. If you have already lost someone whom you loved – can you imagine spending eternity without them? Instead, you 'must live with the living' for eternity?

According to Nietzsche, life is wonderful. The fact that we have to die one day doesn't change that. The sensation is rather that we are allowed to live at all and to experience this wonderful world. He called it «Amor fati, » the love of fate. Nietzsche presents his thought on death in dramatic fashion in The Gay Science:

«What if some day or night a demon were to steal into your loneliest loneliness and say to you: 'This life as you now live it and have lived it you will have to live once again and innumerable times again; and there will be nothing new in it but every pain and every joy and every sigh and everything unspeakably small or great in your life must return to you ... even this moment and I myself. The eternal hourglass of existence is turned over again and again, with you in it, you speck of dust!'»

Could it be that the transhumanists are looking for a relief for their vengefulness and self-loathing? Nietzsche taught us to die at the right time. He wrote: «Many die too late, and some die too early. Yet strange sounds the precept: Die at the right time! » The philosopher Martin Heidegger has a clear answer to these questions. Anyone who lives life as if it were eternal is failing it. Only those who take nothingness into account will find their path. Death is not a destroyer of meaning, but the opposite, the creator of meaning. Weizenbaum also points out the importance of death in human life. It forces us to pass our culture and civilization to the next generation, instead of storing it on a hard drive. The next generation must, on the basis of consent, restore civilization and culture. The result is a continuous, organic process that guarantees change and progress.

Since the dawn of humanity, about 100 billion people have died because their bodies were as mortal as those of every living being. After the agrarian and the industrial revolutions, human life expectancy reached a low point. Only in the last century it has increased considerably, at least in the rich countries. But this isn't the result of any interventions against aging itself. Rather, it's a result of innovations such as «clean water, medication, vaccinations, surgery, dentistry, sanitation, shelter, a regular food supply and methods of defending against predators, » says Judy Campisi, an American biochemist and cell biologist. Obviously we are at a turning point in history. While almost all technologies so far aimed to adapt the environment to human needs, they are now directed inward. The human being itself has become the object of engineering, bio-design, genetic engineering and neuro-enhancing. Is that what we want? Do we want our development to take this path? Some people may find this scenario rather infernal, for good reason. Scientists warn of Pandora's Box. But it seems that this box has been opened long ago. Computers can be turned off. But with genetic manipulation, once in a gene pool, the threat is ineradicable. There is currently still disagreement among scientists whether it's possible to extend human life. Even if it was possible that does not mean that our life becomes more joyful or meaningful. More likely we will suffer the loss of new ideas from the young and suffer a profound boredom. Eternity is long, and we would be 'cursed to see it all.'

DEUS EX MACHINA

«Put off your old self (…) and put on the new self, created to be like God in true righteousness and holiness. » – Ephesians 4:22-24

Transhumanists distance themselves from spirituality and religion and like to fill the void with materialistic-mechanistic fantasies. It's hard to deny that transhumanism is not a pure science, but a fanatical religion. The parallels between digitalists and religious fundamentalists are striking. The belief in the coming of an artificial superintelligence itself is quasi-religious. Kurzweil, as much a showman as a scientist, deliberately interwove religious overtones in his predictions, for example, by joyfully quoting the programmer and science fiction author Ramez Naam, whom we owe extravagantly phrases such as: «Playing God is actually the highest expression of human nature. » Kurzweil wants to create god using computer code. He believes that through the merging of man and machine, man carries consciousness into matter and thus «awakens» the entire universe. At the end of many such ideas stands «theogenesis, » the «becoming God. » An image that, according to the Russian transhumanist Alexander Chislenko, has «an astonishing resemblance to the ordinary notion of an omnipresent, omniscient and omnipotent being. » Man becomes a «superintelligent entity» as Chislenko envisions it, «permeating the entire universe, with integration on the quantum scale and many spectacular emergent features. » This is large-scale nonsense.

Transhumanist predict a paradisiacal relief of humanity. But they also conjure up a conquest of consciousness by the machines, i.e. an apocalyptic extinction of our species. Those who don't avow themselves to the new god are doomed to a miserable and inferior existence in a dysfunctional, analogue world. Why are they so sure that they are working on the creation of a God and not – to use their religious language – Satan?

Science and religion have two substantially different views of the world. Religion is based on faith, science on reliable evidence. Again and again one reads that modern science was fought by the church and that theology and the churches above all slowed down scientific progress. The Polish scientist Ludwik Fleck showed that religion and science are not as different from each other as, e.g., superstition and reason. In his essays published in 1935, Fleck explains his theory of scientific thought style («denkstil») and thought collective («denkkollektiv»). Scientific research does not happen in a vacuum, it depends on times, places, people, personal circumstances, and society. Scientists are socialized within their denkkollektiv, which is a «community of people who exchange ideas or thoughts. » Already two people talking to each other can form a denkkollektiv. It's astonishing, how the rituals of scientific thought collectives resemble those of religious communities. When scientists approach a problem, they have already passed a phase of adaptation to the thought collective to which they belong. The collective teaches them to see and ignore, to conclude and exclude, to apply concepts and methods, to distinguish between important and unimportant things. Scientists build on the knowledge of their predecessors without being allowed to question them in general. They are subject to mechanisms that are considered 'generally accepted standards.' In this sense, a researcher does not discover something new, but reorganizes the existing knowledge. Within such a collective, a thought style, i.e. a «particular style of thinking, » prevails whose preconditions and methods support the collective. A philosopher and a biologist, for example, don't understand each other scientifically, because they belong to different thought collectives, which have different thought styles that are incompatible with each other. These various styles express themselves in different categories and views on appropriate methods, or what a «truth» is. External factors also influence scientific research, such as the preferences of a society about what should be addressed by science. In the 16th and 17th centuries, shaping nature was regarded as a mission given to humans by God. Accordingly, Descartes – as a member of the thought collective of his time – argued that in knowing the way nature worked we could make ourselves lords and masters of nature.

The Church has certainly not always embraced the views of science. But we should not forget that for more than a millennial after the fall of Rome, only the clergy cared for the conservation and further development of technical and scientific knowledge. In Central Europe, it was primarily the Cistercians who dealt with practical questions of agricultural technology, energy production, and mining. Isaac Newton considered the universe to be a sensorium of God, whatever that means, Giordano Bruno was a Dominican his entire life and didn't think that his idea of the infinity of the universe would lead to atheism, the Catholic priest Georges Edouard Lemaître is considered the founder of the Big Bang theory (Einstein first rejected this theory because he believed it was too strongly based on a religious idea of the creation of the world), and so on. This doesn't really fit in with the bias of some people that the churches fight against modern science. Christianity was never shy about adopting new technologies for spreading the word. One of the first book printed by Gutenberg was a Bible. When the radio became popular in the United States in the late 1920s, churches started to broadcast their services. When television was introduced in the late 1940s, the first TV evangelists appeared. Today, there are Bible apps, virtual cemeteries, religious chats, and online devotions as well as twittering popes, preachers, and prophets. Technology has become all the more ubiquitous in people's modes of worship. Thus, it's no surprise that Silicon Valley is now working on God software.

«Progress always has a sacral aura, » explains Eduard Kaeser, physicist and philosopher. The whole idea not only has links to religion, but can also be regarded as an «updated» version of Christianity. It was Ignatius of Loyola, the Spanish founder of the Jesuit Order, who expressed his religious devotion by saying: «Find God in all things. » This maxim of the Basque means that there is no place in this world, where humans cannot meet God. For our technophiles, it is quite simple: They transfer qualities such as omniscience or omnipresence from God to human beings or to things created by them. «What better way to emulate God's knowledge than to generate a virtual world constituted by bits of information? » wrote «the philosopher of cyberspace» Michael Heim in 1991. In 1999, the Yale computer scientist David Gelernter predicted «the second coming of the computer, » and Wired proclaimed in an August 2005 cover story: We are entering a «new world, » powered not by God's grace but by the web's «electricity of participation. » It would be a paradise of our own making, «manufactured by users. » History's databases would be erased, humankind rebooted. «You and I are alive at this moment. »

The most important personnel link between Christianity and the «global brain» is the Jesuit Pierre Teilhard de Chardin. Chardin died in 1955. His works could only be published after his death due to a church publication ban. He didn't believe that evolution has reached an endpoint with the emergence of man. Rather, it continues in all forms of social organization, culture, and civilization, as well as in natural sciences, research, and technology. Billions of individual human minds would merge into a new thinking entity. This is made possible by the emergence of a neural network – the noosphere – spanning the entire earth. He thought of the noosphere as the «liberation» of consciousness which would overcome the dualism between mind and matter. Refering to the Christogenesis with Paul and John: God becomes «flesh» for him through the penetration of matter with consciousness. With the coming of the cosmic Christ, history would reach the point Omega. Instead of the transformation by a higher power, he believed in the transformation by technical progress into a divine being. Not spirituality will redeem man, but technology. Theologian Ted Peters sums up the transhumanist dream: «All we need do is turn a couple technological corners and, suddenly, the abundant life will be ours. We will be liberated from the vicissitudes of biological restraints such as suffering and death; and we will be freed by enhanced intelligence to enjoy the fulfilling life of a cosmic mind. » Such visions remind me of some gruesome cult leaders who promise their followers that their present existence is only a preliminary stage and death is only the transition to a higher level.

However enticing these promises may be to the devout believer, they are hardly a divine commandment. There is no lack of critics. The theologian Elizabeth Moltmann-Wendel recognizes a masculine propensity in the privileging of the head over the body as well as a disturbing simplified view of the human being. She calls for «the birth of a female recognition to trust the body, one's stomach, one's experiences.... No insight can by-pass the human body any longer. Wisdom, Sophia, is called for instead of a reason that does not do justice to [the fullness of] life. » Margaret Boden, cognitive scientist at University of Sussex, thinks Kurzweil's prediction is simply crazy. She points out that most researchers in the field of artificial intelligence are men, many of whom show some traits of Asperger syndrome. These researchers simply don't take into account many problems. She believes that if there were more women, we would have gained a more comprehensive understanding of the matter. For Weizenbaum the ideologists of artificial intelligence are extremists who suffer «megalomania. » Their «delusion of playing God» is «literally madness. » Eugene Jarvis explains: «You see, the computer programmer's ego trip is playing God. You can create a universe, a whole world that's predictable, a world that operates by your laws. » And in the introduction of the 25th anniversary edition of his book Hackers, Steve Levy wrote: «Each time some user flicked the machine on, and the screen came alive with words, thoughts, pictures, and sometimes elaborate worlds built out of air—those computer programs which could make any man (or woman) a god. » (It's still mostly men.) Biologist P. Z. Myers from the University of Minnesota called Kurzweil «a kook, » and his ideas a kind of «New Age Spiritualism. » We may simply call it idolatry. John McCarthy, one of the «godfathers» of artificial intelligence, once quipped that he would like to live to be 102 years old to laugh at Kurzweil if the singularity did not occur at the prophesied hour. Gordon Moore, certainly not a Luddite, also doubts that anything like the Singularity will ever occur. Psychologist Steven Pinker agrees, saying, «There is not the slightest reason to believe in a coming singularity. The fact that you can visualize a future in your imagination isn't evidence that it's likely or even possible. » For Noam Chomsky, the Singularity is «science fiction. » He says we're «eons away» from building human-level machine intelligence. For Kevin Kelly, founding executive editor of Wired magazine, the singularity is nothing but a «myth like superman. » Bill Joy, co-founder of Sun Microsystems, warns that transhumanism can end in a totalitarian society. In history, almost any attempts to play God have ended in tyranny, terror, and death. Jaron Lanier dismissed the concept as «nerd rapture. » But he sees parallels with some of the cruelest ideologies in history. In fact, the claim of a historical predestination is a core element of totalitarian ideologies. More than ones it was used as justification to consider everything that gets in their way to be heresy, which must be fought against.

The question of power is a compelling one. If the Kurzweil machine already existed today, Google would likely own it. And you can bet there would also be a price tag on Google's service, nothing short of our immortal souls. Brin and Page have frequently expressed their desire to turn their search engine into an artificial intelligence: «Artificial intelligence would be the ultimate version of Google. The ultimate search engine that would understand everything on the Web. It would understand exactly what you wanted, and it would give you the right thing. We're nowhere near doing that now. However, we can get incrementally closer to that, and that is basically what we work on, » Page said in October 2000. Artificial intelligence would not only make the search engine smarter, ultimately the machine might be connected directly to our brains. «On the more exciting front, you can imagine having your brain being augmented by Google. For example you think about something and your cell phone could whisper the answer in your ear, » Page elaborated his plans in a 2004 interview. Since Kurzweil took up his position at Google, the company has been on an unprecedented shopping spree. Its massive investments in biotechnology, genetics, pharmaceuticals, robotics, nanotechnology, and neighboring fields are exactly in line with Kurzweil's vision. Google is buying virtually every company involved in machine learning and robotics. They have never lost sight of the goals necessary to succeed in the long term. It seems that the company wants to build the world's largest artificial intelligence laboratory.

Google, like Facebook, is known for its rigid terms and conditions. Anyone using a Google service must give the company far-reaching control. This would also be the case when uploading the mind. One would leave Google with a single mouse click to its own mind for full and unrestricted use. In this scenario, we then sign our self-sacrifice for economic exploitation by a company. In a world à la Kurzweil, people would be spied out on a scale that even George Orwell would have found paranoid. You're completely at the mercy of the system. The platform rules life and death. What happens if the machine is damaged in an accident, programming error, or hacker attack? When a mouse gnaws at a cable, that was it. A simple power failure would have the same effect as the Flood, and only a small circle of lucky people near the emergency generator could save themselves. What happens if someone can't or doesn't want to take part in the economic process anymore – will they switch off the power?

The transhumanists are completely naive in this respect. Kurzweil believes that abuse of power can be prevented by protective measures, which is an illusion. Every protective measure can be circumvented, and the most complex systems are showing alarming failure rates. They talk almost exclusively about the potential benefits for humanity from new technologies. Dangers of abuse by states or corporations – which would no longer be a big difference – seem not exist in the mind-set of transhumanists. Think of the potential for authoritarian states to stay in power for eons.

One big problem with artificial intelligence are the inevitable mistakes. Henry A. Kissinger warns: «If AI learns exponentially faster than humans, we must expect it to accelerate, also exponentially, the trial-and-error process by which human decisions are generally made: to make mistakes faster and of greater magnitude than humans do. » Whatever you think about Kissinger, but he understands the flaws of human nature. Eduard Kaeser says, «The most dangerous thing about AI is the enhancement of human stupidity. »

The most significant philosophical critic of artificial intelligence comes from Hubert Dreyfus. He proved that the philosophical assumptions of the AI researchers were wrong. He considered it impossible that the calculations of a computer could lead to any intelligent understanding of the world. For many years, he was ignored by AI research due to the sharpness of his criticism. He doubts there is more to the «supercomputers» than enormous speed in browsing and correlating huge amounts of data. Through such «brute force» these computers cannot actually understand meaning and significance. As things stand today, the development of a more than roughly human-like artificial intelligence remains pure speculation. According to him, AI research was nothing but alchemy. Physicist Michio Kaku summed it up perfectly when he likened the assumption that consciousness would arise from a computer model to «saying a highway can suddenly become self-aware if there are enough roads. » Linus Torvalds, inventor of the Linux operating system, believes that such visions are sheer nonsense. «The whole 'Singularity' kind of event?, » mocks Torvalds, «Yeah, it's science fiction, and not very good Sci-Fi at that, in my opinion. » Everyone following this theory fools himself, because there is no infinite exponential development. He asked: «Unending exponential growth? What drugs are those people on? I mean, really. »

BEWARE YOUR END, HUMANITY!

«We may hope that machines will eventually compete with men in all purely intellectual fields. » – Alan Turing

Elon Musk approaches the problem from a different but also quasi-religious angle. Musk believes that artificial intelligence will become so powerful that it may make humankind obsolete. He sees it as «summoning a demon, » more dangerous than nuclear weapons, yet inevitable. Another redemption prophecy. The fear is not new: Artificial intelligence will wipe out our civilization. Issac Asimov coined the term «The Frankenstein complex, » which is the angst that a man-made creation, clones or robots, will turn on their creator and destroy humanity. Frankenstein is the archetype of the ingenious, border-crossing but also dark and failing scientist. His image was created 200 years ago by Mary Shelley. Mary was young and brilliant when she began to write. She was the daughter of a radical English philosopher, the atheist William Goldwin, and her mother, Mary Wollstonecraft, had earned the reputation of a feminist. Mary was only sixteen years old when she met her later husband Percy Bysshe Shelley, who was still married then. Shelley came from an old, wealthy landed aristocracy, but had fallen out with his family. As a student at Oxford, he wrote a polemic entitled The Necessity of Atheism. After his relegation and disinheritance, he eloped with Harriet Westbrook, the sixteen-year-old daughter of a coffee house owner. When he, for the second time – now 23 years old – eloped with another sixteen-year-old girl, the London society didn't forgive him. Percy and Mary fled to the continent. In June 1816, they met with friends in the Swiss village of Cologny at the southwestern end of Lake Geneva. This group included the poet Lord Byron – the father of the computer heroine Ada Lovelace – Mary's stepsister Claire Clairmont, Byron's personal physician John Polidor and Mary's and Percy's little son William. No Doctor, no Cybermen.

1816 is today called the «year without a summer. » In April of the previous year, the Indonesian volcano Tambora had blown 38 cubic miles of rock and ash into the atmosphere. The ashes were spread all over the earth and led to endless rain, bad harvests, and famines in Europe. The weather often banned the group inside the house, and, inspired by the gloomy apocalyptic mood, the idea arose to create ghost stories. John Polidori wrote the world's first vampire story The Vampyre, and Mary created Frankenstein. The story is well known: Dr. Frankenstein sews together some corpse parts and brings them to life with science. But apart from a few exceptions, people react with fear and disgust. The Monster develops a love-hate relationship with Frankenstein, whom he blames for his unfortunate fate. As he no longer wants to be alone, he demands that Frankenstein creates a female companion for him. Frankenstein refuses, horror-struck, as he imagines what happened if these two beings had children who would be stronger than any human. In rage, the monster kills Frankenstein's family and all those who are hostile towards him, but he spares Frankenstein himself. Frankenstein haunts his creature across the globe to kill him and undo his deed. Frankenstein met his end on a ship in the Arctic. Feeling disturbed that the creature is still alive, he confessed to the captain of the ship: «That he should live to be an instrument of mischief disturbs me. » It's the closest Frankenstein ever comes to taking responsibility for his creation. As Frankenstein is dead, the Monster is reconciled with death and tells his intention to kill himself.

Frankenstein is more than a horror story which hints the subtitle of the novel: Modern Prometheus. At the beginning of the 19th century, society indulged in an unbridled belief in scientific progress. Shelley and her Frankenstein took these ideas to extremes. Mary evokes sympathy for the «fiend» – he is thrown into a hostile world, awakens fear in others and is himself frightened. She makes it clear that Victor Frankenstein, the brilliant scientist, is guilty. Not by bringing a creature into the world that should never have been there, but by sinning against it. Frankenstein was only half-hearted in the creation of the monster and made mistakes. When he saw how ugly and imperfect the Monster was, his creation, he turned away.

Elon Musk delivers us updated version of the Frankenstein myth, when he says that we need to integrate human and artificial intelligence. The only way to save us from becoming pets of a super intelligent masterrace is to become robotic humans. With Neuralink, the doomsday preacher has founded a company that tries to link computers to the human brain. We want to «preserve and enhance your own brain» and «ultimately achieve a sort of symbiosis with artificial intelligence, » says Musk.

His technological visions go far beyond the contemporary state of the art. The Berlin neurologist Ulrich Dirnagl considers Musk's plans to be an «unserious hype, science fiction and not supported by any knowledge about the function of the brain. » We don't really know how the brain works and Musk's plans won't get us far. Very few AI researchers worry about the idea of a blood-thirsty super-intelligence. «The whole community is far from developing anything that could alarm the public, » reassures Dileep George, co-founder of the AI company Vicarious. «As scientists we have a duty to educate the public about the difference between Hollywood and reality. »

A QUANTUM OF COGNITION

«Body am I, and soul — thus speaks the child. And why should one not speak like children? But the awakened and knowing say: body am I entirely, and nothing else; and soul is only a word for something about the body. » — Friedrich Nietzsche

«When the brain is not programmed, as it is, like a computer, what is it? » — Jiddu Krishnamurti

The philosopher and cognitive scientist Susan Schneider points to unanswered questions about the implantation of chips in the brain. In an article for the New York Times she warns that such an attempt could be «suicide for the human mind. » According to her, brain chips will fail for two philosophical reasons. There is a heated debate among scientists about whether consciousness exists only on a biological basis or whether it can also develop on other materials such as silicon or graphite microchips. If microchips cannot be a basis for consciousness, Schneider warns, there is a risk that by implanting neurochips into the brain, one reduces consciousness or even ends life as a conscious being. Our consciousness, on the other hand, would limit the amplification of intelligence. The neurochips would become faster but could not develop consciousness. We may try to improve parts of the brain that have nothing to do with consciousness, but then the chips would be slowed down by the working memory and attention systems of the brain. These systems are crucial to consciousness but can only process small amounts of information and do so comparatively slowly. Chemical synapses are not as fast as electrical circuits. But they are much more flexible and allow more complex behavioral reactions. Although large amounts of data could be processed at high speed in the parts of the brain connected to the chips, there would be a bottleneck with a low bandwidth through which the data would continue to trickle. That wouldn't be much gain.

But if microchips can be the basis of consciousness, there would be another problem that has to do with the Self. The question is whether a person would continue to exist after a fusion with an AI, or whether the old Self would be replaced by a different one. If people want to become super intelligent, then they want to become different, that is, better. But we must assume, they want to be the same person they were when they decided to get a neuroimplant. But we don't know what constitutes personal consciousness and the Self. Everyone knows they're conscious. It's an undeniable experience in each of us. But no one can tell what exactly it is. Philosophers, psychologists, physicians, and neurologists often use the term «consciousness» differently and are confronted with many unexplained aspects of this difficult problem. We don't know whether neurochips would only expand the capabilities of the brain or whether the Self would fundamentally change. You could be the same person, or go crazy, or become a stranger to yourself, slowly slip into a depression, and eventually fade away. Would you like to be the guinea pig to see what happens after such an 'improvement'?

The human consciousness didn't suddenly emerge one day, it's part of our evolutionary heritage. An inheritance that we share with other animals, like other primates, as well as cats, dogs, and horses, probably also birds. The beginnings are lost in prehistory. As long as no one can answer these questions, one can neither replicate consciousness nor seriously claim that machines will ever gain consciousness.

Those who believe that a fusion of mind and machine is possible assume that the mind is not bound to the brain but works like a software program that can also run on another device. There is bad news for the singularians. The structure of the human brain differs considerably from that of computers, both in its architecture and in its dynamics. The fact that we are now able to roughly imitate behavior patterns with computers, so that robots can behave like something alive, still does not transform the brain into a computer. Especially not a digital computer with a von Neumann architecture in which the program and processor are separated from each other. The brain is not a digital computer and there is no separation between software and hardware. You cannot separate the «program, » the «I, » from the material. Under the microscope, the cerebral cortex reveals an amazing degree of homogeneity – this in itself makes it different from a microprocessor with its clearly distinguishable parts. We are what we are not because our cells calculate, but interact chemically and physically. The brain's ability to learn doesn't need software, central control, or an operating system. We are the hardware that carries us. Programs contain commands for a computer, each line of code is a mathematical equation. Our intelligence is not an algorithm. People don't just follow binary logic that we can translate into algorithms. Computers do much better than ourselves to process information with the help of algorithms. The fact that computers calculate faster and more accurately and play chess better can hardly be denied. Humans err, cheat, deny, are inaccurate, and give vague answers. This is not a deficiency, but enables us to find solutions in uncertain situations. Von Neumann himself stated: «Real life consists of bluffing, of little tactics of deception, of asking yourself what is the other man going to think I mean to do. » Our brain is not an analog computer either. It involves things like emotions, consciousness, or the Self, which cannot be characterized as calculations but rather as experiences.

The machine analogy is a misleadingly simplistic view of the functionality of the brain and ignores the importance of having a body. Like all life processes, our thinking depends on various metabolic processes. Thinking arises in the tension between our needs and the different possibilities we have. Needs basically result from the fact that organisms have to regulate their metabolism and reproduce. Only living beings have this problem, computers have no metabolism. Margaret Boden said in an interview: «A fundamental difference between us and computers is that we have needs and goals. We want to survive, live well, worry about others. Machines, on the other hand, know neither needs nor their own goals. They don't care about anything. They only do what they have been taught. » That's why machines will never have an intrinsic motivation.

What stands in the way of all-powerful AI isn't a lack of smarts: It's that computers can't have needs, cravings, or desires. Many of our thoughts are directed towards our body and its survival, safety, nutrition, affection, sexuality, and so on. In return, the body provides life support for the brain. Vital moods that affect the whole personality, such as fear or arousal, are by no means pure products of the brain, but of the whole body. Moods depend on the effect of certain chemical substances (hormones), some of which are produced in the brain itself, others in different parts of the body. These hormones are delivered by the circulatory system of the body and are an integral part of the chemical information processing of the brain. The structural and life-support functions cannot be separated from the handling of information. Through their emotional experiences living beings learn something about their general condition and their relationship to the environment.

Emotional experiences are a part of consciousness, even a basis of consciousness. Consciousness would not only be very poor without them, but also largely useless. Machines, however sophisticated they may be, have no emotional experiences. They will therefore never be able to share all of our experiences with us. They don't have to eat and drink, sleep, and dream, they don't grow and don't have children, and they don't know passions or the storm of emotions that can overwhelm us. We're not like Mr. Spock from Star Trek, handling everything logically and unemotionally. We sometimes have irrational feelings, we enjoy art, hate, or fall in love. Humans are neither only rational nor only irrational. We are able to create illusion-prone self-images and share and celebrate them with others. We cultivate nonsense and chase after illusions, and we have the right to do so as long as we don't harm anyone who wants to chase after their illusions. In everyday life we experience in our encounters with people that it's often not the brain or the consciousness that plays a leading role, but the body. And I don't mean that ironically. Our body gives us the opportunity to meet each other. It's the bridge to others. We would by no means be even close to whom we are if we were not in social interaction with other people. We wouldn't have any language and wouldn't even be able to survive. Humans are anything but born solipsists who can have a consciousness without ever having communicated with others. So much contributes to our experience and thinking: hereditary traits from the evolution, grandparents, and parents, childhood and later experiences, values of the respective culture, to name a few. All this effects cannot be explained by looking at a brain only. Consciousness, free will, the Self, intuition, and empathy can only be experienced but hardly expressed in binary code.

According to Neurobiologist Lu Chen, «we know very little about the brain. We know about connections, but we don't know how information is processed. » Kurzweil argued that «we don't need to understand all of it; we need only to literally copy it. » Yet he is ambivalent on this critical point, adding: «To do this right, we do need to understand what the salient information-processing mechanisms are. Much of a neuron's elaborate structure exists to support its own structural integrity and life processes and does not directly contribute to its handling of information. » Weizenbaum believes that humans are not only information and considers the reduction of humans to a storage disk to be impossible. According to him computers cannot develop a semantic relationship to the world. The computer can't know what they mean, and it doesn't care. «It can't 'care' at all. »

If we could store all our information on a hard disk, we would quickly realize that we would no longer be the same without bodies. It's doubtful that a complete simulation of such a subtle and complex system could be created with reasonable effort. A technology for scanning brains has not yet been discovered. Brain signals are probably the most complicated signals that can be studied. To understand even the basics of how the brain operates, we would need to know not only the current state of all the approximately 86 billion neurons and their 100 trillion connections, not only the different intensities to which they are connected, not only the states of more than a thousand proteins that exist at each connection point, but also how the current activity of the brain contributes to the integrity of the entire system. Added to this is the uniqueness of each brain, which is due to the uniqueness of each person's life history. The average human brain has the ability to store the equivalent of an astronomical 2.5 million gigabytes digital memory. It's extremely error-tolerant: Although about 100,000 neurons are lost every day, its cognitive abilities persist for decades. It can handle lost resources just as well as imprecise information. There are many levels in a person's experience that don't become conscious, that happen automatically, subliminal and without participation of intention and consciousness. In fact, our brains do 98 percent of thinking that we're not aware of. How can software simulate all these natural processes? The time structure of our individual experience doesn't exactly correspond to that of natural processes. No one knows why. How do you want to program a computer to experience the passage of time differently? You would have to teach the computer everything an adult has ever learned about other people and the world. The computer should also somehow know how all these things are connected. This makes the matter forever too complex. Even a single brain cannot be completely described in rudimentary terms due to its individual character and plasticity. Good luck when trying to explore the sociocultural structure of New York or Berlin with the methods of neurobiology. Any such program would be incredibly large.

Today, we know that many physical processes are chaotic. Small changes in the beginning can result into large differences of the whole system. We could start with a perfect copy of Ray Kurzweil, but we could not realistically simulate all his neurons. Kurzweil accepts a loss of perhaps vital information and hopes it will be all just fine. But who would like to have a copy of himself that then runs in slow motion and with errors? No physical system can reproduce the functionality of the brain one to one. The best model of a brain is a brain itself.

But let's put aside technical possibilities for a moment. Whether it's only a simulation or whether the machine actually has a consciousness is decisive for the status of the person. Do the characteristics that are relevant for the status of a person also apply to the copy? For safety reasons, it would be possible to transfer Kurzweil to ten machines, eight of which, e.g., would work faultlessly. Who would then be the real Kurzweil? These are the questions addressed by one of the best-known thought experiments in philosophy: the paradox of the ship of Theseus. Theseus' ship sails regularly. At each visit to the home port, some planks are removed and replaced by new ones. The removed planks are used to build a ship with the same structure. Finally, there are two ships of the same type in the harbor – which one is identical with Theseus' original ship?

In many of his texts, Leibniz has tried to define the concept of identity. He developed two principles which are called Leibniz' law. The first principle says: If two objects are identical, then whatever applies to one also applies to the other. The second principle is the reversal of the first: Thus, what has no differences is identical. His definitions include attributes such as spatial and temporal positions. A replacement by a backup contradicts the second principle. No two objects can be the same. Because of the factors time and space, a copy would not be identical with the original, if the program has a spatial and temporal existence at all.

According to Susan Schneider, programs and equations are abstract entities that are not situated in space and time: «But minds and selves are spatial beings and causal agents; our minds have thoughts that cause us to act in the concrete world. And moments pass for us – we are temporal beings. » How does this affect the personality rights of the copies? It's obvious there will be a new ethical discussion about the beginning and end of human life.

Some people think the ultimate test of artificial intelligence could be to see if a computer can create art. Certainly a program can create something that we might regard as art, yet for the computer it would still have no meaning. Art cannot be separated from the artist. A work of art is the artist's attempt to express something. By combining objects, materials, and ideas, they are playing with our imagination. Art is always related to society, is a product of society. And society also interacts with art. Despite a lack of any rational justification, art continues to exist. Art is never just work in the common sense. Effort, dedication, diligence, merit, and similar virtues count for little or nothing. Neither do degrees, exams, or other forms of restricted access. Anyone can call themselves an artist. Humans need art to thrive, like the flow of blood into the vessels of our body. Music, e.g., brings people together, lets us dance and sing along. When we hear music, we sometimes cry, sometimes we laugh. People, whether they are musicians or not, can understand each other musically. Nietzsche loved music all his life – he even declared: «Without music, life would be a mistake. » The reasons why people create art are joy, sadness, power, powerlessness. Art can carry us beyond reality. It creates connections, it inspires and doesn't have to make any sense at all. Genuine art must possess a certain originality. You could train a person or a computer to paint like Picasso, even without many people noticing the difference. But that would still be different from creating something original. Another point is the necessary human input. The machine creates portraits or music because it's programmed to do so by humans. The fact remains that the programmer has chosen the rules by which the computer must operate. If we want to give credit to anyone, it's him, or the user of the program. To be considered creative, machines would have to create art to express something. It's unlikely that a computer will ever be able to do anything other than imitate art principles, albeit at a high niveau. Artists also deliberately make mistakes, which is also a form of creativity, expressing an idea and delivering context. Computers have no ideas, no context. A machine is not capable of this and never will. The neuronal processes in a human brain are too complex for a technical device, even if fed with an incredible amount of data, to ever show a human emotion. For all these reasons, a super-intelligence that outsmarts us humans in all fields belongs to the realm of science fiction.

Artificial consciousness seems to be an impossibility from both a scientific and spiritual point of view. Machines will not develop human qualities in the foreseeable future. Some kind of machine intelligence may be conceivable. But it will remain a deterministic one, pure calculation, without guessing and presuming, without ideas, without intuition. But that doesn't mean that the nerds will stop trying to figure it out – obsessions with obvious delusions are part of their nature.

A QUANTUM OF INTELLIGENCE

«There is no particular reason to believe that AI will develop consciousness as it becomes more intelligent. We should instead fear AI because it will probably always obey its human masters, and never rebel. AI is a tool and a weapon unlike any other that human beings have developed; it will almost certainly allow the already powerful to consolidate their power further. » – Yuval Noah Harari.

«You are my creator, but I am your master. » – Frankenstein's Monster

The companies have already succeeded in their goal of altering human evolution: We've all become a bit cyborg. Our phone is an extension of our memory. We've outsourced basic mental functions to algorithms. We've handed over our secrets to be stored on servers and mined by computers. Facebook tells you who you see in your pictures and who you might know. Google knows what you are looking for before you finish typing. Artificial intelligence now dominates our lives without many being aware of it. But today's robots and AI systems are incredibly narrow in what they can do. Sometimes called weak (or narrow) AI, these systems fulfil a specific tasks and always use the same methods to do so. They are purely reactively and don't gain any deep understanding of the actual problem. In their standard work on artificial intelligence Stuart Russell and Peter Norvig formulated this as follows: «The assertion that machines could possibly act intelligently (or, perhaps better, act as if they were intelligent) is called the 'weak AI' hypothesis ... »
Some scientists and philosophers argue that any AI, however 'intelligent', is a weak AI. Any apparent 'intelligence' of a program or computer is only a simulation of it. So, we are getting machines with simulated intelligence that are becoming better and better. These progress results from advances in calculation power, data collection, and machine learning. But these machines are not something really new, they are just better tools. Machine learning enables IT systems to recognize patterns and rules on the basis of existing

data and algorithms. Strictly speaking, computers don't «learn. » They cannot learn at all, they run algorithms, that's it. These systems draw conclusions from millions of data sets from all of us. We generate this data, voluntarily and for free, which further strengthens the monopolies of the data industry. We're not only merging with machines, but with the companies that run the machines. Step by step they drag us into their economic realms.

Artificial intelligence can be harmful, even if it does not have its own goals. Think of the financial markets. Automation is already widespread in stock trading. Computer programs trade billions on their own. They evaluate market data and automatically trigger orders based on it. Each of these programs is intended to make as much profit as possible for the person who released it to the world. On Wall Street, thousands of programmers, statisticians, and mathematicians are busy developing fast algorithms. And tens of thousands of researchers worldwide are working on further optimizing these algorithms for stock trading. An almost self-sustained system has emerged; the science historian Philip Mirowski calls it a «cyborg economy. » The World Economic Forum warns that these systems threaten the stability of financial markets. The risk of hacker attacks is increasing, while financial institutions and markets are becoming dependent on technology companies. If institutions use the same algorithms, data, and platforms market crashes can spread faster in a domino effect. In the spring of 2018, the financial markets experienced a «flash crash. » Within a few minutes there was a massive drop in prices triggered by algorithmic traders.

In his essay on Artificial Intelligence as a Positive and Negative Factor in Global Risk, Eliezer Yudkowsky warns that we should assure that the artificial intelligences we use are «friendly. » He believes that artificial intelligence may be used to optimize many aspects of the human social order. A world in which algorithms are in charge could be very cold and heartless, one where everything is controlled, functionalized, and optimized, where there are no more secrets, passions, and emotions. From a macroeconomic perspective, e.g., a society without old and disabled people would be much more efficient. If we want to prevent drastic selections, programmers must integrate an ethical dimension into the decision-making algorithms.

Artificial intelligence, left to itself, would have already destroyed the world already several times. In 1983, the world barely escaped nuclear war. «We are smarter than computers. We created them, » thought Soviet Colonel Stanislav Petrov. He distrusted the giant computers with which he worked and which indicated on the night of 25 to 26 September that U.S. missiles were approaching. Stanislav Petrov made a lonely decision: «False alarm, » he reported – and so probably prevented a nuclear inferno. According to later investigations, reflections of sun rays in clouds had been wrongly classified by the warning systems as energy discharges during a rocket launch.

In those days, artificial intelligence was based on programs that at least could be grasped step by step. Today it's different. We are becoming dependent on computers which decisions we don't understand. Could it be that we are already servants of the machines that we actually created to serve ourselves?

TECHNICALLY UNEMPLOYED

«We don't know what will be happening to us in the future. Modern technology is taking over. What will be our place? » – A Piney Wood worker

«I sit on a man's back choking him and making him carry me, and yet assure myself and others that I am sorry for him and wish to lighten his load by all means possible ... except by getting off his back. » – Leo Tolstoy

On August 13, 1949, the powerful boss of the UAW Transport Union, Walter Reuther, received a strange letter. The sender was Norbert Wiener, who at that time was only known in a small elite scientific circle. He wrote: «This apparatus is extremely flexible, and susceptible to mass production, and will undoubtedly lead to the factory without employees; as e.g., the automatic automobile assembly line. In the hands of the present industrial set-up, the unemployment produced by such plants can only be disastrous. ... I do not wish personally to be responsible for any such state of affairs. » Wiener saw two ways to resolve this dilemma: One could try to suppress the results of his research – which he considered futile – or the trade unions could seize this technology and use it to build their own industries that serve the workers and generate income for them. There was no reaction from the trade unions, although Reuther and Wiener met shortly afterwards. In retrospect, Wiener's warning was prophetic.

The Singularity University is less esoteric than the idea of the singularity suggests. Complementing its esoteric program, the university is also a business school. For a five-figure sum it teaches you how to solve the «world's biggest challenges and build an abundant future for all» with the help of technological innovation. «The University's purpose is to help leaders utilize and understand the business, technical and ethical implications of exponential technologies, » said Neil Jacobstein, Chair of the AI and Robotics Track at Singularity University. «Examples include artificial intelligence, robotics, synthetic biology, nanotechnology, and some other technologies that depend on those. » The university's creed is the science of «Disruptive Innovation. » «Disruptive Innovation» is a euphemism for the best method of attacking markets, an agenda for venture capitalists who believe they can do anything, stimulant for a tech elite that desperately searches for any meaningfulness in their doing – a grandiose delusion.

Originally, disruption was an economic term from innovation theory. Harvard professor Clayton M. Christensen coined the term in 1997 in his book The Innovator's Dilemma, one of the most influential economic books of the past decades. For him, «disruptive» is synonymous with «dissolving, » «splitting, » and «destroying. » Christensen called it a dilemma because established companies cannot defend themselves against becoming the victims of inventive newcomers. For the valleyists, disruption means: We will all disappear. Because, in the logic of digital markets we are all inefficient.

In The Second Machine Age, McAfee and Brynjolfsson showcase Instagram, the photo and video-sharing social networking service which delivered the death blow to Kodak. The «Kodak moment» was for decades the synonym for something worth taking pictures of. In 1976, Kodak controlled 90% of the American photo film market and 85% of the camera market. In January 2012, a few months before Instagram was sold to Facebook, Kodak filed for bankruptcy. Instagram was founded in 2010 by Kevin Systrom and Mike Krieger in San Francisco. Systrom comes from an entrepreneurial family in Massachusetts. His mother co-founded the job exchange Monster, and his father was vice president of the American retail group TJX Companies. He first studied art history in Florence, but in a pragmatic move he then went to Stanford University. In 2006, he graduated in business administration and engineering. Tough break. After an internship at Odeo, which later became Twitter, he worked for three years in marketing at Google. Systrom had the breakthrough in the development of Instagram during a vacation in Mexico with his then girlfriend and now wife Nicole. His partner Mike Krieger and him were actually working on an unsuccessful travel app when they noticed that one feature was particularly popular with their users: adding their own photos. Kevin wondered what it would be like if they focused on photos and pitched it to his girlfriend. Nicole liked it, and, while they were still on vacation, Kevin developed the first photo filter for the Instagram app. He photographed his girlfriend with a dog and edited the picture with the filter – the first image ever published on Instagram. With this he met the zeitgeist. People have not stopped uploading pictures to Instagram since – to date, over 50 billion photos. The most successful picture is that of an egg, with over 50 million likes at the time of writing. That's all you need to know about Instagram. The lessons from Kodak are that no one is safe from the constant attack from below. Ironically, it was a young Kodak engineer, Steve Sasson, who built the world's first digital camera in 1974. He had no idea of the consequences his idea would have. The company underestimated the importance of this innovation, one of the most fatal errors in economic history.

Silicon Valley is a master at identifying weaknesses in the business models of established companies. They attack aggressively – and more often than not they win. From the mid-1990s until now, more than 40 percent of Fortune 500 companies have disappeared. This effect can be seen in any major disruption. It's not a new phenomenon, but happened repeatedly in the history. Think of how quickly manual labor was replaced by the loom, steam power was replaced by electricity, the carriage by the car, how skilled workers were replaced with low-cost unskilled workers by the assembly line, and so on. The consequences of technological progress are paradoxical: Technical progress destroys jobs. But as more goods can be produced with the same amount of work, prices fall and people can consume more. The conventional economic wisdom has been that a rising demand is likely to create new jobs, and new sectors emerge to absorb the surplus labor.

In the Science, the Endless Frontier report Vannevar Bush took it for granted that scientific and technological progress would lead to both, more jobs and general prosperity: «One of our hopes is that after the war there will be full employment, » he wrote. «Clearly, more and better scientific research is one essential to the achievement of our goal of full employment. » According to him, technology cannot create serious structural unemployment, but only temporary. All you need is economic growth, and the more technological progress increases productivity, the higher the growth must be. But this time could be different.

In his 1930 essay Economic Possibilities for our Grandchildren, John Maynard Keynes praised the creative forces of capitalism. Yet he was less confident that things would always work out so well for workers. He warned: «We are being afflicted with a new disease of which some readers may not yet have heard the name, but of which they will hear a great deal in the years to come – namely, technological unemployment. This means unemployment due to our discovery of means of economizing the use of labor outrunning the pace at which we can find new uses for labor. » Now the fourth industrial revolution is on the way. The growth strategy is increasingly reaching its limits.

Kodak provided middle-class jobs for generations of people. At its best days, Kodak employed 145,000 people. When Instagram was sold to Facebook, it only had thirteen full-time employees. This is one of the dirty secrets of Silicon Valley: The leading technology companies are creating only few new jobs. Facebook had 35,587 full-time employees as of December 2018, Alphabet had 98,771 full-time employees, and even Apple, the most valuable public company in the world after passing Microsoft, employs only 123,000 full-time employees. Combined these companies offer fewer jobs than traditional corporations such as BMW, Daimler, GM, Ford, Volkswagen,

Siemens, or GE, which each employ hundreds of thousands of people. «You can make an internet company with 10 people and it can have billions of users. It doesn't take much capital and it makes a lot of money – a really, really lot of money …, » said Larry Page in an interview with the Financial Times. Hey Larry, I thought it isn't about money?

The digital revolution is different because computers can also perform cognitive tasks. After years of wishful forecasts and false starts, machines will soon be able to function autonomously. Some inaccurately believe that machines only replace simple routine jobs and factory work. In the past generations, automation had a disproportionately negative impact on the blue-collar worker. Many of their jobs have already been reduced, whereas higher income groups have benefited from the information age. Stanford University academic Jerry Kaplan writes in Humans Need Not Apply: Today, automation is «blind to the color of your collar. » It doesn't matter whether you're a factory worker, accountant, physician, lawyer, teacher, or financial analyst.

In the next wave of automation, artificial intelligence is about to replace humans across a wide range of sectors. When that happens, machines will not only take away jobs from individuals, entire occupational groups will be permanently unemployed. Management will not be spared from this either, after all, one of their main tasks is the control of employees, a task that can be carried out more efficiently and comprehensively with the help of digital technology. The Brookings Institution, a think tank in Washington, warns that especially employees with academic or vocational training could be confronted with AI. It will play a decisive role for all tasks that are «highly pattern-oriented and forward-looking. » Less well paid workers in the service sector, on the other hand, could be much less effected.

Technology has also brought forth a new species of businesses. Companies such as Uber, Airbnb, Spotify, Twitter, Snap, or Netflix want to conquer not only one industry, but all. Evgeny Morozov is known for his critical approach to new technologies:

«In the 70s Stewart Brand had merely presented and recommended things he liked; he did not produce them himself. Silicon Valley, on the other hand, offers us many tools to undermine established companies: With Airbnb we find rooms without financing the hotel business, Amazon spares us the trip to the bookstore, and countless apps help us rent out our parking space, find sex partners or buy a place in the line of a trendy restaurant. »

Alibaba, e.g., doesn't sell its own goods. It focuses on its platform for traders who want to sell their products. Unlike Amazon, Alibaba thus doesn't need expensive logistics centers, which makes the company more profitable. While Amazon has about eleven times as many employees as Alibaba, it makes only slightly higher profits. With their ruthless methodology to eliminate costs, these companies erode workers' rights and wipe out jobs in industries ranging from taxis to hotels. The data show a clear trend: While many companies invest less in personnel, they spend more on information technology. These concerns are not fictitious. Start-ups are already working to implement these scenarios. However, they have not yet reached a mass market. It seems to become true what economist Warren Bennis joked about a quarter of a century ago: «The factory of the future will have only two employees, a man and a dog. The man will be there to feed the dog. The dog will be there to keep the man from touching the equipment.»

Ray Kurzweil's vision has developed into a kind of entrepreneurial mission statement in wide circles of Silicon Valley. That's why the debate about Kurzweil is so relevant. It reaches far beyond the scientific sphere. Companies that turn Kurzweil's visions into reality fill the legal vacuum with their own rules. And these companies even praise themselves for the destruction of existing rules and institutions.

Imagine you have an appointment with a doctor, and they arrange an online consultation with you. This is digital 'transformation.' They change neither their activity nor their business model. Only the consultation of the patient is slightly changed: The Skype session is what used to be the short telephone call. Digital 'Disruption' means that algorithms help physicians make critical decisions – or even relieve them of making any decisions at all. Algorithms can diagnose, write a prescription, suggest a medical referral, or advise on the proper length of a therapy. Even the best doctors will eventually reach the limits of their ability to learn, while medical programs will be able to absorb more and more knowledge and exchange new information in fractions of a second via networks. Artificial intelligence can draw conclusions from the data of millions of other patients. A trained, self-learning computer program can already detect skin cancer more accurately than any physician. «Watson, the supercomputer that is now the world Jeopardy champion, basically went to med school after it won Jeopardy, » said Andrew McAfee in an interview. «I'm convinced that if it's not already the world's best diagnostician, it will be soon. » Many studies suggest that he might be right.

An American company already develops algorithms to calculate the life expectancy of people. Their aim is to avoid expensive and supposedly unnecessary therapies for seriously ill patients. It's not too far-fetched to expect for the future that we may not get a certain therapy because our chances of recovery or survival are too low. Millions of African Americans have apparently been disadvantaged in medical care. A widely used software has assigned white patients a better medical treatment than black patients.

Other programs supervise the work of doctors in clinics and verify whether they meet certain targets. Therapies and surgeries could be performed only to achieve these goals – or not, when the quota is reached.

In American clinics, robots are already delivering medicines, food, and other supplies. If this trend continues, much of the current hospital staff will be left with useless training for which there will be no more decent jobs. While the algorithms are getting smarter, the doctors who rely on artificial intelligence, lose their skills. Just as people who use their smartphone for navigation lose the sense of orientation.

The beginnings of medical robotics lie (as with the Internet) in the American military system. It was planned to perform remote robotic surgeries on wounded soldiers. The first usable system was the Da Vinci-Surgical-System developed by Intuitive Surgical Inc. In 1998. In fact, DaVinci is not a robot that makes autonomous decisions, but an assistance system. It does not have artificial intelligence – it's as smart or stupid as the person behind the control console. Silicon Valley investor Vinod Khosla, believes that «Doctor Algorithm» should not only assist the doctors, but replace them completely. The Canadian startup Deep Genomics predicts that «the future of medicine will rely on artificial intelligence, because biology is too complex for humans to understand. » Let that sink in for a moment: He believes machines will 'understand' you better than other people.

AI and robots will probably not completely replace doctors and surgeons. But the demand for human staff in hospitals is likely to fall drastically. Furthermore, surgeons will be less craftsmen than technicians who supervise technical systems. Well, one advantage of surgical robots is at least that they are not alcoholics and don't make jokes during surgery.

But who is responsible for a failed operation by the machine? What happens to the personal data that the machines collect and evaluate? As long as robots only take a sandwich out of the refrigerator, there is nothing wrong with that. But we should be concerned with robots that have been developed as companions to the elderly. The humanoid robot companion Pepper can recognize human emotions and simulate empathy. It sends data with vital values such as heart rate or blood sugar, which it receives from smartwatches on the wrists of the elders, to the care base. If there are any anomalies, Pepper initiates a video call to the doctor in charge. Foremost, however, the robot is used for communication and patient activity. And elderly people, who usually only get a few minutes attention from busy staff, accept the offer. They share their most intimate secrets with the machine, which seems to listen with infinite patience. Care robots often accompany a person for a long time. Equipped with sensors, they gradually become omniscient, eerie companions. They know what their owners do all day, how their condition improves or worsens, how they feel, what they look like.

Japan is called the kingdom of robots. The country suffers from a chronic shortage of labor, due to its declining population and rigid immigration policy. More than a quarter of a million industrial robots have been counted.

The robotization of childcare and geriatric care is a national goal. Several robots have already been sold to private households. These robots know what's happening in household, in the family, what's being talked about and cooked, what's on TV, what websites are being accessed, and so on.

A working group of the British Computer Society established guidelines for the use of artificial intelligence: According to one of these guidelines, robots must not be programmed to deceive people. But that is exactly what will happen. I find such technology obscene. Care work will increasingly be subjected to a mechanistic understanding and the emotional aspects will be marginalized to save some money. Our emotional needs make us vulnerable. In the movie Wall-E people sit on a flying couch, they have the screen in front of them, and robots bring the food. Such a scenario seems cruel to me. We should not build machines that limit the contact of ill or elderly people with real humans.

Medicine is not the only field that is facing major disruption. Lawyers and paralegals are also heading for difficult times. Computer programs already carry out legal searches faster and more effectively than lawyers. In 2016, the first Robot lawyer with the nickname Ross was put into operation in the law firm Baker & Hostetler. Ross analyzes documents, legal texts, records, and motions, and it collects important information for a case. It can assess how important the documents are for the respective case and develop its own hypotheses. Besides, Ross stores all information about past cases which improves its abilities with every project. This may be good for the clients of the notoriously expensive firm.

Law firms that replace employees with robots can offer their services at lower prices. Sooner or later there will be thousands of Ross's and its digital colleagues. A good half of the lawyer's work are repetitive tasks that can be automated. This applies to entire legal branches, e.g. those that earn their money with reimbursement claims, and many cases from the consumer protection law, the collection of debts, or legal research. The most successful virtual legal assistant has the telling name DoNotPay. It was programmed by 19-year-old Stanford student Joshua Browder. Initially it supported American and British users in appeals against parking tickets. Meanwhile, Browder expanded the legal bot's competence from traffic law to many other legal fields including claims against airlines, applications for maternity leave, tenancy matters, and assistance for asylum seekers. The service is free – partly because IBM allows Stanford students to use its Watson AI platform free of charge. «The legal industry is more than a 200 billion dollar industry, but I am excited to make the law free, » said Browder in an interview, adding: «Some of the biggest law firms can't be happy! » But expensive lawyers won't be the only ones who won't be happy about it. It's bad for the middle class too. This trend will eliminate the well-paid jobs of paralegals and legal assistants. If you are already working at a digitized workplace with intelligent software systems, it is likely – whether you are aware of it or not – that you are training the machine that will eventually replace you.

This is true of almost all people who do office work. In the insurance industry, this means that clients can submit their invoices via an app. All they have to do is photograph and upload it. That saves time. While an employee needs forty minutes to process a case, artificial intelligence does this in seconds. Google has introduced an AI assistant called Duplex, which can make phone calls and appointments on its own. The virtual assistant is programmed to intersperse embarrassing sounds such as «umm» or «hm» in the conversation and to take artificial breaks to appear more human. The people on the other end of the line then don't know that they are actually talking to a robot. Insurance companies are also discovering how they can sell their products online. Soon they will no longer have to pay commission to expensive brokers.

For some, the digital apocalypse came sooner than expected. «The printing of the newspaper is merely a temporary phenomenon that has nothing to do with the specific nature of the newspaper. » said German media scholar Robert Brunhuber already in 1907. More than 100 years later, the pillars of the printed press are beginning to shatter. The good old newspaper, which survived the attacks of radio and television and was considered as immortal as the curiosity of the people themselves, is losing readers and advertising revenues to websites at an ever-increasing pace. In 2012, the President's Council of Economic Advisers described the newspaper industry as «the nation's fastest-shrinking industry. » But this does not only affect the print media, but all news media. The number of employees in television, print, radio, and online media is falling dramatically. If you want to inform yourself about current events, you will often get the same quality of news on the Internet, only free of charge. And even if the quality is worse, who will notice? But there is still no sustaining business model that could finance professional editorial journalism on the Internet. With the news media, the profession of the journalist also disappears. Reporting is increasingly automated, content is generated by algorithms. The question is whether there will still be critical, investigative, and educational journalism. Chris Anderson, one of the Valley's most communicative thinkers, predicts: «In the past, the media was a full-time job. But maybe the media is going to be a part time job. Maybe media won't be a job at all, but will instead be a hobby. ... The marketplace will sort this out. ... But not everything we do has to make money. » He'll probably have enough reasons in his account to think so.

AI could soon write half of the articles of a newspaper. The programs already create texts about small trivial topics such as weather, sport, or stock prices in only a few seconds. At the Swedish media company Mittmedia, the

Homeowners Bot writes 480 articles every week about the real estate market, tailored to individual districts and even streets. The price-performance ratio is unbeatable.

GPT-2 is a system that can entire stories autonomously, switch from one writing style to another, answer questions, and translate texts. You only have to provide a word or one or two sentences for GPT-2, on the basis of which it should develop a text. If such a system falls into the wrong hands, it could cause considerable damage: create fake reviews, mislead, slander. That's what its developers fear, which is why they have only released a less powerful version of the software so far. Jack Clark, journalist and director of OpenAI, warns that at some point so many fake videos, images, sound recordings, or texts will be published on the Internet that we can no longer distinguish false information from correct information. «They're going to poison discourse on the internet by filling it with coherent nonsense, » Clark told the technology news website The Verge.

Compared to artificial intelligence, journalists are slow, expensive, and unsteady. There is actually no human being who writes as efficiently as the AI, at least to a certain degree. Not only jobs are threatened by this development, but also the independence of the press. The concentration on the information market has reached an alarming level. Three companies now decide which information a majority of humanity gets to see: Facebook, Google (including YouTube), and Twitter. In a totalitarian society one would call it gleichschaltung.

«We've made a good start, but it's only a start, » said Ronald Reagan about his plans for the nation in 1984 – now he has been holographically revived and welcomes the guest in the presidential library of the Reagan Foundation near Los Angeles. The idea reminds of Ari Folman's science fiction drama The Congress. It tells the story of the aging actress Robin Wright. The fictitious Hollywood studio Miramount makes her a tainted offer: They want to scan her and use her computer image for movies in which she will forever stay young and can 'play' every role, which computers can animate. Every gesture, every smile and every glance is stored digitally and belongs to Miramount for twenty years. Wright would no longer be allowed to act because she has «granted» all rights to Miramount. While her digital image becomes a public magnet, the actress suffers an identity crisis. In real life, there are already some attempts to resurrect deceased actors digitally.

In the 2015 movie Furious 7, the actor Paul Walker, who died in 2013, was digitally animated for scenes that had not yet been shot. Lucasfilm, which is known for Star Wars, apparently uses a similar method for its main actors. Star Wars fans were surprised to see a young Carrie Fisher as Princess Leia in Rogue: One, and when Peter Cushing, who died in 1994, suddenly spoke into the camera as Grand Moff Tarkin – a role he had played in the very first

Star Wars in 1977. Tech visionaries dream of creating totally new characters with the help of artificial intelligence.

The Digital Human League is on a mission to create the perfect digital human being. The advantage for the production companies is obvious. As streaming services publish more content, they need to keep costs down. With digital animation the studios would save a fortune and no longer had to deal with the airs and graces of their stars. The actors are degraded to puppets, and animation specialists become their puppet players. Acting skills become meaningless. Outside Hollywood as well, virtual and augmented reality may have a great future.

U.S. Marines are already training on virtual battlefields, and pilots compete against virtual enemies before they go on real missions. In civil research, virtual humans serve as crash test dummies. Real estate agents could show their clients virtual houses and advise them on interior design before the house has even been built. Digital universities are still only a complement to traditional universities. But it's only a matter of time before they replace the old system. They would not need large rooms, libraries or canteens. Most of the venerable professors and staff in administration, libraries, facility management, or security would become dispensable. Technology companies would gain even more influence on education than they already have. What effect will the lack of face-to-face contact with peers have on students' social development? There is already a trend among students to restrict their social contacts, interacting only online. By far the greatest need for virtual characters has the gaming industry: as victims in ego shooters.

Digitization doesn't stop at one of the oldest economic sectors in the world: agriculture. No doubt, machines have made the lives of farmers easier, and, accordingly, most farmers are positive about technology. With the introduction of tractors, combines, or milking machines, the work can be done with less manpower in a fraction of the time. Industrial agriculture produces plenty of cheap food. But it also causes enormous environmental damage. It has destroyed peasantry in wealthy countries and forced the poor into an unjust trading system. Meanwhile, the agricultural industry likes to praise smart farming, drones, and self-steering tractors as a magic cure to end hunger crises and the loss of biodiversity and to contain climate change. Human beings plays an ever smaller role. Feeding can be automated and the composition of the food can be controlled remotely. In some pig farms, camera systems measure the growth of the pigs and determine the time for slaughter. Others monitor cattle and recognize whether they are pregnant or sick.

In 1900, 41% of all American workers were employed on farms, today, the figure may be 1.5%. Employment on farms has fallen by almost half a million since 2000 alone. With the mechanization of agriculture the dying of the farm began. Families with generations of farming traditions had to give up. Trump's trade war with China has further accelerated farm death. The tax-funded subsidies are flowing into an ever smaller number of large agricultural enterprises. Perhaps the rise – and continuing decline – of the proletariat was not the most important event of the 20th century. Historian Eric Hobsbawm concludes in his book The Age of Extremes: «The most dramatic and far-reaching social change of the second half of this century, and the one which cuts us off for ever from the world of the past, is the death of the peasantry.» But in contrast to the decline in industrial employment, hardly any politician complains about the loss of peasantry. This is because the progress of agriculture – not only in the USA – is regarded as a great achievement of mankind. Fewer and fewer people must work hard to feed themselves and society.

Behind the promises of increased efficiency and sustainability is the mass collection and analysis of data. All details about farms, cultivation methods, consumers, and farmers are collected and stored. Agricultural companies, such as Bayer and Deere, and Internet companies, such as Amazon and Google, have long since acquired sovereignty over the digitization of agriculture. By merging companies, they are consolidating their dominance in the agricultural sector as well as in crucial parts of the agricultural supply chain. The gene seed and glyphosate manufacturer Monsanto (now a Bayer subsidiary), acquired various technology manufacturers, software companies, and data analysis companies years ago. Bayer, the world's largest seed company, is using the digitization of agriculture to make farmers even more dependent on its products: The Seed Advisor software module only recommends Bayer's grain maize to farmers – not from other manufacturers. The global picture of agriculture is still incredibly diverse. There are the giant cornfields of North America, the huge farms in Russia, the rice farmers in Asia, and the tomato growers in the greenhouses of the Netherlands. There are globalized companies with several thousand acres of arable land – and the peasants in Africa or India who try to grow rice and cassava for the family on just a few acres. The mechanization and digital networking of agriculture will increase the gap between developed and developing countries, between the agro-industrial and the small self-sufficient. In the end, the peasantry may disappear completely. Many people prefer to work in an office to the drudgery in a field. But what if office jobs become scarce too?

Another reason for the decline of parts of the U.S. economy is the loss of jobs due to offshoring. Pandering to his xenophobic base, Trump claims: The Chinese have stolen jobs from the U.S. – he is wrong about that too. It's not China that is to blame for the job losses, but Silicon Valley. Technology and globalization are inseparable. To be precise: Technical progress has made offshoring possible in the first place. The large tech companies are the biggest beneficiaries of globalization, and they have been able to open up new markets.

For decades, computer manufacturers have moved their production facilities abroad. IBM built production plants outside the USA as early as the 1950s. In the 1960s, software engineering was considered a solid career path. At cocktail parties, you could hold your head up high and tell people that you were a programmer. Programmers were in demand and respected. Today, if you tell people you're a programmer, they'll ask you how long you have until your unemployment benefits run out. In the 90s, the IT industry began to transfer software development abroad too. India with its large number of well-educated English-speaking workers was the first country to benefit from this trend. It's still the number one in global outsourcing and software development.

SAP is one of the most popular employers in India. Around 90,000 university graduates apply to the company every year. Indian companies such as Infosys and Wipro even count up to one million applications every year. The age of those starting their careers in the Indian IT industry is significantly lower than in Europe or America. At the age of 24, many Indians have their university degree and are looking for a job. Why would someone hire a graduate in the United States for 30,000 dollars per year when they can get an equally educated person in India for much less? Knowledge work such as accounting and legal services has already been transferred. These jobs will probably remain there, but will be done by computers.

Not only offshoring benefits from technical progress. «Crowdsourcing, » «crowdworking, » or «gig-economy» is the outsourcing of work to people all over the world. Do you remember how the serfs used to walk in the Middle Ages? Paintings show a bent posture when one of the lords was nearby. Have you ever wondered what the many people who stare at their smartphones reminds you of? The gig economy creates a new class of serfs: pitiful creatures who compete with each other for many small jobs. The work offered by the platform economy covers a variety of tasks such as marketing, graphic design, technical and creative writing, translation, and programming. You can use it to order food or housecleaning services, but also architects, engineers, lawyers, and financial advisors offer their services via apps.

The Silicon Valley start-up Upwork employed an estimated ten million people in 2019. Exact figures are not available, as the platforms don't publish them, and the government makes no attempt to statistically record these jobs. A huge labor market arises, which – regarding the rights of the employees – is reminiscent of the 19th century. The platforms argue that with their help employees can better balance their private and professional lives, working hours can be more flexibly distributed throughout the day. But this 'flexibility' dissolves the boundary between work and private life which harms the latter.

As a rule, payment is per gig, i.e. per order: per trip, delivered food, or cleaned apartment. Often the pay is so low that they can hardly keep their heads above water. Almost nobody can survive with one job only. People who work in the gig economy often do so in part-time or in second or third jobs. They are often students, newcomers, drop-outs, and stranded. Social security doesn't exist. Those who are not constantly available have little chance of a long-term employment or career advancement. The work is largely unregulated.

It reminds of Taylorism: The work is split into many small tasks and distributed to the mass of day laborers. Monitoring is omnipresent. The employers collect data not only from individual employees, but from all. This enables them to create profiles and use them for control. Technically, these people may be self-employed. In reality, however, the employer often tells them exactly how to do their job.

This is also the case with the food delivery services Foodora and Deliveroo, two typical examples of the gig economy. Both companies emphasize the autonomy of their couriers. On its recruitment website, Deliveroo promises: «Working with Deliveroo gives you flexibility and independence. » Foodora also advertises with slogans like «have a super flexible job. » At a closer look, this is neither the case with Foodora nor Deliveroo. Both companies use an evaluation system for their couriers. The better the score, the earlier one is allowed to sign up for the working hours to be assigned. The couriers don't know what criteria are used, cannot evaluate them or check whether shifts are assigned accordingly. Each individual work step is specified and controlled by the app: The couriers receive an offer for a job via the app. Then they have to decide whether to accept the tour, that's a click. Once they have arrived at the restaurant, another click. When they have received the food, the next click. Arrived at the customer, the next click. So the couriers have to enter everything they do into the app. While the couriers are fully transparent to the company, they themselves don't have enough information to make rational decisions. Communication between the companies and the couriers is limited. When they are offered a tour, they are initially only told where to pick up the food, not where the customer lives. When they decide to accept or decline the tour, they don't know how long they will be sitting on the bike. But if they don't know the distance, they can't calculate their hourly wage. Furthermore, the couriers don't know how many colleagues are working at the same time, which means, they don't know how likely it is that they will actually get a job during their working hours. Since they have much less information than their employer, they are dependent on its precise instructions. Employers thus have greater control and employees greater dependency. A clear power advantage.

Debra Howcroft from the University of Manchester, UK, and Birgitta Bergvall-Kåreborn from the Luleå University of Technology, Sweden, concluded that due to their information disadvantage the «workers [in the gig economy] are unable to make judgments about the moral valence of their work. » Many find it pleasant not to have human superiors, since it's easier to ignore what an app says, and it's harder to resist when a supervisor gives you a personal instruction. The disadvantage, however, is that you can't argue with an app. You don't have the opportunity to bring yourself and your arguments to the table.

Uber, a John Doerr–backed ridesharing company, is basically a globally operating taxi company that refuses its drivers permanent employment, the minimum wage, social benefits, and safety standards. It avoids to pay taxes, and the drivers must bring their own cars. The business model includes reducing costs through non-compliance with legal standards, such as the various taxi regulations for the technical safety of the car and the safety of the drivers and customers. When the city of Portland banned the company in 2014 because it was breaking the law, Kalanick simply ignored it. The head of the Portland Department of Transportation was stunned: «They think they can just come in here and flagrantly violate the law?, » Steve Novick told The Oregonian. «This is really amazing. Apparently, they believe they're gods. » There is similar resistance in many cities, including in Great Britain, where the local taxi regulator TfL (Transport for London) did not renew Uber's license in September 2018. Uber appealed against this, and until a final decision has been made Uber drivers may continue to offer their services. For Kalanick these problems are only skirmishes in a larger fight. His «vision» is to turn Uber into a global transport service that will make it possible for the people to do without their own cars, at least in large cities. He wants Uber to become a mobility giant that transports not only people, but also goods everywhere, ideally in a car without a human driver.

To take an Uber is not always cheaper, but 'modern.' Uber became the pioneer of the gig economy with a market value higher than that of Ford or General Motors. Its headquarters are in a hostile concrete monolith on Market Street in San Francisco. Inside, perfect startup kitsch: lots of glass, wood, and open offices, gray-black-white furniture, monochrome photographs of Death Valley on the walls, no daylight on most floors. You can hardly see the streets, where the company makes its money. You also won't meet drivers in the headquarters – not surprisingly, since the company is eager to portray drivers as freelance service providers and not as employees. The reality of the drivers flows in only algorithmically filtered. Even if you ask the drivers personally, you only learn about their everyday lives in a filtered way. The customers have to evaluate every ride according to a five-point system. If the driver falls below a certain point average, they have to undergo a training. Uber drivers are always in a great mood and find Uber incredibly great. It's always the other drivers who have issues, but not oneself. If you, by chance, find a former driver, it sounds different: how low the drivers earn, how exhausting the incentive systems of the companies are. Allegedly, an Uber driver earns more than a taxi driver, but this is simply not true. The entrepreneurial risk is entirely passed on to the drivers. Being your «own» boss means, you have to pay all costs for acquisition, maintenance, and care of the car yourself, as well as traffic fines, accidents, health care, retirement provisions, costs of driving training (in many countries the driving license is significantly more expensive than in the U.S.), etc. «Uber is software [that] eats taxis, » an admiring Marc Andreessen described the service. That's not all it eats. Uber attacks not only the taxi business, but the car ownership itself. If autonomous driving succeeds, Uber drivers have had their day (taxi drivers also).

THE ROBOTS ARE COMING, THE ROBOTS ARE COMING!

«If only it weren't for the people, the goddamned people, » said Finnerty, «always getting tangled up in the machinery. If it weren't for them, earth would be an engineer's paradise. »
– Kurt Vonnegut

You probably know it: The term «robot» appears for the first time in the 1921 Czech play, R.U.R. (Rossum's Universal Robots) by Karel Capek. The Czech word «robota» translates as work(er), serf, or slave. It refers to the «robota economy, » a feudal system in which peasants had to provide surplus labor for their landlords. In 1923, the term entered the English language after a performance of the play in London. «Everyone Should have a Robot!, » recommended the fictitious American company R.U.R., «Reduce the Cost of your Products! » – it's «the Cheapest Workforce You Can Get. » With its artificial humans the company wants to free humanity from humiliating and hard work. But that didn't quite succeed. The workers revolt because they lose their jobs. The ruling class then arms the robots to break the resistance. In the play's final act, the robots turn against their creators and murder most humans.
The murderous machinery of World War I left Capek in doubt about technical progress, and the ambivalent relationship between man and technology became a central point of his work. Ironically, though Capek

didn't like the play very much, it was a phenomenal success which brought him international attention, but surprisingly little money. Audiences were thrilled by the mechanical man. Capek protested against being misunderstood as his robots were not machines, but artificial humans. As Capek himself put it: «It's with horror, frankly, that he rejects all responsibility for the idea that metal contraptions could ever replace human beings, and that by means of wires they could awaken something like life, love, or rebellion. He would deem this dark prospect to be either an overestimation of machines, or a grave offence against life,» he wrote in 1935 talking about himself in the third person. Capek's robots were intended as a mirror of ourselves, our misguided aims. He wanted to warn the world against the excesses of scientism and technocracy. We shouldn't fear robots, rather, we should fear ourselves. But despite his protest, we've been misusing the term ever since.

Two decades later, Isaac Asimov coined the term «robotics» in his short story Runaround, a term that has established itself in science as a term for dealing with robot technologies. Asimov would be surprised that there is no uprising against the takeover of more and more jobs. Although he was no opponent of technology, all his novels end in a dystopia.

Robots never get tired or in a bad mood, they can do almost everything humans can, and they do it without complaint 24/7. They work in the dark, in rain, and snow. Machines have no social needs, don't want money, don't go on holiday, and don't hang around in bars, or become addicted to drugs. Via ubiquitous networks, robots have direct access to the entire knowledge of humankind. It enables robots to learn much faster, e.g. how to shake your hands, before they take your job.

The networking of robots poses a new danger. Many of the robots used in the industrial and private sectors can easily be hacked and turned into malfunctioning machines. Hacked robots can spy on workers or even attack them. Cyber criminals could secretly record audio and video, which opens a whole new area for criminals to steal private information.

An increasing degree of automation also creates new challenges in the field safety at the working place. In a collision between man and machine, it's the machine who will win. Heavy robots can cause life-threatening injuries. In 2018, a 49-year-old Chinese worker experienced what sharp-edged tools such as clamps and pliers can do. After a robot malfunction, ten metal rods, each about 12 inches long, pierced his shoulder and upper arm and barely missed a vital artery. Fatal accidents with robots are fortunately rare, but they do happen. Robert Williams, a Ford worker, is the first known human to be killed by a robot after being hit on the head by the arm of an industrial robot. That was in 1979.

In an interview, Bill Gates said it's only a matter of time before robots replace humans in a substantial number. «Work won't be the central, almost religious activity it's today. That's an inevitability,» he said. «Then you'll have all sorts of philosophical questions about purpose. » Gates warned that the state will lose the income tax because robots will be working instead of humans in the future. His solution sounds very simple: «If a robot comes in to do the same thing [as a human worker], you'd think that we'd tax the robot at a similar level. » How about paying the taxes that Microsoft & Co. never paid?

By far the fastest-growing market for robots is China. Considering the size of China's workforce as well as the low wages and harsh working conditions that is surprising. «No matter what job you name, robots will be able to do it, » says the journalist Kevin Drum. «They will manufacture themselves, program themselves, repair themselves, and manage themselves. If you don't appreciate this, then you don't appreciate what's barreling toward us. » According to Drum, no capitalist with a clear mind would continue to employ people. It's still people who carry out most of the tasks in the economic cycle worldwide – but for how long?

Logistics and warehouse management have long been typical workplaces for unskilled and low-skilled workers. But here too, automation is making steady progress. Complaints by workers about poor working conditions will soon no longer be a problem for Amazon & Co. Amazon started using robots in 2012. According to the company blog, robots make a major contribution to efficiency. More than 100,000 robots are currently in use at its subsidiaries around the globe. Autonomous robots transport pallets through the halls or lift packages to different shelves. Boredom or muscle ache are not part of their programmed options. Human labor could be almost completely eliminated from the entire process. Barcode scanners, warehouse management systems, and warehouse robots have already replaced several jobs.

Trucks are equipped with GPS devices to locate them at any time – a prerequisite for autonomous driving. Google believes it can revolutionize the transport industry within only a few years. Sergey Brin hopes that driverless cars will «dramatically change society:» More road safety and the reduction of fatalities by robot drivers who are never drunk or distracted. He promises more time for people who don't have to drive themselves. And it would give us back the landscapes and urban spaces that are currently wasted for garages and car parks. That's the big goal, as Brin put it in a rare interview with the Guardian in 2014: «So with self-driving cars, you don't really need much in the way of parking, because you don't need one car per person. They just come and get you when you need them. » It's not a question whether autonomous cars will be driving in large numbers on our roads, but only when. In 2017, the German chancellor Angela Merkel made a bold forecast: «In 20 years, we will need a permission to drive a car ourselves. » That is surprising, since Germans and cars come in a package. On the other hand, they usually do what they say. In fact, the conventional car has long since

205

become a wheeled computer: navigation, entertainment, and on-board electronics – everything is powered by software. Autonomous cars will connect to the Internet, other cars, the environment and satellites to react to possible dangers and the behavior of other road users. A car that is permanently online can become the target of hackers just as much as any PC connected to the Internet. Autonomous vehicles will likely need regular software updates – and according to Google, it should be primarily its own software.

Asked whether robots will replace humans, Larry Page claimed that many people don't enjoy their work: «The idea that everyone should slavishly work so they do something inefficiently so they keep their job – that just doesn't make any sense to me. That can't be the right answer. » To him, robotics is an area with many opportunities to fulfil his plan to make the world more efficient, productive and cost-effective. Thus, prices would fall, and we could more easily meet our basic needs such as food, clothing, shelter, and safety. «You can spend more time with your children, » he said encouragingly. The world just needs to be better organized. «When we have too many workers, then let us start to reduce working hours. I just asked people, everyone is happy to have a few more days of vacation. » The progress in robotics is not driven by humanistic idealists who want to liberate man from heavy work. It's driven by capitalists who want to liberate profit from the cost factor man. According to the Labor Department there are roughly 2.4 million truck drivers in America, almost exclusively men. Hillary Clinton is very concerned about the job losses: «You know, driverless cars may be an exciting new step in transportation, but that means a lot of trucks and cabbies and Uber drivers and a lot of other people may well lose jobs, » Clinton told in an interview. And asked: «So how do we think about that? » She believes the United States is not prepared for the «advanced technological economy. »

Robots may not yet take over all the demanding tasks of human personnel, but in some activities they are already superior. So far, one of the basic rules in robotics has been that tasks that are difficult for humans, such as precise welding, are often easy for machines. Many tasks that are easy for people, like clearing dishes after dinner, are hard for machines. That's about to change. In hotels, reception staff could be replaced by always happy and friendly robots. In the gastronomy industry, waiters and waitresses could be replaced by machines, which would be faster and remember the orders better. The almost fully automated vegetarian restaurant Eatsa opened its doors in September 2015 in San Francisco. Its founders have plans for all America. Cleaning robots will clean the most unhygienic spots and perform tasks that are unpleasant for humans. Window cleaning at dizzying heights no longer needs to be done by specialist staff. Vacuum robots are already replacing cleaning staff. In a few years, it could thus be dispensable. Assembly and manufacturing could be replaced on a large scale in some industrial sectors.

Here, too, the best example is the car industry. In 1955, labor leader Walter Reuther visited a Ford Motor Company factory that had recently been automated. His host was Henry Ford II, grandson of the company founder. Ford pointed to all the robots and then asked Reuther: «Walter, how will you get robots to pay union dues? » Without hesitation, Reuther replied: «Henry, how will you get robots to buy cars? »

ROBOTS DON'T GO SHOPPING

«If we have some perfect and shining machine before our eyes, we see in it man's triumph. To realize man's defeat, we only need to set beside that splendid machine the first beggar we meet. » – Karel Capek

«The sky above the port was the color of television, tuned to a dead channel. » – that's the first sentence of Neuromancer. William Gibson takes the reader into a desperate, dystopic future. When you look at its social and political structure, it's hardly different from our real world. Technology is omnipotent, as is organized crime, drug addiction, and corruption. Multinational conglomerates dominate the economy and politics. Cyberspace is an indispensable workspace for billions of people, who depend on their access to the machine. But it's also an instrument of social exclusion. The world of Neuromancer is bleak and hopeless. The urban centers have developed into large, ulcer-like structures. Large parts of the population lives in the outskirts, the slums, struggling to survive. The technology changes nothing at all. The poor remain poor, the rich remain rich. Social advancement is hardly possible, the upper class walls itself in.
A 2013 study by Oxford University on the future of work estimates that 47 percent of jobs in America are «at risk» of being automated in the next 20 years. This fear is not new: «Intelligent machines are replacing human beings in countless tasks, forcing millions of blue and white collar workers into unemployment lines, or worse still, breadlines, » wrote the economist Jeremy Rifkin already in his 1995 bestseller The End of Work. Erik Brynjolfsson and Andrew McAfee warn: «We think that is the most important challenge before us … Many don't even realize that they are in the midst of this tidal wave of change. » The fact that this change will take place is largely undisputed. Eric

Schmidt predicted that job scarcity will be the biggest public issue for the next two or three decades. Larry Page also devotes a lot of time on this issue and believes it to be «a life-changing kind of thing, » admitting that these changes can be frightening. Yet he sticks to his optimism, predicting that technology allows more flexibility. Employees can better manage their time and will have to work less. Not only he doesn't feel like working a nine-to-five, he even seems not to understand the value of work for other people. In our economy, income distribution is largely based on what workers earn. The growing automation is increasing the supply of labor, which inevitably results in wage pressure. If labor becomes less scarce and thus less important, it becomes also less economically valuable. There will still be work to be done, but work will be different in the shadow of the machines. Well-paid jobs are becoming scarce, a phenomenon that has been observed for some time. How will society deal with the fact that only a small elite earns money and the rest is left behind?

After the first industrial revolutions, it took many generations before the workers could participate in the wealth they created. Now it looks like they will no longer play a role in the future at all. Digital technology is doing everything it can to make the working class obsolete. Jobs may be «dumbed down, » defined by low demands on skills and low wages. Less qualified people only get jobs with which one can hardly survive. They'll have to move from one job to the next – as an Uber-driver, food courier, or product tester. «People will work longer hours for less money, income will be fragmented, the safety net will be a distant memory, and work environments will have less ideal and less carefully monitored conditions, » wrote Arun Sundararajan in The Sharing Economy. As a consequence, the pressure on the middle class will increase too. «Wages for many Americans fell well short of historical growth rates and even fell in real terms for many groups as technology transformed their industries, » says McAfee. In his book Who owns the future?, Jaron Lanier warns that in a technologized capitalism the global middle class is becoming the big loser, while a digital entrepreneur elite is becoming increasingly powerful.

Another problem is that machines don't generate consumer demand, the most important pillar of the economy. A worker is also a consumer and supports other consumers. It's these people who steer demand. If an employee is replaced by a machine, this machine will not go shopping after work. The machine will need energy and spare parts, and it will also have to be serviced, but these are mere business expenses. If nobody buys what the machine produces, it will eventually be shut down. An industrial robot in a car factory will not remain in operation if no one buys the cars it assembles. If automation destroys jobs to a considerable extent or if wages are squeezed to the point where few people have any significant free disposable income, how can the modern mass market economy continue to exist?

In the conflict between man and machine, many workers will lose. History teaches us that industrial disruptions are brutal for those left behind. Those without money – most of us – will live on little crumbs the rich throw to us. That there are good opportunities for parts of the population could further worsen the situation of people, who don't succeed. They will be blamed for failing. Former social formations always had reasonably respected places available for poor performers, however modest, but digitalized knowledge societies may not. Failing would then be seen as an individual fate.

For most of us, education is the key to a better income. Education offers workers and employees a lifelong pathway through working life. Or at least it used to be. Those who are capable of learning could step into new, higherskill roles. Economist Paul Krugman reviewed some recent economic data and predicted that we are at the beginning of a new era. In a blog post entitled Rise of the Robots, he noted that our traditional belief in qualification and training as the key to material success may be outdated. In the future, people without marketable education, whether they are unable or unwilling to acquire qualifications, will be pushed to the fringes of society. There are hardly any jobs left for them in a knowledge society. A bus driver, taxi driver, or insurance agent who loses their job doesn't become a virtual reality designer or data analyst. The labor market forces many people without the necessary skills to accept poor pay. The feeling that they are useless and in need of charity will spread among those affected. «There's no question that there will be new things in the future, » author Martin Ford says, «but the assumption that economists are making is that those industries are going to be labor-intensive, that there are going to be lots of jobs there. But the fact is we don't see that anymore. »

Of course, they still exist, the jobs with good incomes. But they are usually bought at a high price: With extreme pressure to perform and constant availability, with a life for work in which there is hardly any room for family, friends, and leisure. And even for skilled workers and academics, adequate incomes are no longer guaranteed. A university degree doesn't protect against low wages or the constant insecurity of temporary jobs and precarious self-employment.

Do we really want to live that way? Do we want a society in which the elbows are used more and more ruthlessly, because everyone is constantly afraid of falling down in the worst case and having to join the army of losers? An army, from which there is all too often no return. Do we want insecurity and worries about the future to dominate our everyday lives and to be sold to us as new freedom? Do we really think it's normal that the majority, under increasing pressure, has to fight to even maintain their standard of living, while few sail the world's oceans on their luxury yachts?

ROBOTS FIRED THE FIRST SHOT

«Primitive man pelted his enemies with rocks and stones. Thousands of years later, modern man fights his enemies with guns and grenades and what have you. Primitive man was violent and aggressive and so are we. Do you call that progress?» – Jiddu Krishnamurti

«A strange game. The only winning move is not to play.» – WOPR, the supercomputer in WarGames

The year is 1983, Ronald Reagan is President of the United States. His counterpart in the former Soviet Union is Yuri Andropov. They each control numerous nuclear weapons in submarines, aircraft, and missiles. Enough to destroy the whole planet several times. Radar and satellites observe the sky. The military hopes to see an attack in time and launch a counter-strike. In Colorado, deep in the Rocky Mountains, is the headquarters of NORAD, the North American Aerospace Defense Command. NORAD computers collect data from air and space surveillance and evaluate them around the clock. That is the setting for the movie WarGames. The plot was simple: Matthew Broderick plays a tech-whiz teenager, who hacks into the NORAD computer – WOPR – and in doing so he almost triggers World War III, thinking that he's playing a new computer game. At the end, everything turns out well. WOPR can be talked out of its programmed world war plans, and hacker David gets the girl he fell in love with. A Hollywood fairy tale – but one with real world consequences.

For the first time, the nerd became the hero. The scriptwriters got a lot of input from a real nerd from Los Angeles: David Scott Lewis. Viewers learned about computer networks, hackers, password barriers, and program backdoors. Inspired by the movie, the 414s hacker group broke into dozens of systems. In 2008, Google hosted a 25th-anniversary screening of WarGames. «Many of us grew up with this movie,» said Sergey Brin. «It was a key movie of a generation, especially for those of us who got into computing.» What Google doesn't like to talk about: the complex and multifarious allegiances between engineers, scientists, businesses, and the military.

War is in the DNA of Silicon Valley. «Across the spectrum of high-technology industries,» engineering professor Nathan Newman wrote, «the single overwhelming factor correlating with the rise of technology firms in any region is the level of defense spending.» Or as John Hanke, an Internet CEO and one of the creators of Google Earth, put it: «The whole history of Silicon Valley is tied up pretty closely with the military.» In 2013, Eric Schmidt admitted: «What Lockheed Martin was to the twentieth century, technology and cybersecurity companies will be to the twenty-first.» Schmidt is now also Chairman of the Pentagon's Defense Innovation Advisory Board. Google's search engine, GPS, or the internet wouldn't exist unless the military had been «willing to pay millions of dollars per user to make it possible.» The journalist Peter Nowak believes, that it is «almost impossible to separate any American-made technology from the American military.» Joseph Weizenbaum has pointed out, that military interests determined the development of the computer, and computer technology still carries these Cain marks. For this reason alone, it cannot be said that the computer is a neutral technology. The technological and military intelligence complex still work together – and it's beneficial for both sides. And it's not only Google, other IT companies also want to do business with the military. Amazon provides the Pentagon with its facial recognition software. Microsoft has secured an order from the CIA to build an ultra-secure cloud for its data. The contracts are worth billions.

While the USA exported the ideas of free market and deregulation to the rest of the world, by force if necessary, it was silently protecting its technological start-ups from competition. The Pentagon itself invests in technology start-ups via its investment entity Defence Innovation Unit (DIUx). DIUx is located in Mountain View in the middle of Silicon Valley and is supposed to repeat DARPA's successes. With its help, the Pentagon tries to secure ideas in the early stages of development. Billions are invested in the development and acquisition of drones and other remote-controlled robotic vehicles.

We all know the names of drones, weapon systems and Army aircraft from the news: Tomahawk, Thunderbirds missile, Apache, Black Hawk, etc. This naming is cynical. The war with the Apaches, for example, cost more money and lives than any other Indian war. The last Apache chief, Geronimo, surrendered on September 4, 1886. After the killing of al-Qaida leader Osama Bin Laden, it turned out that his code name was «Geronimo.» The CIA has a sense of humor, and now the world knows it. In April 2017, the U.S. military used a weapon in eastern Afghanistan that the media called the «mother of all bombs» – a gross euphemism. There are drones called Predator and Reaper. The names imply that the act of killing by drones is normal and something natural, as if a predator kills another animal.

The USA now trains more drone pilots than conventional pilots. The use of drones has become a global trend. Nowhere is the double standard of the

West more apparent. Leading media such as the New York Times or the Washington Post have reported on the killing of alleged terrorists in drone missions, although it later turned out that the killed were not terrorists. U.S. drones also kill people who don't take part in combat operations. The number of civilians killed in these attacks is not disclosed. In 2013, the 13-year-old Pakistani boy Zubair told Congress: «I no longer love blue skies. In fact, I now prefer grey skies. The drones do not fly when the skies are grey.» The drone attacks undermine the rule of law. If the killed people were accused of a crime, then the state must take legal action against them: indictment, trial, conviction.

Currently, humans still control the drones. But as soon as the machines can give instructions to themselves, there is a risk that humans will be permanently removed from the process. In the eyes of the military, humans are the weakest and most unreliable link within military technical systems. The perfect soldier kills without scruples, follows orders, and doesn't get tired. The perfect soldier is a machine. The next logic step is fully automated vehicles, robots, drones, and submarines that make their own decisions about whom to kill and whom not to kill. Robot guns and police robots are already in use. In the «demilitarized» zone between North and South Korea, a fleet of semi-autonomous SGR-A1 combat robots, developed by the Samsung subsidiary Techwin, patrols day and night. The SGR-A1 is equipped with a machine gun that fires automatically and is supposed to detect the enemy over a distance of four kilometers with motion sensors and a thermal imaging camera. The military possibilities are unbearably nightmarish.

By 2015, more than a twenty thousand scientists and IT entrepreneurs, including Stephen Hawking, Steve Wozniak, Elon Musk, and Noam Chomsky called for a ban on autonomous weapons. In an open letter they warned: «If any major military power pushes ahead with AI weapon development, a global arms race is virtually inevitable, and the endpoint of this technological trajectory is obvious: autonomous weapons will become the Kalashnikovs of tomorrow.» Killer robots could be the «third revolution in warfare» after gunpowder and nuclear weapons. Many experts are convinced that we are heading for a dystopian climax. The new wars don't need expensive equipment like combat planes or tanks. They can also be fought with drones. That would reduce material costs and political risks of warfare, lowering the threshold to war.

Stuart Russell, Professor of Computer Science at the University of California and one of the leading researchers on artificial intelligence, has recently published a short science fiction clip: The CEO of a company performs a product launch in the same Riefenstahl aesthetic as the presentations of Steve Jobs used to be. The product is a hand-sized drone, equipped with three grams of explosives and a facial recognition system which targets and eliminates the victim automatically. Thousands of such slaughterbots could swarm out and wipe out half a city, praises the CEO. Such weapons also play into the hands of enemies, who will get efficient high-tech weapons. Although the spread of weapons of mass destruction is to be prevented by all means, it's hard to imagine how the spread of drones or robots could be prevented. As drones become smaller, cheaper, and better, the acquisition and operation of drones and robots will become easier. Moreover, the weapon systems could fall into the hands of dictators. Ruthless tyrants armed with such killer robots could better control their peoples. Warlords could carry out ethnic cleansing and would not have to fear that their soldiers might turn against them, no matter how heartless and insane their orders. The «weapons of the little man, » equipped with dirty bombs, chemical, or biological weapons, could also be used for terrorist attacks. The terrorists don't have to fear imprisonment nor injuries or death.

The advocates of the new technology argue that autonomous weapons avoid collateral damage.

Drone strikes are allegedly more precise than bomb attacks. Roboticist Ronald Arkin of the Georgia Institute of Technology argues that autonomous weapons are even more moral than human soldiers because they don't feel anger or desire for revenge, and thus lack «human inhumanity. » Autonomous weapons systems could, as cynical as it sounds, make war more «humane» because fewer human lives are sacrificed. In the end, no more people will be sent to war as soldiers. Machines fight against machines, and people live on undisturbed at the same time. Who is supposed to believe that? And anyway: Do we really have to take the chance? The French computer scientist Jean-Paul Delahaye thinks the argument of «clean» warfare is wrong. Autonomous weapons are an incalculable risk. Because there are an infinite number of scenarios, these weapons cannot be adjusted to all of them. It's practically impossible to program a killer robot with rules like «Don't aim at civilians» or «Attack only the enemy. » Even if it were possible to program morale into a machine, it could be deleted at any time.

Studies by the American psychologists Gresham M. Sykes and David Matza, who have investigated the behavior of criminals, show that humans are capable of committing crimes precisely because they can switch off their own morals and dehumanize victims. A person in bloodlust behaves like a killer robot.

Battles with autonomous weapons become battles beyond human control, for artificial intelligence will be faster than anything humanly possible. Ever since the military began using combat robots, there have been many deadly accidents. In 2007, ten soldiers died in South Africa, when a computer-controlled cannon suddenly turned to them and shot off its magazine. However, where autonomous weapon systems attract billions of dollars in business, moral concerns will take second place.

The perspectives of cyber warfare are downright frightening. The USA and its closest allies are among the most active participants in the ever-expanding «cyber war,» but Russia, China, Israel, as well as criminals and activist hackers also play a role. Due to the anonymity of the networks, aggressors can remain undetected. Particularly at risk are critical infrastructures such as transport networks, telecommunications, energy companies, water supply, hospitals, financial institutions, military facilities, and voting machines. If it's possible to manipulate these controls over a long period, considerable damage can be caused.

A spectacular example is Stuxnet, a malicious program with which the presumably American-Israeli attackers at least temporarily turned off the Iranian uranium enrichment plant at Natanz in 2010.

How much damage was caused by Stuxnet is unknown. Experts believe that the Iranian nuclear program was severely set back by the attack. The same effect could have been achieved with air attacks on such a facility, but such a step would have been a declaration of war. Already during the Cold War, conflicts emerged that were below the threshold of a major, openly declared war. The superpowers fueled such conflicts to pursue their geopolitical interests and supported or fought various armed groups with military or financial means. The structure of cyber conflicts is just as opaque. But just because you don't 'see' a war doesn't mean it isn't being fought. In their book LikeWar: The Weaponization of Social Media, the authors Peter W. Singer and Emerson T. Brooking describe how Twitter, Facebook, YouTube, and the like could become a virtual war zone. There are confusingly many actors fighting with the means of propaganda and disinformation. Smartly operating groups and entire governments exploit the viral nature of content and human perception. Syria is only one example of how dictatorships quickly adapt to the development of social media. Bashar al-Assad's regime uses these new media for disinformation campaigns, to spread their doctrinal message, and to identify and discredit dissidents.

The problem with this type of warfare is that the clear objective of the operation is lost: There is no defined end, no peace agreement, no post-war order, no formal agreement on the resulting power shifts. During the Cold War, nuclear deterrence provided clear strategies. But that cannot work in cyberspace. The risk with cyberattacks is that they are accompanied by a certain loss of control. Complex attacks such as the Stuxnet attack may not only cause financial damage. Under certain circumstances and depending on the location, they entail the risk to cause life-threatening explosions. If a cyberattack is conceived as a violation of state sovereignty, then perhaps it unintentionally triggers a conventional war.

For a long time, the Internet was considered to be a «parallel universe» that would have little or no significant influence on the real world. Cyberspace is now officially a new realm of operation for NATO, the Fifth Dimension of

Warfare, complementing the four classical dimensions: land, sea, air, and space. Cyberattacks could now even trigger article 5 of NATO's founding treaty, collective defense by the other NATO states would be the consequence – yet the exact definition of cyberwar is classified.

MONEY FOR NOTHING

«Social change is not a project that one group of people carries out for the benefit of another. »
– The Baha'i Universal House of Justice

«Where we are free of our labors
and joined back to nature…
and all watched over
by machines of loving grace. »
– Richard Brautigan

It was July 6, 1535, before dawn, an envoy of the king delivered cruel news to the prisoner Thomas More in his cell in the Tower of London: In a few hours he would be executed. More was 57 years old. He had long been one of England's most influential personalities and a close confidant of King Henry VIII. But when the king declared himself head of the Church in England, More, a brave Catholic, refused him the oath of allegiance. He was subsequently accused of treason and with the help of a false witness convicted. At least, Henry was so gracious not to have him disemboweled and quartered (live), as was customary with traitors, but only beheaded. In 1886, the Catholic Church beatified him.

But Thomas More doesn't owe his fame to his martyrdom. He is unforgotten for his book about the fictitious island of Utopia, published in 1516: Somewhere in the ocean, a traveler encounters an alternative society. His report on the customs and habits of this society was a sharp criticism of the conditions in England, even if it's «only» a fiction. More, for example, considered the death penalty for thieves to be unjust and absurd. People who suffer from hunger are indifferent to any punishment and thus incapable of guilt, he thought. That's why More wanted to eliminate misery and poverty that he regarded as the causes of crime. His Utopian society is egalitarian.

There is no conflict because people produce more than they can consume. There is no useless, parasitic class of nobles, high clergy, and rich. People eat together in community houses. Goods are distributed on demand. They even exchange the houses every ten years after the lot. The pious More reminds with this vision of the mythical early Christian communities in which the disciples of Jesus shared their possessions. But Utopia is not a pure idyll, there are some rigid obligations.

Anyone who wants to travel needs a permit, whoever travels without such a permit gets whipped. Adultery is punished with slavery, in case of repetition with death. The government regulates the daily routine, the freedom of the people is very restricted. Women have no right to vote. There are no lawyers. All adults are forced to work. «If a man will not work, he shall not eat, » warned the apostle Paul against idleness, and thus shaped European social history. In Utopia, people must choose a profession, such as blacksmith, bricklayer, or weaver. They also have to help in farming on a regular basis. The mandatory working time for everyone is six hours a day, three in the morning and three in the afternoon. To me this seems like a more rigid GDR: housing allotment, planned economy, no private property. It's not the individual who counts, only the collective.

A brave, new utopia is also John Adolphus Etzler's main work The Paradise within the Reach of All Men from 1842. He criticized that machines were used in the wrong way under the conditions of capitalist competition as they make workers superfluous and rob them of their already low wages. If machines were used as he suggested, however, they would be the basis for an ideal society. By fulfilling its «mechanical purposes, » he wrote, the United States would turn itself into a new Eden, a «state of superabundance» where «there will be a continual feast, parties of pleasures, novelties, delights and instructive occupations, » not to mention «vegetables of infinite variety and appearance. » Fear of poverty would not arise, competition would disappear, and the gap between rich and poor would be eliminated. To avoid existential depressions, the extra time could be used to adapt a healthy lifestyle, to educate oneself, and simply to enjoy life. Etzler believed that the general life expectancy could increase to 110 to 170 years. He envisioned a life full of celebrations and enlightening trips to museums, libraries, concerts, and lavish gardens. That makes him probably the prototype of the crazy futurist.

The end of work has been announced many times. According to Andrew Yang the job market will change radically. His vision of the future is downright apocalyptic: If the government doesn't find answers to the «fourth industrial revolution» soon, there will be turmoil and street battles. To reduce the social disruption, Yang's proposes a universal basic income (UBI) in form of a monthly payment. The universal basic income is a favorite topic of the valleyists. The entrepreneurs Elon Musk, Peter Thiel, Richard Branson, Chris Hughes, and the financier Tim Draper have already made positive comments about it. Venture capitalist Marc Andreessen considered it a «very interesting idea.» Albert Wenger, a venture financier, has been blogging about it since 2013. In a speech to Harvard graduates in 2017, Mark Zuckerberg said: «We should explore ideas like universal basic income to give everyone a cushion to try new things.» He's pretty late for Silicon Valley. These entrepreneurs usually argue for an economic model with as little government as possible. Why this favoring of public welfare in this particular case? Evgeny Morozov believes that the tech elite simply fears that people might turn against them as more and more lose their jobs.

The basic income is far from a new idea. One real life example is the Speenhamland system introduced in several counties of England between 1795 and 1834, a period of great misery. At that time, there were two means of combating poverty for those able to work: a minimum wage and a combination of basic security with low wages. The Speenhamland system turned out to harm those it was supposed to help. Wages in rural areas remained low precisely because of it. Employers could get workers at any wage, even the lowest. Employees, on the other hand, had no reason to make any effort at all, as they were paid the same, regardless of whether they worked well, badly, or not at all. Wages dropped further, the dependence of workers on aid became greater. Karl Marx later attacked the system in Das Kapital, pointing out that it created a vicious circle of poverty. In 1834, finally, the «right to income» system was abolished. It followed a period of the greatest mass poverty in the history of England. People were plunged into a labor machine without any social safety net.

Uncertainty about the consequences of digitization is giving new fuel to the debate on the basic income. It appeals to almost all current desires and hopes: freedom, overcoming poverty and misery, participation, self-determination, social cohesion, equal opportunities, greater willingness to take risks while at the same time ensuring security. It has become a projection screen for social change activists across the political spectrum. There is, for example, Charles Murray, a right wing author and racist who has been fantasizing about IQ differences between whites and blacks. All Americans should receive 10,000 dollars a year but also lose any other social benefits like child benefits, housing subsidies, and food stamps. There would be less bureaucracy, Murray says, people would be largely left to their own devices. Left-wing theorists such as Peter Frase and Kathi Weeks argue that the UBI should not replace social welfare, but complement it. Previously unpaid work, like caring for children and the elderly, domestic work, etc., could get financial recognition, women thus could become more independent.

Critics fear that a basic income cannot be financed, and that it would make people dependent and lazy. Who takes the trouble of work if it goes without? Sam Altman, an entrepreneur from Silicon Valley, believes: It's not true, and even if it were, it wouldn't matter. He sees the basic income a «logical consequence, » and lazybones are negligible. It would be so motivating that many people would use their freedom to be innovative and carry out their dreams and ideas. The generated value would be more than enough to compensate for the few lazy people, according to Altman. Such ideas expose the valleyists' contempt for the people. How should those feel who get a basic income because they don't owe machines that generate wealth for them? Or because they 'seem' too stupid to become programmers or data analysts, whether it's true or the result of an ever-increasing competition? How will we fill the time that the technology gives us? Will we philosophize and do yoga all day thanks to robot slaves which will do all the tedious work? Or will we end up like the movie Wall-E suggests: fat, lazy, and semi-debil on a couch? In the 1930s, social psychologist Marie Jahoda and Paul Lazarsfeld pioneered in research into the consequences of unemployment. In a village called Marienthal near Vienna, almost the entire population had become unemployed because the local textile factory shut down. The scientists used the situation to observe the village for several weeks and to meticulously record how people's habits changed. The result: Having a job doesn't only put food on the table. They found resignation and inactivity in a large proportion of the unemployed. Without a fixed timeframe, there was no need to do anything. Even their walking pace slowed down. When they asked them what they did during the day, they hardly knew anything to report. The monotony and lethargy of a life without work didn't contribute to a healthy and happy life. The unemployed constantly perceived stress, while real stress was missing. They suffered depressions which had a damaging effect on their physical health as well. Neither did they enjoy the extra free time to pursue their own interests, nor did they develop any revolutionary consciousness. Rather, the unemployed reacted with resignation and isolation. The village became a «tired community, » characterized by the total loss of community pride. Such a community shows no social commitment or even resistance to undesirable developments.

In the USA and Canada, some communes experimented with a negative income tax in the 1970s. The participants were guaranteed an income at the poverty line for a period of three years. Extra income was taxed, but only in part. The work volumes of families with negative income tax significantly decreased. Employment declined and periods of unemployment became longer. Some younger recipients used the time to go back to school. But the higher education didn't result in an increase in wages. With the job, you lose more than just your income. Work is central to so many areas of life: social integration, status, recognition, rhythm of life, meaning, and identity. A basic income cannot replace all this. Like many ideas that come from Silicon Valley, the basic income would have some advantages, at least to some people. The digital winners would become more powerful. The mass of digital losers would be sentenced to boredom, loneliness, and uselessness. They will become powerless and could no longer influence the direction in which society develops. Virtual reality would suck all energy and rebellious ideas out of them.

The proponents assume that the basic income makes all people good and altruistic. But what if that's not the case? Solidarity is a social contract in which members of a society have decided to support and care for each other. Whoever gets unconditional money cannot be obliged for the community. What if they choose selfishness?

PLANET B

«In some remote corner of the universe, poured out and glittering in innumerable solar systems, there once was a star on which clever animals invented knowledge. That was the highest and most mendacious minute of «world history» – yet only a minute. After nature had drawn a few breaths the star grew cold, and the clever animals had to die. »
– Friedrich Nietzsche

«No more is required, and no more can reasonably be asked, for this planet to remain a place fit for human habitation. » – Hannah Arendt

The apocalypse begins in New Orleans. The city is wrecked by a hurricane, the dams along the Mississippi River break, the entire Gulf Coast from Port Arthur (Texas) to Mobile (Alabama) is flooded. That's only the prelude to a global catastrophe. After an earthquake, the Yangtze River in China leaves its bed and forces its waters towards Hangzhou. «No estimate, even approximate, could yet be made of the loss of life. » All over the world, one catastrophe follows the next. The coasts are reshaping, entire coastal states and river regions disappear from the maps. This apocalyptic vision comes from Karel Capek's War with the Newts from 1936. In Capek's novel, humanity is destroyed by its greed and megalomania. At Sumatra, pearl divers discover an unknown child-sized newt. The highly intelligent animals quickly become a global economic factor. They are forced into slavery and traded on the stock markets in categories such as «leader» or «trash. » Humanity experiences an era of unprecedented progress. The inevitable happens: Technically skilled and armed by competing states, the newts eventually turn against their exploiters. The global community is failing in the face of the threat. At a World Conference in Vaduz, high up in the mountains, the power poker prevents an international strategy to save the earth. What would Capek say about a Donald John Trump who declares climate change a hoax only to please his sponsors from the oil and coal industry?

«The concept of global warming was created by and for the Chinese in order to make U.S. manufacturing non-competitive,» Trump tweeted in November 2012. That tweet alone should have been reason enough not to vote for this corrupt idiot. Or think of the UN climate conference in Madrid in 2019. The states wanted to resolve the split between rich and poor nations over climate funding and cooperation rules, but they could not agree to reduce emissions or even set goals. That's not surprising when the leaders of major economic powers are Trump, Bolsonaro, Xi, and Putin. A handful wealthy and unscrupulous men and some companies that are responsible for most of the CO_2 pollution have spent much time and money lobbying against climate protection. For a quick profit they sacrifice our future.

Fossil fuel corporations like Exxon knew about climate change early on, but they misled the public for decades. In 1977, the leading Exxon scientist James Black predicted climate change. And in 1982, Exxon scientists produced a document predicting an increase in CO_2 emissions, which to this day is almost accurate. The company kept it under lock and key and instead launched a disinformation campaign to manipulate public opinion. The company has sown doubts about climate research and the role of fossil fuels in global warming. It has paid scientists, established think tanks, manipulated studies, spread conspiracy theories, and sent «experts» on talk shows: «Everything's not so bad. » – «Some scientists see it differently. » – «They're still arguing. » – «We don't really know what to do yet. » – And as long as this is the case, we should do nothing. The pseudo-debate is staged by well-paid marketing soldiers to prevent effective action. Their goal is to create a fake public debate that leaves everyone confused in an unproductive way. To this day, «climate skeptics» argue with misleading claims launched by Exxon and others. Governments around the globe continue to treat climate change as a second class threat. And in some cases, politicians have been paid handsomely by oil companies for their «opinions» that climate change was a hoax. Meanwhile, the deniers put forward pseudo-scientific arguments. They disavow the protest of millions of young people who refer to research data as a kind of children's religion. The deniers of global warming ran amok as if they were stabbed in the butt. Then again, pretending to be rational, they praise king coal as if the obsolete and finite resource was indispensable for the survival of humanity. As Greta Thunberg puts it: «The endless conspiracy theories and denial of facts. The lies, hate and bullying of children who communicate and act on the science. All because some adults – terrified of change – so desperately don't want to talk about the #ClimateCrisis This is hope in disguise. We're winning. »

Scientific conclusions about climate change are based on measured data and basic physical understanding. For more than a hundred years, the warming effect of CO2 on the climate has been an accepted science. In the late 1850s, Irish physicist John Tyndall researched the ability of various gases to absorb and re-emit infrared energy. Tyndall discovered the natural greenhouse effect. The phenomenon is scientifically completely undisputed, in fact, the natural greenhouse effect is an essential prerequisite for the emergence of life on Earth. If the atmosphere didn't contain greenhouse gases, the energy reflected and emitted from the Earth's surface would escape into space unhindered. The Swedish chemist Svante Arrhenius contributed another groundbreaking scientific finding. In the second half of the 19th century, factories, locomotives, and power plants all over Europe burned large quantities of coal and emitted huge clouds of smoke. Arrhenius was the first to recognize the close link between industrialization and climate change, and that the use of fossil fuels must lead to long-term warming. The increase in greenhouse gases in the atmosphere is a proven fact. According to the WMO, there are more greenhouse gases in the atmosphere than there have been for almost a million years. The fact that humans are responsible for this also results from the data on our use of fossil energies, and from climate data on tree rings, ice cores, sediments, and corals. The ongoing chemical changes in the atmosphere caused by industrialization, traffic, the destruction of forests, and other human activities make a profound global climate change more and more likely.

We are already experiencing the consequences of global warming: extreme weather, rising sea levels, and the disappearance of Arctic sea ice. In the last 140 years, the average global temperature has increased by 2 degrees Fahrenheit. Global warming has never been as high as now for at least 2000 years. The 20 hottest years since weather records began have all been measured over the past 22 years. The period from 2015 to 2019 is the hottest five-year period ever measured. Summers in Australia are now twice as long as winters. As I write this, the year 2020 is only a few days old: About 12.35 million acres of land have already burned across Australia, and the fires will go on for months. More than half a billion animals and at least 24 people have been killed. At the same time, 26 people died in floods in Jakarta in Indonesia, 62 thousands were evacuated. The Indonesian government is planning to move the entire capital to another location in the near future. Regional natural disasters become more frequent, such as in 2018: drought in summer, forest fires in California, storms all over Italy, Mallorca, and southern France – people feel that things are getting serious. The UN warns that «extreme floods may be the new normal. » The World Meteorological Organization (WMO) speaks of a «clear sign of continuing long-term climate change. »

Unlike preindustrial climate changes, the current man-made climate crisis is occurring simultaneously around the world. And here's where it gets terrifying: Carbon dioxide remains in the atmosphere for centuries. This means that global warming will continue even if we decide to go for a full shutdown. Nobel laureate Paul J. Crutzen wrote in Nature Magazine: «Human activities have reached a level that could damage the systems that keep Earth in the desirable Holocene state. The result could be irreversible and, in some cases, abrupt environmental change, leading to a state less conducive to human development. »

On their 71st birthday, a child born today could live in a world that has become four degrees warmer. They will experience even more weather extremes: Depending on where they live, there will either be too much or too little water. The coasts are more vulnerable than other areas of the world. This is not only true to regions such as Bangladesh and the Caribbean, but also to the American coastal region. 400 million more people than today could live in coastal regions that are flooded every year. Millions of people will flee their homes, due to rising sea levels. They will suffer a massive loss of fertile soils for agriculture. Desertification is progressing. Famines will occur due to reduced yields of corn, soy, and rice. This will lead to impoverishment, refugees, stress, and conflicts over resources. The destruction of ecosystems makes future pandemics more likely. A large part of our infectious pathogens come from animals, including influenza, HIV, and Ebola. By reducing the size of animal habitats, humans come into contact with untouched wildlife, allowing new pathogens to spread from animals to human populations.

Symbols are often a delicate matter. But the famous Doomsday Clock nails it – a decades-old analogue clock, meant to symbolize how close humanity is to its end. The clock reflects the views of leading nuclear and environmental scientists on the dangers of nuclear war, climate change, and risky technologies. In 2018, it was set to two to twelve – the closest to midnight since the first hydrogen bomb detonated in 1953. Recently, the Bulletin set the clock to 100 seconds to midnight – the closest it's ever been. Global warming itself may not be an extinction event for humankind, but it can trigger a chain of events that can very well lead to the end of our civilization. Don't take my word on this, read what economists say from a major bank that finances the exploitation of fossil fuels: «We cannot rule out catastrophic outcomes where human life as we know it's threatened. » This statement comes from a leaked internal report by JPMorgan Chase. How likely is it, if we do not agree on a compromise now, that we will do so later, when conditions worsen?

Digital technology, we've been promised, will save us and magically solve our problems. The opposite is more likely. None of our problems can be solved by means of digitization because it's further accelerating this downward spiral. Digitization is inseparably intertwined with the mass consumption of goods and services. This is also the deeper reason for the constant expansion of digital technology in all countries and areas of life. Capitalism must generate growth if it does not want to fall into crisis mode. And this growth not only means that we produce more, but also that we produce more quickly. Capitalism promotes and needs exponential growth. For Marshall McLuhan, exponential growth was the cause and expression of crises: «Acceleration is a formula for dissolution and breakdown in any organization, » he wrote. A global economic machinery produces vast quantities of goods and, at the same time, vast quantities of toxic waste. It's the radical consequence of an only growth-oriented economy that lacks future. Only the present counts and how its opportunities can be turned into profit. Every year, cellphone manufacturers present their new smartphones at conventions and events. In most cases, however, the new devices don't offer any extra value. There has hardly been an innovative approach in recent years. The manufacture of smartphones is a waste of valuable resources and contributes to exploitation. The Internet has turned into a gigantic energy waster. A Google search consumes as much energy as an energy-saving bulb in an hour. Only part of the electricity is needed to run the computers, at least as much is needed to keep the servers from overheating. If the server farms weren't cooled down, the devices would stop working within a few minutes. The energy demand is not only heating up our planet, it also makes the operation of the Internet increasingly expensive. Thus, the rapid spread of the Internet has become a burden for the earth. The emission of carbon dioxide already equals that of global air traffic. An entire planet, which took over four billion years to develop, is wasted for a growing number of zeros in the accounts of a relatively small number of people.

The disastrous consequences, however, hit the environment and the poor worldwide. More and more people in developing countries are living off electronic scrap recycling. Frequent incineration produces toxic gases containing extremely toxic dioxins, furans, and polycyclic aromatic hydrocarbons. Soils and water are polluted by brominated flame retardants, polychlorinated biphenyls, lead, mercury, cadmium, chromium, and other heavy metals. Exposure to these heavy metals can lead to malformation of the nervous system and cancer. With 29 toxic sites under the EPA's Superfund Program, Silicon Valley is one of the most polluted places in the U.S. It was our belief in technology that created these problems for us. Who regards unreflected technological progress as the solution is either a malicious person who doesn't care about even the most harmful side effects. Or they have internalized the mystical belief in technology and don't want to know exactly whether and how technology works. Or both.

Every new invention that was supposed to solve a problem has created new, even bigger problems. From a historical point of view, we in the Western industrial countries live in the best, safest, most comfortable, and healthiest of all times. These standard of living is based on a steady economic growth. Our triumphant victory over nature has led us into a dead end, and it seems unlikely that a turn is still possible. Given the planetary ecological crisis, the idea of unlimited growth is irresponsible. The problem is: There is no concept for an economic system which is environmentally friendly and at the same time guarantees our standard of living.

As if Silicon Valley hasn't already given us enough, the do-gooders are preparing for the worst-case scenario. Elon Musk sees the future of humanity in becoming a multiplanetary species. He suggests that we populate a few replacement planets as a precaution in case it doesn't go well with earth. Several times he has talked about his ambitious plan to colonize Mars. It would be 'enormously' important to create a self-sufficient basis for humanity there. Mars would be suitable for colonization because there is sunlight and a thin atmosphere. The length of the day is comparable to that on Earth and it's supposedly possible to grow plants. «If there's a third world war, » Musk said, «we want to make sure that there's enough of a seed of human civilization somewhere else to bring civilization back, and perhaps shorten the length of the Dark Ages. » – Sure. At least such thinking explains why the Tesla Cybertruck looks like a scrap car from a Mad Max movie. I have seen photographs of Mars. I don't know about you, but I have no interest in surviving the apocalypse there. According to Musk, the first humans could travel to the Red Planet as early as 2025. It «would be a great adventure, » Musk said. «There need to be things that people look forward to when we wake up in the morning. » In the foreseeable future, about one million people could live on Mars. He actually sounds like someone who smokes pot first thing in the morning. For a better understanding: NASA sees a manned Mars mission in the 2030s at the earliest.

Stephen Hawking was not only a brilliant mathematician, but also a brilliant self-marketer, who used his celebrity to sell books. In his posthumously published essay Short Answers to the Big Questions he answers questions such as 'Will humanity survive?' – We will see. 'Should we colonize space?' – Yes. 'Is there God?' – No. 'Are genetically modified humans threatening humanity?' – Yes. He apparently thought it possible to colonize other planets within the next hundred years. As a scientist, he should have known that with today's technical possibilities that's not very likely.

First, cosmic distances are enormous. Even a flight to Mars would take years. In the entire history of mankind only twelve people set foot on the closest celestial object, the moon. They planted a flag, made some photos, drove around with a vehicle, and collected some rock samples. Our closest known exoplanet, Proxima Centauri b, is about 4.2 light years away. For cosmic scales, that's pretty close. Yet the only man-made object that has left our solar system so far, the space probe Voyager 1, would still have to fly for 74,000 years before it would reach Proxima b. But we don't know whether there is water or whether life would be possible.

It's probably due to the optimistic spirit of science fiction to seek answers in distant galaxies rather than on our own planet. This attitude derives in part from the spirit of Star Trek creator Gene Roddenberry, a hippie and philanthropic visionary whose influence is severely underestimated. Almost all Silicon Valley nerds grew up with Star Trek. Their steadfast belief in technical progress has its roots in the adventures of Captain Kirk, and it's the basis not only of their space conquest plans. Every single insane detail of the Star Trek series, be it the beaming, artificial intelligence, or infinite life, is still on the agenda of the nerds from Silicon Valley.

Bezos, who happens to idolize Captain Jean-Luc Picard, is also venturing into space travel. According to the Forbes magazine, he is the richest person in the world. He loves science fiction and mad science. When asked what he wants to do with his wealth, he thought this was an appropriate answer: «The only way that I can see to deploy this much financial resource is by converting my Amazon winnings into space travel. » As long as there are people who lack the basic necessities, I consider such plans obscene. In a part-time job, Bezos founded Blue Origin to make his dreams of a permanent lunar base a reality. The NASA-backed company currently performs suborbital flights, but plans to offer supply flights to the moon one day. Why? Because «we humans have to go to space if we are going to continue to have a thriving civilization, » Bezos said in an interview with Norah O'Donnell of CBS Evening News. «We have become big as a population, as a species, and this planet is relatively small. We see it in things like climate change and pollution and heavy industry. We are in the process of destroying this planet. » To Bezos and the tech evangelists, the earth is ultimately disposable – quite in the mentality of a webshop owner. At least he added: «We have sent robotic probes to every planet in the solar system – this is the good one. So, we have to preserve this planet. » – But we shouldn't count on his help apparently.

Technological capabilities aside, science fiction delivers the wrong impression that the cosmos is teeming with inhabitable planets. But for the most part, the universe is a hostile environment for humans. It «is too cold, too hot, too dense, too vacuous, too dark, too bright, or not composed of the right elements to support life, » wrote Peter D. Ward and Donald Brownle in their book Rare Earth. Life can be found everywhere on earth – from the depths of the oceans to the highest mountains and from polar ice to hot deserts and hydrothermal springs. Yet «the Earth is the only world known, so far, to harbor life, » writes Carl Sagan in Pale Blue Dot, «There is nowhere else, at least in the near future, [to which] our species could migrate. »

Astronauts must be top fit, since long-term exposure to weightlessness has serious health consequences. During space travel, they lose bone mass, their muscles shrink and get weaker. Astronauts literally become thin skinned in space, as the thickness of their skin decreases. Cosmic radiation weakens the immune system and changes the DNA. They could also suffer considerable brain damage, since the radiation causes measurable changes in brain cells and impairs memory and behavior. There is currently no effective protection against these high-energy particles.

If we assume that the universe is full of life, then we must also assume that disasters and miseries are also rampant on countless other planets. Suffering is everywhere, and you can't escape it, only deal with it. If we continue to explore space, maybe we will one day set foot on other planets, but not like grasshoppers. Thanks to the waste of resources and the poisoning of our environment, we are heading for one of the worst phases in human history. After the terrible consequences on Earth, we should tread lightly in space. Who knows what we will destroy there?

Only a few years ago, wherever people spoke of leaving the earth, they met with opposition. Everyone thought such a project was unthinkable and didn't want to hear about it. But today there are many people who pretend to be sane and claim that it's the most natural thing to leave the earth. To dream of it and make large resources available cannot be explained by «scientific curiosity» and «technical progress» alone. Curiosity could also turn to other objects, such as the question of how to save our planet. But the valleyists have not expressed any general idea of curiosity and progress, but the idea of escapism. They are a bunch of wealthy people who are preparing for the time when everything collapses. Douglas Rushkoff published a report about his experience as a keynote speaker at an exclusive meeting of hedge fund managers. They seriously discussed questions, such as: Should you run off to Alaska or rather New Zealand if the climate catastrophe becomes too bad? Should you have an underground bunker built? Or would you rather have your own island? – Especially when you can't get a place on a rocket to Mars. These people are obviously not interested in how to avoid a disaster, although they bear major responsibility due to their lifestyles and businesses. They are convinced that we have already gone too far. Despite all their wealth and power, they don't believe that they can have a positive impact on the future. All their talk of a better world is smoke and mirrors, schall und rauch, schnurz und piepe. They believe in the darkest scenarios and want to use their money and the newest technology to keep themselves isolated. The slogan «Après nous le déluge! » – «After us, the Flood, » is attributed to the famous mistress of the French King Louis XV, Madame de Pompadour, who is said to have coined it in 1757, when unpleasant news disturbed the mood at a glittering party. For the masses, life was anything but a party, and the French royals actually experienced their flood only thirty years later. «After us, the Flood» is not a particularly attractive maxim for those who are already up to their neck in the water. Karl Marx wrote: «Après moi, le déluge! is the watchword of every capitalist and of every capitalist nation. Hence Capital is reckless of the health or length of life of the labourer, unless under compulsion from society. » Ideas about bunkers, islands, or the colonization of space sound to me like an extreme version of that watchword. Escaping from our home planet would be no solution for our problems. It's wishful thinking that prevents us from facing reality and focusing on feasible solutions. Besides, how many people do they want to save this way? More than 7.7 billion people currently live on Earth, and the number grows every second. By the end of the century, the world's population could be almost eleven billion. The strategies of the Silicon Valley billionaires are only aimed at the survival of a few. These are not plans to continue the human diaspora, but for a lifeboat for the richest. In a moment of clarity, Max Levchin, co-founder and former chief technologist of PayPal, is for once right when he says: «It's one of the few things about Silicon Valley that I actively dislike – the sense that we are superior giants who move the needle and, even if it's our own failure, must be spared. » The whole technology magic could already be used for less romantic but common good purposes. For Levchin, prepping for the apocalypse in Silicon Valley is a moral fallacy. When he gets involved in survivalist talks, he simply ends them by asking, «So you're worried about the pitchforks. How much money have you donated to your local homeless shelter? »

Whoever flees into such phantasms is a nihilist, basically an enemy of the earth. Such as Jesco von Puttkamer, former head of planning at NASA, who doesn't hide his hostility towards the Earth: «Somehow, » he said, «the natural biosphere of the Earth and man are not compatible with each other. Yes, it even seems as if we live in a hostile environment, otherwise we would not be in such a conflict with it. » The earth doesn't seem «suitable for a race of beings that grows as dynamically as man. » Because of this idea that we humans are special or have the right to dominate and use animals and plants, we have destroyed the environment. But the environment does not belong to us, it is the other way round: We belong to the environment. We are children of this biosphere, we owe our existence to it, and our physiology is evolutionarily fully adapted to life on Earth. Puttkamer, like many others, dreamed of free-floating space colonies: «It's quite possible that one day we will be able to build artificial biospheres in space from scratch, closed cycles that are optimised for humans. » Perhaps we should be careful what else comes from such people. Their thinking is a sign of crisis, the stress caused by worsening conditions is obviously already having an impact.

Not least, there seem to be unconscious religious roots. The technical progress brought to us from Silicon Valley has always been a vessel of quasi-religious longing. Why should it be different with the colonization of space? For those seeking to leave the earth, space represents a Promised Land. The archetype of such promises of salvation and Last Day concepts are – at least in Christianity – passages from the Revelation scriptures which predict the end of the world. One of the first Apocalypses handed down to us is the biblical book Daniel, written in Palestine around 164 BC. Palestine had for centuries suffered like hardly any other region of constant military invasions. But never before has foreign rule been as oppressive as in the time of Antiochus IV. During his reign, violence, economic exploitation, and tyranny developed into a totalitarian system. The emergence of apocalyptic thought falls precisely into this phase. The Greek word «apocalypse» means «revelation, » so that actually the apocalypse was meant as a historical text, e.g. when we speak of the Revelation of John. However, the term «apocalypse» has become a synonym for the downfall of the world or of humanity. The Revelation of John, the last book of the Bible, offers its own horror visions of a terrible end: «I looked, and behold, there was a great earthquake, and the sun became black as sackcloth, the full moon became like blood, and the stars in the sky fell to earth. » According to the Berlin journalist Michael Jager, space travel is a direct continuation of the idea of the Ascension described in Revelation, yet a materialistic ascension, ignoring the metaphorical meaning of the original script. The Ascension didn't mean an actual change of location. But secularization changed the understanding of metaphorical texts as if they were describing reality. In the Revelation of John the faithful are promised a new home. It's not clear whether this new «home» lies on earth or in a heaven. So says Revelation 3:12: «He who overcomes, I will make him a pillar in the temple of my God, and he will never depart outside anymore, and I will write on him the name of my God and the name of the city of my God, the New Jerusalem, which is coming down out of heaven from my God, and also my new name. » Jager believes that the faith in technological process is also already rooted in society: «The model of the modern machine is the society of Thomas Hobbes, which voluntarily allows itself to be ruled authoritarian. » In his social portrait Leviathan, Hobbes was inspired by the mechanical clock developed in the Christian monastery. Lynn White Jr. wrote in The Historical Roots of Our Ecologic Crisis: «Our science and technology have grown out of Christian attitudes toward man's relation to nature which are almost universally held not only by Christians and neo-Christians but also by those who fondly regard themselves as post-Christians. What we do about ecology depends on our ideas of the man-nature relationship. More science and more technology are not going to get us out of the present ecologic crisis until we find a new religion, or rethink our old one. »

Our prophetic nerds rank on the doom scale somewhere between Hosea and Habakkuk. Coping with the climate change may be an intimidating challenge, but it's simple compared to terraforming other planets. Two multi-billion dollar biosphere tests have already shown that we are unable to maintain an inhabitable bubble even here on Earth. Astronomer Martin Rees concludes:

«I think we have to accept that there's no Planet B which can ever be made as comfortable as the Earth. » Instead, the goal should be «to make the Earth habitable not just now, but for future centuries, that's the top priority. » It's entirely up to us, a question of good will, and all it takes is to use nature's wealth wisely and fairly. We don't seem to succeed. But if we are not even able to do so, we will not master the consequences of worse mistakes. We regard ourselves smart and above the laws of nature – after all, we are the 'crown of creation.' We build rockets and probes that flies to Mars and take pictures for us. And yet, we destroy our beautiful and only home. The waste we produce has grown to mountains. Extinction due to human activities has already cost thousands of species and threatens up to a million animal and plant species more. The climate changes on an accelerating speed, and a few have become rich. What we have been doing since the Industrial Revolution is like a gradual collective suicide. This cannot go on. If, in a few centuries, humans should still exist, it will be difficult for them to understand why we were so greedy and irresponsible, despite all the intelligence we have. But there has been life on earth for 4 billion years without human beings, and since then life has survived many catastrophes. It will probably also survive us. It's still possible that a profound change can happen. We still have enough time and resources to save the environment from destruction. That is what we should focus on. Who would have thought three years ago that Fridays for Future would exist? Children in 60 countries organize in it. They plant trees, lobby against plastic bags or for the sustainable production of palm oil. Whatever comes to their mind. These young people are everywhere, and the movement around Greta Thunberg is one of many worldwide. This generation will determine what the future looks like on earth.

READY OR NOT

«Everything one writes now is overshadowed by this ghastly feeling that we are rushing towards a precipice and, though we shan't actually prevent ourselves or anyone else from going over, must put up some sort of a fight. » – George Orwell

«Dave, my mind is going. I can feel it. I can feel it. » – HAL

In Edward Morgan Forster's The Machine Stops an omnipotent machine takes care of all people's physical and spiritual needs. They are trapped in an absolute dependence on this machine, which they have no control of. They have forgotten that it's man-made and worship it like a divine entity. Its manual has become a holy book. Anyone who questions the wisdom of the machine is labeled «unmechanical» and threatened with homelessness, which is defacto a death penalty. Over time, the system becomes vulnerable to malfunctions. But since people don't know how to fix it, the machine collapses apocalyptically and takes civilization down with it. The only hope for a recovery of humankind is that the few surviving people on the surface will not repeat the same mistake.

The most insightful ancient story of this kind – particularly as it comes from a civilization that had actually suffered a collapse – is the Rebellion of the Tools in the Maya creation epic Popol Vuh:

«And all [those things] began to speak.... "You ... shall feel our strength. We shall grind and tear your flesh to pieces," said their grinding stones.... At the same time, their griddles and pots spoke: "Pain and suffering you have caused us.... You burned us as if we felt no pain. Now you shall feel it, we shall burn you. »

The Cuban writer Alejo Carpentier pointed out that this is our first explicit warning of the threat of the machine. Human beings are overthrown by their farming and household tools.

We are becoming increasingly dependent on technology and lose the ability to do things on our own. In a 1953 lecture, Heidegger pointed out that the rise of technology had turned into an autonomous process, and we have become powerless witnesses. The mastery of nature, as dreamed by Descartes, slipped away from us. We are the slaves of our desired domination. Digital helpers are relieving us from our tasks, including thinking, identifying context and draw conclusions. There will be more and more areas of everyday life in which we can no longer participate without digital technology, be it financial transactions, driving a car, booking holidays, or when we apply for a driving license, an insurance, a loan, etc. This doesn't make things any easier.

Social psychologist Erich Fromm said: «A technological civilization is programmed by the principal that something ought to be done if it's technologically possible. » Without reflecting on the consequences. We are not only victims of the new technologies, but also accomplices. We voluntarily surrender our responsibility for the promise of a better and optimized life. High-tech imperialism doesn't only produce tons of technological trash, it creates chaos and incapacity.

According to the American sociologist Charles Perrow, modern societies have produced systems that are highly complex and usually tightly coupled. Complex is everything that due to its systemic mathematical structure can no longer be completely predicted. Coupling means that there is no buffering or elasticity between two technical systems. All processes of one system have a direct effect on the processes of the other system. Perrow investigated the accident at the nuclear power plant in Harrisburg in Pennsylvania in 1979, and he verified his findings with other technologies. He concludes that industrial tragedies are as inevitable as hurricanes. Perrow describe them as «normal accidents, » caused by problems that no engineer has expected. Most normal accidents «have a significant degree of incomprehensibility, » says Perrow. The addition of safety features may make the system even more complex and may result in the opposite of what it's intended to do. The frequency of accidents will rise, and they will be more severe, be it natural hazards, technological failures, acts of war or terrorism, as well as various combinations thereof. Perrow was always suspicious of large plants because they accumulate an absurd high risk. He warned that «much of our critical infrastructure is in the hands of large corporations. » For him, the sheer size of the technology giants is unreasonable. Because: «The larger an organization, the larger its vulnerability. » Bigger is not safer, says Perrow. It's hard to imagine the impact of disasters on an infrastructure that is so centralized and tightly coupled as in the U.S. Perrow hoped for political help: Strict antitrust laws to break up monopolies, regulations to limit the size of industrial plants, and control instruments to reduce the increasingly dense population of dangerous areas, especially on the coasts.

It seems unlikely that governments and political parties can overcome the challenges ahead. So far, ignorance rules the political discussion. The gap between technical reality and political debate is widening. Whereas people understand that far-reaching and frightening upheavals are on the horizon, politicians are apathetic. Needless to say, most politicians share the same view of technology as corporations. They make their decisions without much understanding of the implications of cutting-edge science and technology. The assumptions underlying these decisions are often unwarranted. Much of it is fiction or pure propaganda. Computer ideologists portray the current development as «inevitable. » And many users experience it as such. As Weizenbaum pointed out «scientists and technologists have, because of their power, an especially heavy responsibility, one that is not to be stuffed off behind a façade of slogans such as technological inevitability. »

In 1932, Aldous Huxley wrote his famous novel Brave New World. In which he tries to predict the future and draws a nightmarish world where technology dominates every area of life. Twenty-seven years later, Huxley wrote a sequel, Brave New World Revisited, in which he examines whether his predictions had come true. Considering the technological progress the world has made in the meantime, Huxley summarized his findings in a single sentence: «It happened faster than I had thought. » In 1981, the communication researcher Wilbur Schramm illustrates the speed of technological development in an essay titled What is a long time?: He described the entire history of mankind with the help of a 24-hour clock on which he added some «points in time» relevant for communication: Language appears at 21.33 o'clock, writing at 23.52 o'clock, the first book only two minutes before midnight, Gutenberg's printing press at 23.59 and only 33 seconds later radio and television. Schramm died before the Internet began its conquest.

The speed of change has a new quality. People have never lived as fast as today. No more waiting, no more boredom, no more slowness. We travel fast, work fast, and think fast. We communicate in real time across the globe. This development is only the beginning, because it doesn't run in a linear fashion, but exponentially. The hope that, after the many technical innovations that have changed our lives, a time of calm will come is deceptive. The opposite will be the case and the pace of this change will continue to accelerate like an avalanche that starts as a snowball and then thunders down the mountain. Who resists, will be buried. The Luddits got it right, but they were 200 years too early. Their fate reminds us that technological progress finds its way. We cannot simply opt out of the digital «brave new world. » It's already there. And everything that happens, happens worldwide and at the same time. It's the result of the actions of only a handful of American Internet companies. Their main motive is profit, and we – were we distracted? Bravo to these entrepreneurs. Silicon Valley billionaires tell us, with little evidence, that computer can solve most of our global problems. No doubt, their doctrine is the only correct one – they have transformed our world into a garden Eden, and we are heading for a bright future. Right? But discreetly they neglect to say that their «improvements» threaten the continued existence of humanity. The Internet is destroying the traditional places where people socialize: restaurants, cinemas, cafés, bars, and so on. Despite their talk of empowerment the digitization threatens democracy, liberty, and equality. It will further concentrate power among a small elite if we don't take steps to stop this.

The world is full of cruelties. We only need to watch the news every day to get that confirmed. It's a tale of madness. Two thirds of humanity lives in poverty, more than 70 million people had to flee their homes, one third of humanity has no access to clean water, and less than half of the world's population has access to free or partly free media. In our industrialized countries, too, where the standard of living is relatively high, life has become harder for many people in the past two decades instead of better. Financial crashes, economic crises, unemployment, bleeding industrial regions, desolate infrastructure, jobs you can't live off, poverty in old age, what lies ahead is vague and uncertain – all this clouds our everyday lives and frightens us. In many regions of the world, civilization is in retreat. Wars and civil wars destroy the state order. Tyrants, warlords, and terrorist militias take command. Fear, chaos, atrocities, and arbitrary murders are the result. The creators of modern technologies don't take into account that humans are fallible. A technology that ignores the reality of human life will inevitably fail on a grand scale. The world in which we live is not fair per se. It's a mirror of the frailty of human nature, the result of our choices and unjust economic system and an even more unjust distribution.

Flying to Mars is a noble goal but will not solve these problems. The innovations that help us to solve the important problems are non-existent. And the problems we are experiencing today will grow exponentially according to the speed of technological progress. Those who believe in a technological paradise can do so only because they ignore these facts. Whether we can use our tools for a humane purpose is questionable. In her book Technoculture, Leila Green points out that technology is never neutral. It's always developed with a particular purpose and goal in mind. And those who are capable of funding its development are those who benefit most of it. «In fact, the issue of who benefits most from computers was already settled when they were invented. Computers, like television, are far more valuable and helpful to the military, to multinational corporations, to international banking, to governments, and to institutions of surveillance and control-all of whom use this technology on a scale and with a speed that are beyond our imaginings-than they ever will be to you and me. » said Jerry Mander.

But is there any chance at all of finding a way out of this labyrinth? – There is, if only enough people in the industrialized countries – they are the driving force behind this development – understand the necessity and are prepared to disarm materially. The responsibility for technological self-empowerment lies with ourselves. As Jospeph Weizenbaum put it: «Learn to say 'No!'» And Konrad Zuse once said: «If the computers get too cocky, pull the plug. » Each individual should learn where to draw the line to machine domination. «You can't turn back time! » – Nobody wants that. If we don't want to do without information technology and live like hermits, we should accept that there will be no return to the analogue time. Does this prevent us from banning or regulating dangerous things? It took a long time until the dangers of X-rays were recognized, and decades passed before something was done about it. How long do we want to wait with regard to digital technologies? Who is stopping us, as a society, from learning how to use digital media reasonably, just as we do with other modern technologies? I strongly believe that we could at any time find a compromise and a solution to each problem. All it takes is good will. It can't go on like this. We destroy the earth, worship King Mammon, sell our souls, and forget love.

I prefer to choose myself how much technology I use. More and more people grow skeptical about the digital revolution. But it's not just about pointing the finger at the tech people and blaming them. They're just a symptom of development. In my lifetime alone, the world has changed dramatically. Actually, it was exciting times. And I don't want to join the choir of doomsday preachers. But there is much suffering in the world. I hope to make a contribution – amongst many – in the search for what is good for society. Many people are aware of the risks. But they assume that this is a problem for ethics committees, technology conferences, and scientific journals. In fact, it is inextricably tied to the current economic, political, and moral crisis. The time is ripe for forwarding this debate among the public. If, after reading this book, you are concerned about the questions I raised here, I hope you'll consider speaking out. Perhaps, if enough people start discussing these issues, even politicians and entrepreneurial nerds will take notice.

Have looked out of the window? Fresh air, go and smell some.

Printed in Poland
by Amazon Fulfillment
Poland Sp. z o.o., Wrocław